D0265214

# THE REPTILE AND AMPHIBIAN
# KEEPER'S DICTIONARY

# The Reptile
# and Amphibian
# Keeper's Dictionary

AN A–Z OF HERPETOLOGY

DAVID C. WAREHAM

**BLANDFORD**

A BLANDFORD BOOK

FIRST PUBLISHED
in the UK 1993
by Blandford
(a Cassell imprint)
Villiers House
41/47 Strand
LONDON
WC2N 5JE

DISTRIBUTED IN THE UNITED STATES
by Sterling Publishing Co., Inc.
387 Park Avenue South, New York, NY 10016–8810

DISTRIBUTED IN AUSTRALIA
by Capricorn Link (Australia) Pty Ltd
P.O. Box 665, Lane Cove, NSW 2066

BRITISH LIBRARY CATALOGUING-IN-PUBLICATION DATA.
A catalogue record for this book is available from the British Library.

ISBN 0-7137-2318-1

TYPESET BY Pure Tech Corporation, Pondicherry, India.
PRINTED AND BOUND IN FINLAND

(W) 639.376 W

# CONTENTS

# PREFACE

The aim of this book has been to compile clear, concise and informative definitions of the terminology commonly encountered by herpetologists when discussing or reading about reptiles and amphibians. It is intended for all who have an interest in these animals, from the amateur hobbyist, who may be faced with what can be a somewhat frightening technical term or scientific expression, to the professional zoologist who may become confused occasionally over the exact meaning of a particular term. It will, it is hoped, also be a useful source of reference to all others who are actively or passively involved in some aspect of herpetology – keepers, curators, breeders, researchers, students, teachers etc.

The dictionary contains over 2000 fully cross-referenced entries, including all the basic technical terms relating to the external features of reptiles and amphibians (e.g., femoral pore, parietal scale, supralabial gland), all the herpetological families (e.g., Bufonidae, Iguanidae, Viperidae), biological processes (e.g., aestivation, spermatogenesis, thermoregulation), selected biographies (e.g., Bellairs, FitzSimons, Smith), herpetological slang (e.g., hoody, milked up), and many other terms and expressions of relevance to herpetologists, from the fields of anatomy, ecology, zoogeography, behaviour and husbandry.

The headwords are arranged in alphabetical order and wherever a particular term contains more than one word the order of those words remains the same. For example, 'metatarsal tubercle' appears under M and not under T as 'tubercle, metatarsal'. Words appearing in small capital letters within the definitions are themselves defined elsewhere in their correct alphabetical position. Synonyms, where appropriate, are included in parentheses immediately after the headword.

The self-explanatory illustrations support and supplement the text by enhancing the interpretation of a particular term, and a list of abbreviations in current herpetological use appears at the front of the book. Obviously with a book of this size it has been impossible to include every single herpetological term ever devised but it hopefully contains most of those in everyday usage, and some others which are perhaps not quite so familiar.

As with any compilation, this work has relied almost entirely upon the work of others who have contributed to the science of herpetology over the years. They are too numerous to mention but without them this book would not have been possible. Thanks too are due to all the many friends and colleagues who have offered much help, advice and encouragement during the book's progress and who suggested terms for possible inclusion. Again they are too numerous to mention individually but they know who they are. My thanks to them all.

*David C. Wareham*
*Radcliffe*
*Manchester*

# ABBREVIATIONS

| | |
|---|---|
| AAZPA | American Association of Zoological Parks and Aquariums. |
| ad. | Adult. |
| ARAZPA | Australian Regional Association of Zoological Parks and Aquaria. |
| ARKS | Animal Records Keeping System. |
| ASRA | Association for the Study of Reptiles and Amphibians. |
| BHS | British Herpetological Society. |
| BI | Bicolour. |
| BRC | Biological Records Centre. |
| C, °C | Celsius, degrees centigrade. |
| c/ | Clutch of (followed by number of eggs). |
| CBSG | Captive Breeding Specialist Group (IUCN). |
| CITES | Convention on International Trade in Endangered Species (of wild flora and fauna). |
| CoEnCo | Council for Environmental Conservation. |
| COGBAZ | Council of Governing Bodies of Australasian Zoos. |
| CPR | Captive Propagation Rescue. |
| CRES | Centre for Reproduction of Endangered Species (Zoological Society of San Diego). |
| CREW | Centre for Reproduction of Endangered Wildlife (Cincinnati Zoo). |
| DICE | Durrell Institute of Conservation and Ecology. |
| DoE | Department of the Environment. |

| | |
|---|---|
| DTH | Daytime high. |
| DTL | Daytime low. |
| ECR | Excitement colour reaction. |
| EEC | European Economic Community. |
| EPA | Environmental Protection Agency. |
| ESR | Excitement secretion reaction. |
| f. | Female. |
| FLS | Fellow of the Linnean Society. |
| FFPS | Flora and Fauna Preservation Society. |
| FSC | Field Studies Council. |
| FZS | Fellow of the Zoological Society (of London). |
| IHS | International Herpetological Society. |
| imm. | Immature. |
| ISIS | International Species Inventory System. |
| ITE | Institute of Terrestrial Ecology. |
| IUCN | International Union for the Conservation of Nature (and natural resources). |
| IZY | International Zoo Yearbook. |
| juv. | Juvenile. |
| L (Linn.) | Linnaeus. |
| LD | Lethal dose. |
| LD50 | The minimum amount of venom that results in the death of 50% of test subjects. |
| m. | Male. |
| MVP | Minimum viable population. |
| NCC | Nature Conservation Council. |
| NCT | Nature Conservation Trust. |
| NERC | Natural Environment Research Council. |
| NIC | National Institute for Conservation. |
| NOAH | National On-line Animal Histories (European version of SPARKS). |
| NPS | National Park Service (USDI). |
| NSHP | Nutritional secondary hyperparathyroidism. |
| PST | Preferred substrate temperature. |
| PVA | Population viability analysis. |
| RJMG | Reptile Joint Management Group. |
| SMCC | Species Management Coordinating Council (ARAZPA and COGBAZ). |
| SMP | Species Management Programme (Australian version of SSP). |

| | |
|---|---|
| sp. | Species (sing.). |
| SPARKS | Single Population Analysis and Record Keeping System. |
| spp. | Species (pl.). |
| SSC | Species Survival Commission (IUCN). |
| SSP | Species Survival Plan (AAZPA). |
| ssp. | Subspecies. |
| SSSI | Site of Special Scientific Interest. |
| SVL | Snout–vent length. |
| TA | Tactile alignment. |
| TAG | Taxon Advisory Group (AAZPA). |
| TAR | Thermo-activity range. |
| TC | Tactile chase. |
| TD | Tricolour dyad. |
| TL | Total length. |
| TM | Tricolour monad. |
| TP | Tricolour pentad. |
| TRAFFIC | Trade Records Analysis of Flora and Fauna in Commerce. |
| TSCA | Tail-search copulatory attempt. |
| TSD | Temperature-dependent sex determination. |
| TT | Tricolour triad. |
| TTE | Tricolour tetrad. |
| UNESCO | United Nations Educational, Scientific and Cultural Organisation. |
| USDA | United States Department of Agriculture. |
| USDI | United States Department of the Interior. |
| USFWS | United States Fish and Wildlife Service. |
| UVR | Ultraviolet radiation. |
| WCI | Wildlife Conservation International (New York Zoological Society). |
| WCMC | Wildlife Conservation and Management Committee (AAZPA). |
| WWF | Worldwide Fund for Nature. |
| ♂ | Male. |
| ♂♂ | Males. |
| ♀ | Female. |
| ♀♀ | Females. |

# DICTIONARY

# A

**ABDOMEN** 1. The region of the body, usually the hindmost section, which contains the reproductive system and the major part of the digestive system; the belly. 2. The complete undersurface which, in limbed amphibians and reptiles, is the area lying between the fore- and hind legs and, in limbless forms, between the throat and the CLOACA; the VENTER.

**ABDOMINAL** Pertaining to a scale or LAMINA on the undersurface of a reptile which, in lizards, is any scale lying on the abdomen and, in snakes, is any one of the enlarged VENTRAL scales. In chelonians, the abdominal is either of the pair of laminae lying third from the rear on the PLASTRON.

**ABDOMINAL GLAND** 1. An enlarged gland situated inside the cloaca in male urodeles, which in certain species may serve to stimulate the female during courtship. 2. In the casque-headed skinks (*Tribolonotus*), any one of a number of glands, each located beneath an abdominal scale, and a feature unique among lizards.

**ABERRANT** Abnormal or diverging from the usual or normal form. Among reptiles and amphibians, an aberrant individual exhibits, in one way or another, a feature or features uncharacteristic of its species. A snake that shows the characteristics of albinism, or one that has a pattern defect where spots are replaced by stripes, are examples of aberrants.

**ABSCESS** A localized gathering of pus, often caused by bacteria and occurring on various parts of the body. In tortoises, abscesses are usually present mainly around the ears and, in small lizards, they generally occur in the area of the CLOACA. In other reptiles, abscesses can occur almost anywhere, but particularly on the head in snakes.

ABUNDANCE   In reptile and amphibian ecology, abundance refers to the density of specimens, less commonly to species, within a specified area.

ABUNDISMUS   A variety of MELANISM in which the specimen displays one or more alterations to its basic species pattern, e.g., an increase in the number of black markings in normally non-black areas, whilst not being entirely black as in true melanism.

ACANTHOCEPHALA   Spiny-headed worms. A phylum of parasitic worms that, with a hook-equipped proboscis, securely fasten themselves in the intestines of a host. Adults of the genus *Acanthocephalus* are sometimes found in water snakes, and those of the genus *Neoechinorhynchus* are frequently found in tortoises.

ACARIASIS   Tick and mite infestation that occurs as ENDOPARASITOSIS but most often as ECTOPARASITOSIS. Newly captured reptiles, particularly snakes, tortoises and varanids, are often infested with ticks, but the most significant ectoparasitosis in reptiles is caused by the blood-sucking mites, *Ophionyssus*, which occur on snakes.

ACARID   A small arachnid of the order Acarina. A mite or tick.

ACARIDOMATIUM   Sometimes found in early literature relating to the pocket or pouch formation at the rear of the limb insertions of certain lizards. Literally, 'mite house', referring to the mites which sometimes dwell within these pockets.

ACCESSORY ABDOMINAL PLATE   Has been used to describe the foremost row of dorsal scales when distinguishing between a smooth or slightly keeled row of scales where, in certain species, the remaining dorsals are keeled.

ACCESSORY FANG   *See* REPLACEMENT FANG.

ACCESSORY PALPEBRAL   Sometimes used to describe any one of the scales that lie between the PREOCULAR and the true PALPEBRAL scales on the heads of certain lizards.

ACCLIMATIZATION   Adaptation. Refers, in herpetology, to the way in which a particular natural reaction is reduced or even eliminated over a period of time. For example, crocodilians and large boids which are used in demonstrations can become acclimatized to their 'appearances' and cease to act defensively. The urge to threaten or flee can also disappear.

ACENTRIC   Having no body, or centre, in reference to the vertebrae of amphibians.

ACINOUS   Relating to any GLAND that is subdivided into small cavities or pouches. In male anurans, the NUPTIAL PAD is acinous.

ACOUSTICO-LATERALIS SYSTEM   *See* LATERAL LINE SYSTEM.

ACROCHORDIDAE   Wart snakes. Family of the Henophidia, inhabiting South-East Asia, Indonesia, Papua New Guinea and northern Australia. Three species in two genera.

ACRODONT   Having teeth fused to the top of the upper jaw margin. Found in amphibians, the tuatara, and certain lizards and snakes.

ACROMIAL   Refers to the CLAVICLE in anurans.

ACROMIAL PROCESS   A small projection directed anteriorly on the cranial border of the SCAPULA and which, in chelonians, becomes quite extensive and lengthened, forming an essential part of the extraordinary PECTORAL GIRDLE found in this group.

ACTIVITY AREA   *See* HOME RANGE.

ACTIVITY RHYTHMS   The intermittent and repetitive pattern in the locomotory activity of organisms. Usually linked to a day/night variation (CIRCADIAN RHYTHM), and occurring both as ENDOGENOUS or EXOGENOUS patterns, and also consisting of different single activities.

ACUMINATE   Ending in a tapering, sharp point.

ADAPTIVE RADIATION   The development of two or more allied groups of animals along completely different evolutionary routes. This type of divergent evolution occurred in the MESOZOIC reptiles.

ADDLED   Term used to describe eggs that fail to hatch.

ADETOGLOSSAL   Free-tongued. Used mainly in reference to the tongues of salamanders of the genus *Plethodon*.

ADHESION SURFACE   Part of a subdigital LAMELLA in lizards, positioned laterally and sustaining many hairlike structures forming a fibrous group at its extremity.

ADHESIVE APPARATUS   *See* ADHESIVE ORGAN.

ADHESIVE ORGAN   Referring to the folds at the hindmost border of the mouth in embryonic tadpoles of anurans. These folds can be horseshoe-shaped, V-shaped or crescentic, or divided into two bilateral parts, and are covered internally with intricate mucus-secreting cells. This mucus enables the tadpoles to adhere to submerged objects. The organ is lost before METAMORPHOSIS.

ADHESIVE PAD   Particular tissue occurring on the toes of certain lizards that has developed in such a way as to enable the animals to hold on to smooth vertical surfaces.

**ADNATE** Referring to two different organs that are closely connected, e.g., the tongue and the floor of the mouth in certain amphibians, chelonians and crocodilians.

**ADNEXUS, pl. ADNEXAE** An additional and supplementary part to a principal organ or structure, e.g., an ovary is an adnexus of the uterus, and the eyelids and NICTITATING MEMBRANE are adnexae of the eye.

**ADPRESS** To press close to or hold against. As a method of determining the relative limb length in urodeles, the fore- and hind limbs on one side are held flush with the side of the body and the length of the extension of the toes, or the distance separating them, is recorded. In anurans the hind limb is brought forward in line with the straightened body and the distance between the nostril and the heel is recorded.

**ADULT (ad.)** In herpetology, an individual which has attained the point in its life from whence its general shape and appearance ceases to alter with age, as opposed to a JUVENILE or LARVA.

**AEROMONAS INFECTION** Probably the most significant bacterial disease to occur in reptiles and amphibians, particularly in those living an aquatic existence. In reptiles, *Aeromonas hydrophila* infects mainly the digestive system, but can also be responsible for abscesses and pneumonia. In anurans, the same bacterium is responsible for the usually fatal disease known as RED-LEG.

**AESTIVATION** A condition of torpor during extended periods of high temperatures or drought; a state of inactivity during which the metabolic processes are greatly reduced.

**AGAMIDAE** Agamid lizards. Family of the SQUAMATA, suborder SAURIA, inhabiting much of the Old World (central, south and South-East Asia, and Africa except Madagascar) and Australia. One species occurs in Europe. Over 300 species in some 30 genera.

**AGGREGATE** An assemblage of from several to many members of the same species amassed in the same place. In reptiles and amphibians this occurrence is generally connected with hibernation, e.g., wintering groups of rattlesnakes (*Crotalus*), or reproduction, e.g., courting groups of frogs (*Rana*).

**AGLOSSAL** Having no tongue. Frogs of the family PIPIDAE are aglossal.

**AGLYPH** A term applied to any one of a large group of non-poisonous snakes that have teeth without grooves, in contradistinction to the opisthoglyphous snakes. Teeth of aglyphous species are solid and unable to transfer venom.

The skull of an aglyph snake possesses solid, relatively uniform teeth which lack the canals or grooves necessary for the conveyance of venom.

**AIR SAC** The hindmost section of the lung of a snake. Besides increasing the efficiency of gaseous exchange within the lung, it could also act as an evaporative cooling surface or assist buoyancy in aquatic species.

**ALARM CALL** *See* MALE RELEASE CALL.

**ALARM REACTION** Any one of a number of responses to sudden exposure to various situations in which the animal concerned feels threatened or in danger. In amphibians, for example, this reaction can take the form of mucus secretion, colour change or urination.

**ALBINO** An animal in which all dark pigment has failed to develop so that it appears white or pinkish. Albinism occurs as a genetic mutation in most groups of reptiles and amphibians.

**ALBUMEN, ALBUMIN** 1. Any of a group of uncomplicated water-soluble proteins that are coagulated by heat and which occur in blood plasma, egg white etc. 2. The white of eggs in certain reptiles; the watery protein solution between the shell and the yolk.

**ALBUMINURIA** The presence of ALBUMEN in the urine; a characteristic symptom of envenomation by Russell's viper (*Vipera russelli*).

**ALLANTO-CHORION** An embryonic membrane.

**ALLANTOIC GILL** The respiratory construction occurring in the embryos of entirely terrestrial plethodontid salamanders which gives them a surface for gaseous exchange within the egg capsule. The gills ATROPHY when the larvae hatch.

**ALLANTOIS** One of the three embryonic membranes of reptiles and higher vertebrates. It arises from the hind gut in the developing reptile embryo and is used partly as an organ of nutrition and respiration and partly as a receptacle for storing waste.

**ALLIGATOR**   Crocodilian of the New World and China, having a broad, flat snout and certain teeth in the lower jaw that fit into pits in the upper jaw, not notches as in crocodiles.

Alligators have teeth on the lower jaw some of which, when the mouth
is closed, fit into sockets in the upper jaw.

**ALLIGATORIDAE**   Family of the CROCODILIA, the alligators and caimans, inhabiting the Americas and eastern Asia. Seven species in four genera.

**ALLOCHTHONOUS**   Term given to an animal that has migrated into, or been transported and released into, a region that is not its usual habitat. The Neotropical *Bufo marinus* is allochthonous, having been introduced into a number of countries throughout the world.

**ALLOPATRIC**   Applied to two or more animal populations that could interbreed but do not as they occupy mutually exclusive, although usually adjacent, geographical regions. Compare SYM-PATRIC.

**ALVEOLAR**   1. Referring to the margin of the jaw where teeth, if present, are situated.   2. Consisting of, or containing, many small hollows, sockets or pits.

**ALVEOLAR RIDGE**   In chelonians, the ridge on the crushing surface of the upper jaw.

**AMBIENT TEMPERATURE**   The temperature of the immediate surroundings or of the environment of a captive animal.

AMELANISTIC   Term describing a specimen that lacks the pigment MELANIN which produces mainly black and brown colours. Reptiles that are amelanistic are consequently paler than normal, although they may have a certain amount of coloration from other pigments, particularly red or pink.

AMINOGLYCOSIDE   In reference to the treatment of reptile and amphibian diseases, a group of antibiotics used for GRAM-NEGATIVE BACTERIAL infections. Gentamicin, for example, is an aminoglycoside.

AMMONIO-TELISM   The physiological condition known to occur in several totally aquatic amphibian species, and the alligator, in which the main product of kidney excretion is ammonia. The majority of aquatic reptiles, such as turtles, excrete equal quantities of both ammonia and UREA, as do several species of amphibians.

AMNION   One of three membranes formed in which the embryo develops within the egg. *See also* ALLANTOIS, CHORION.

AMNIOTE   Any vertebrate whose embryos are completely enveloped in a fluid-filled sac, the AMNION. As this sac evolved, it supplied the essential liquid environment for the embryo, enabling animals to breed in places other than water.

AMNIOTIC CAVITY   A closed, fluid-filled pouch that protects the reptile embryo (and embryos of birds and mammals also).

AMOEBIASIS (ENTAMOEBIASIS, AMOEBIC DYSENTERY)   A PROTOZOONOSIS that can infect reptiles, particularly snakes and lizards but, to a lesser degree, chelonians also, causing slimy and watery faeces, which sometimes contain blood, refusal to feed, regurgitation and the urge to drink frequently.

AMOEBIC DYSENTERY   *See* AMOEBIASIS.

AMPHIBIAN   Any member of the vertebrate class Amphibia, containing the newts and salamanders (URODELA), frogs and toads (ANURA), caecilians (APODA), and sirens (TRACHYSTOMATA). Amphibians have four PENTADACTYL limbs, a moist and scaleless skin, and a pelvic girdle joined to the vertebral column. They are POIKILOTHERMS and differ from reptiles by producing eggs that have no protective shell or embryonic membrane and which, with the possible exception of a very few species, are fertilized externally. ADULT amphibians have lungs and live mostly on land but their skin, which is also used in respiration, is thin and moist and, as body fluids are easily lost, they are usually dependent upon damp habitats. The class Amphibia falls intermediate between fishes and reptiles.

**AMPHIBIOUS**    Able to occupy both land and water. Usually used to describe the lives of most amphibians but is equally appropriate to semi-aquatic chelonians, crocodilians and certain snakes and lizards.

**AMPHI-DICHOTOMY**    In snakes, an ABERRANT condition in which the front and rear parts of the body are duplicated about a single, central trunk.

**AMPHIGONIA RETARDA**    Delayed fertilization. In many reptiles and some amphibians, sperm can remain viable for long periods, even several years, within the female before fertilizing the eggs.

**AMPHIGYRINID**    The name given to any anuran tadpole that has two lateral SPIRACLES rather than one, as in the Aglossa for example.

**AMPHISBAENA**    1. Astounding poisonous serpent of classical mythology with a head at both ends and able to move forwards or backwards.    2. GENUS of worm-like lizards.

**AMPHISBAENIDAE**    Family of the SQUAMATA, suborder Amphisbaenia, inhabiting southern Europe, South America and Africa. Around 120 species.

**AMPHIUMIDAE**    Eel newts. Family of the URODELA, inhabiting southern and south-eastern North America. Three species in one genus.

**AMPLECANT**    Used to describe amphibians that are engaged in AMPLEXUS.

**AMPLEXATION**    *See* AMPLEXUS.

**AMPLEXUS**    The sexual embrace of certain species of male amphibians upon the females. There are two basic types: AXILLARY (pectoral) and INGUINAL (pelvic), and a number of variations, including cephalic, lumbar, lumbo-pubic, neck, and supra-axillary.

**AMPULLA URETERIS**    The swollen and expanded area in the URETER of snakes that acts as a vesicle for the storage of sperm during the mating season.

**AMYOTROPHIN**    A powerful TOXIN, found in the venom of cobras (ELAPIDAE), that destroys muscle and nerve cells.

**ANAGOTOXIC**    Has been used to describe something which has the ability to neutralize the effects of venom, usually in reference to the sulphurous waters of São Pedro in Brazil.

Amplexus, or the sexual embrace of certain amphibians, in which the
male grasps the female, may last from a few hours to several weeks
depending on the species. The pair of frogs illustrated here are engaging
in pectoral or axillary amplexus in which the male grasps the female
around her chest.

ANAL   In reference to the anus; area of the body at and immediately
surrounding the anus.  1. The posteriormost LAMINA, usually
paired, on the PLASTRON of many chelonians.  2. In snakes, the
single, or divided, terminal plate of the VERTEBRAL series. Usually
larger than the VENTRAL scales. Also known as preanal or postabdominal.

ANAL CLAW   *See* ANAL SPUR.

ANAL FOLD   In certain species of frog, a single fold of skin situated laterally and dorsally to the anus. In some species it is paired
and situated laterally to the anus.

ANAL GLAND   A usually paired, bag-like feature located within
the base of the tail in both sexes of snakes, though more prominent
in females, and opening into the VENT, or anus. Used mainly in
defence, it produces an evil-smelling fluid which can sometimes be
sprayed a considerable distance.

ANAL PLATE   The plate, or SCUTE, which covers the VENT. In
most lizards and snakes it is usually quite distinct, being larger than
the other VENTRAL scales.

ANAL RIDGE   Referring to the KEEL on the scales directly above
the anus of sexually mature male snakes of certain species which
otherwise have smooth scales on the rest of their bodies. The anal
ridge is absent in some adult males and may show in females so is
not therefore a reliable guide to sex determination.

ANAL SPUR (ANAL CLAW, PELVIC SPUR)   A remnant of the hind limbs, usually visible on either side of the VENT in the boas and pythons (BOIDAE) and Oriental pipe snake (*Cylindrophis*). In most males the spurs are generally quite large and are often used as organs of stimulation during courtship. In females, they are small or, in some species, absent altogether.

ANAL WART   *See* WART.

ANAMNIOTE   Any vertebrate that is without an AMNION. Amphibians are anamniotes, having embryos and larvae that must develop in water.

ANAPSID   Describing a skull that has no openings in the temporal region. Found in extinct reptiles (Cotylosauria) and in the present-day TESTUDINIDAE.

ANAVENOM   Snake VENOM which, after having been processed in order to remove its toxic properties, is injected into the blood of a living animal where antibodies are then formed, thus conferring an immunity to the anavenom. Blood serum from the immunized animal can then be used in the treatment of SNAKE BITE.

ANCIPITAL   Sometimes seen in early literature and used to describe the laterally compressed tails of certain lizards, newts and salamanders which are double-edged.

ANELYTROPSIDAE   Snake lizards. Family of the SQUAMATA, inhabiting Mexico. MONOTYPIC.

ANERYTHRISTIC   Referring to any specimen that lacks all red pigment so that any red markings normally present in that particular species are absent.

ANGEL, Fernand   1881–1950, French herpetologist, who worked on *Mission scientifique au Mexique et dans l'Amerique Centrale: Etudes sur les reptiles et les batraciens* (1870–1909), *Vie et moeurs des amphibiens* (1947), and *Vie et moeurs des serpents* (1950), amongst others.

ANGLE OF THE JAW   The angle created by the joint of the compound bone of the lower jaw with the quadrate bone of the skull.

ANGLE OF THE MOUTH   The angle created by the connective muscle tissue at the point where the upper and lower jaws diverge. In snakes and lizards the angle of the mouth is covered by the hindmost lower and upper LABIAL scales.

ANGUIDAE   Alligator lizards, glass lizards and related species. Family of the SQUAMATA, suborder SAURIA, inhabiting Europe (including Britain), North and South America, West Indies, south and South-East Asia and the Middle East. 75 species in eight genera.

ANGUIFORM Snake-like; snake-shaped.

ANGULAR GLAND In some chelonians and in crocodiles, the MUSK GLAND situated on the throat on the inside of the left and right halves of the lower jaw.

ANGULATE Having angles or an angular shape. The head of the Pacific boa (*Candoia*) can be described as angulate.

ANILIIDAE Pipe snakes. Family of the SQUAMATA, inhabiting northern South America (one species), and India. Ten species in three genera.

ANISODONT Having teeth of unequal lengths.

ANKYLOSE To fuse together into one; to unite two bones into one. Ankylosis is the type of rigid bony union of tooth and jaw found in most toothed reptiles, except crocodiles. The teeth of most lizards and all snakes are ankylosed to the inner margin of the jawbone or in shallow notches (PLEURODONT). In certain lizard families the teeth are ankylosed to the top of a bony ridge within the jawbone (ACRODONT).

ANNIELLIDAE Legless lizards. Family of the SQUAMATA, suborder SAURIA, inhabiting California and Baja California, Mexico. Two species in one genus.

ANNUAL CYCLE In reference to the lives of reptiles and amphibians, the succession of biological incidents that take place each and every year.

ANNUAL RING *See* RING.

ANNULUS Any ring-shaped space, part or structure, such as any of the external body segments of the AMPHISBAENIDAE family of lizards.

ANOMALEPIDAE Blind snakes. Family of the SQUAMATA, suborder SERPENTES, infraorder Scolecophidia, inhabiting tropical South America. Some 20 species in four genera.

ANTARCTIC The faunal region which, besides the Antarctic continent itself, includes the Falkland Islands, Kerguelen Islands and the southernmost tip of South America. There are no RECENT amphibians or reptiles in Antarctica itself and only a handful (some larva lizards of the Tropidurinae) have spread into Tierra del Fuego from the Neotropics.

ANTE-ANAL LAMELLA *See* PREANAL.

ANTEBRACHIAL 1. Referring to any one of the scales situated on the frontal margin of the upper forelimb (the brachium). 2. Any of the scales situated on the lower forelimb (the ANTE-BRACHIUM).

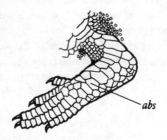

In lizards, the antebrachial scales (*abs*) are situated on the lower forelimb (the antebrachium), extending upward along the front border of the upper forelimb.

ANTEBRACHIUM The section of the forelimb that contains the ULNA and RADIUS bones; the lower forelimb.

ANTEOCULAR *See* PREOCULAR.

ANTEORBITAL *See* PREOCULAR.

ANTERIOR Located at, or towards, the front; of, or near, the head.

ANTERIOR FRONTAL *See* INTERNASAL.

ANTERIOR LOBE The section lying anteriorly to the AXILLARY NOTCH of a chelonian PLASTRON.

ANTERIOR ORBITAL In snakes, the PREOCULAR.

ANTERIOR PARIETAL Used in reference to the first large scale behind the OCULAR in snakes of the ANOMALEPIDAE.

ANTIBOTHROPHIC An ANTIVENIN effective against venoms that are characteristic of the NEOTROPICAL pit vipers other than rattlesnakes; e.g., *Bothrops* etc.

ANTILLEAN Relating to the Greater (Jamaica, Cuba, Puerto Rico and Hispaniola) and Lesser (Virgin Islands to Aruba) Antilles.

ANTIPALMAR Opposite the palm; relating to, or situated on, the back of the forefoot.

ANTIPLANTAR Opposite the sole; relating to, or situated on, the back of the hind foot.

ANTISERUM (ANTIVENENE, ANTIVENIN, ANTIVENOM, SERUM,

SNAKE ANTITOXIN, SNAKE-BITE SERUM) The serum (the fluid part of the blood that remains after clotting) of an animal that has been immunized against a foreign substance and which acts together with the substance against which it has been produced. Serum is processed from the blood of an animal that has received gradually increased amounts of VENOM or ANAVENOM, or a mixture of the two, and, as a result, has become immunized against the VENOM of a specific snake species. Antiserum is produced in horses usually and used in the treatment of ENVENOMATION in other animals including man.

ANTIVENENE, ANTIVENIN   *See* ANTISERUM.

ANTIVENOM   *See* ANTISERUM.

ANURA   The order of amphibians, also called SALIENTIA, that contains the frogs and toads. Most frogs (e.g., *Rana*) live in damp places or are aquatic; many are ARBOREAL. Toads (e.g., *Bufo*), which often have a dry warty skin, are better adapted to drier habitats. Adults have no tail, a short backbone, long powerful hind limbs and are agile swimmers and jumpers. Eggs (SPAWN) of anurans are covered with a protective jelly and, in most species, deposited in water in strings or clumps. The aquatic larva, or TADPOLE, experiences a quick and complete METAMORPHOSIS in which the GILLS are replaced by lungs and the tail absorbed. *See also* AMPHIBIAN.

APICAL   An alternative term for the ROSTRAL when referring to snakes of the genus *Vipera*.

APICAL BRISTLE   *See* TACTILE BRISTLE.

APICAL PIT (SCALE FOSSA, SCALE PIT)   A sense organ set in a small depression on the posterior tip of the DORSAL scales of certain kinds of reptiles. Sometimes called apical pore.

APNEUMONIC   Lungless. Used in reference to salamanders of the genus *Plethodon*.

APODA   The limbless amphibians – CAECILIIDAE, or Gymnophiona – an order of tropical worm-like animals of the class Amphibia.

APODAL   1. Without limbs. Snakes, amphisbaenids and caecilians are apodal. 2. Without feet. Describing lizards that have shortened stub-like limbs, as have certain members of the SCINCIDAE and TEIIDAE families.

APOSEMATIC   Describing the coloration of certain poisonous or distasteful animals which gives warning to possible enemies or predators. Examples of aposematic coloration are seen in the vivid blacks, yellows and reds of dart-poison frogs (DENDROBATIDAE) and fire-bellied toads (DISCOGLOSSIDAE).

**APPENDAGE**   Any projection from the body, or trunk, of an animal, such as a crest, horn or limb.

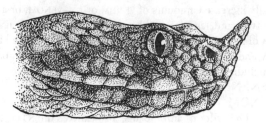

Many reptiles and amphibians have appendages on their heads or bodies in the form of spines, horns, crests etc. Some may act as lures in attracting prey or partners whilst others, such as the 'horn' on the nose of the sand viper (*Vipera ammodytes*), seem to have no particular function.

**APRON**   A pronounced skin fold located on the lower throat in certain species of *Bufo*, which rests upon the folds of the VOCAL SAC when it is deflated.

**AQUA-TERRARIUM**   Type of housing used for amphibious or aquatic amphibians and reptiles. An aqua-terrarium, in contrast to a straightforward aquarium, always has a land area on which the occupants can find shelter or bask etc.

**ARACHNID**   Any one of a class of invertebrates which includes the scorpions, spiders, ticks and mites. Both ticks and mites (ACARIDS) are of significance in herpetology as they are common parasites of reptiles. *See also* ACARIASIS.

**ARBOREAL**   Living in or amongst trees. The term applies also to species that inhabit scrub, bush or rainforest etc.

**ARCTOGAEA**   A major region comprising the four northern zoogeographical regions of the Earth: the ETHIOPIAN, ORIENTAL, PALAEARCTIC and NEARCTIC regions. The Palaearctic and Nearctic regions are occasionally called the HOLARCTIC region as the fauna occurring in both is similar.

**ARENICOLOUS**   Living in sand or inhabiting sandy places. Used to describe such desert species as the sandfish (*Scincopus fasciatus*) and horned vipers (*Cerastes*).

AREOLA   1. A region of small elevated and rounded lumps on the skin, frequently seen on the belly in certain species of frogs, when it is sometimes referred to as 'granular'.   2. The central region of a LAMINA on the shell of a chelonian. It can be either raised or hollow and is the granular juvenile scute from which new growth extends outwards.

ARID   Having little or no rain and referring to the typical climate of a particular region, which decides the state of the soil and flora and fauna within that region.

ARID TROPICAL SCRUB   *See* TROPICAL ARID FOREST.

ARRENOIDISM   Used to describe the condition in which females possess characteristics which are normally typical attributes of males. In *Bothrops insularis*, for example, a proportion of reproducing females have been found to have a HEMIPENIS.

ARRIBADA   A concurrent, mass emergence of marine turtles on to a beach to deposit their eggs.

ARTIFICIAL INSEMINATION   The artificial introduction of semen into the reproductive tract of a female by means other than sexual union. This method has been used successfully in the captive breeding of certain, so-called 'difficult' species where the animals have refused, for one reason or another, to reproduce naturally.

ASCAPHIDAE   Tailed toads. Family of the ANURA, inhabiting Pacific North America. MONOTYPIC.

ASCAROIDEA   Internal parasitic roundworms of the class NEMATODA. Although they are common in many lizards they are mainly found in the BOIDAE (the boas and pythons).

ASCORBIC ACID   Vitamin C present especially in citrus fruits, tomatoes and green vegetables and required in the diet of certain captive reptiles.

ASPECT   The compass direction in which an area of land faces. Reference to the aspect of an area is a significant element in the description of its habitat, particularly in respect of egg-laying sites and HIBERNATION quarters.

ASPERITY   A roughened surface or outgrowth, sometimes used as an alternative to NUPTIAL PAD in male anurans.

ASSERTION DISPLAY   A somewhat weak and casual display in certain lizard species which is not always aimed at another of its own species and, indeed, frequently occurs when no other individuals are present.

**ATELOPODIDAE**   Family of the ANURA, suborder Procoela, inhabiting Central and South America. Over 30 species in two genera.

**ATLASSING**   The collection of information on the distribution of reptiles and/or amphibians in a particular region for use in the compilation of an atlas.

**ATROPHY**   The reduction in size of an organ or part, as a result of disease, poor nutrition or lack of use. The legs and feet of slow-worms (ANGUIDAE) have, for example, through the course of evolution, become atrophied as the lives of these lizards have become more subterranean.

**AURICULAR**   1. Of, or relating to, the auricles of the heart.   2. Of, or relating to, the ear and generally relating to external features. In many lizards the auriculars are modified scales that protrude over the front of the ear opening.

**AURICULAR FOLD**   The fold of skin, which often has spines or enlarged knoblike projections, that lies behind or over the ears of certain lizards.

**AURICULAR LOBULES**   The small projecting scales on the front edge of the ear opening in some skinks. *See also* AURICULAR.

**AUSTRALASIAN REGION**   One of the six zoogeographical regions of the world. Subdivided into three subregions, Australasia consists of the New Zealand subregion; Papua–Polynesian subregion (New Guinea and other South Sea Islands, of which Fiji and the Solomons are herpetologically important); and continental Australian subregion (including Tasmania).

**AUTOCHTHONOUS**   Opposite of ALLOCHTHONOUS. The existence of an animal (or plant) species within its HOME RANGE. The American bullfrog (*Rana catesbeiana*) is autochthonous in its natural range of eastern North America, but in the southern European Alps and Cuba, it is ALLOCHTHONOUS.

**AUTOHAEMORRHAGE**   Self-induced bleeding brought about by the intentional bursting of blood vessels and the rupture of outer surfaces. When boid snakes of the genus *Tropidophis* are threatened or disturbed, blood is oozed from membranes of the nostrils and mouth. Lizards of the genus *Phrynosoma* can eject blood from vessels in the corners of their eyes if they too are provoked or disturbed.

**AUTONOMOUS**   Self-regulating. Used, in Herpetology, to describe reptile or amphibian populations that maintain their numbers independently of outside influence.

AUTOTOMY   Self-division or fracture; the ability to cast off, spontaneously or by reflex, a part of the body and, in Herpetology, usually referring to breakage and loss of the tail. Many lizards and certain urodeles can autotomize their tail if it is seized. In most cases a new tail is grown later, though never quite as perfectly as the original.

AUTOTOMY PLANE   *See* BREAKAGE PLANE.

AVITAMINOSIS   *See* HYPOVITAMINOSIS.

AXIAL BIFURCATION   The duplication of a part of the body along its length, sometimes occurring in chelonians and lizards but most commonly in snakes.

AXILLARY (AXILLARY LAMINA)   The cuticular SCUTE or scutes on the frontal border of the BRIDGE in chelonians.

AXILLARY EMBRACE   *See* PECTORAL AMPLEXUS.

AXILLARY GLAND   A glandular region, noticeable on the chest of pelobatid frogs of the genus *Megophrys*, at the insertion of the forelimb. In *M. hasselli* the gland is flat and rounded, and in *M. monticola* it is tubercle-like and cone-shaped.

AXILLARY LAMINA   *See* AXILLARY.

AXILLARY NOTCH   The indentation in the chelonian shell through which the forelimb extends.

AXOLOTL   The name, of Aztec origin, for any of the several larval salamanders of the family Ambystomidae which inhabit certain Mexican lakes. These larvae may live and breed as larvae (NEOTENY), but, under certain conditions, are capable of resorbing their fins and gills, and finally emerging from the water as air-breathing adult salamanders.

AZYGOUS   Occurring singly. Frequently used in reference to the plates, other than the normal ones present, on the heads of lizards and snakes, e.g., the third INTERNASAL in the genus *Heterodon*, the hognosed snakes (termed 'azygous scale' by various authors).

# B

BACK-FANGED *See* REAR-FANGED.

BAIRD, Spencer Fullerton 1823–87, American naturalist responsible for establishing the herpetological collection at the national Smithsonian Institution in Washington DC. Co-wrote many publications with Charles F. Girard, including *Catalogue of North American reptiles* (1853).

BALANCER *See* STABILIZER.

BALL POSITION A defensive position assumed by certain snake species, including the burrowing python (*Calabaria reinhardtii*), in which the body is coiled tightly into a ball. The tip of the tail is protruded from the coils and, in some cases, waved about in order to distract a potential enemy's attention from the vital and otherwise vulnerable head which is kept hidden in the centre of the ball.

BAND (CROSSBAND) A particular pattern of skin colour that is darker or paler than the ground colour and which transverses the vertebral line. A band may or may not extend onto the ventrals, and may sometimes completely encircle the body. *See also* RING.

BANDY BANDY *Vermicella annulata*, a small nocturnal, burrowing member of the family ELAPIDAE, subfamily Elapinae, inhabiting most regions of Australia except southern Western Australia, northern parts of the Northern Territory, and the far south-east. A striking snake banded with black and white rings which usually encircle the entire body.

BARBA AMARILLA *Bothrops atrox*, one of the largest and most notorious species of PIT VIPER in the world. A member of the family VIPERIDAE, subfamily Crotalinae, inhabiting Central and South

America, and reaching up to 2400 mm in length. Responsible for a high incidence of snake bite throughout its range. Often wrongly referred to as the FER DE LANCE.

BARBEL    Any one of several small, fleshy downward-pointing projections on the throats and chins of certain chelonians, e.g., *Kinosternon*, functioning as a tactile organ. Such barbels also occur on the perimeter of the mouth in larvae of *Rhinophrynus* toads.

Fleshy, sensory barbels occur on the chins and throats of some chelonian species and their presence or absence can be important in the identification of these reptiles.

BARBOUR, Thomas    1884–1946, American zoologist and director of Harvard University's Museum of Comparative Zoology. Initiated, with Leonard Stejneger, the *Checklist of North American amphibians and reptiles* (1917).

BASIHYAL VALVE    The lower of two muscular folds, or plicae, in the rear of the mouth of a crocodilian. Its function, in combination with the upper fold (VELUM PALATI), is to prevent water from entering the glottis when the mouth is opened below the surface.

BASILISK    1. A legendary monster, part snake and part cock; a cockatrice or fabulous reptile hatched by a serpent from a cock's egg, the glance and breath of which were supposed to be fatal.    2. An American lizard of the family IGUANIDAE, genus *Basiliscus*.

BASKING    A rather loose term used to describe the behaviour of a reptile or amphibian when exposing itself to the direct or diffused rays of the sun. THERMOREGULATION may or may not take place during periods of basking which are used for other functions, such as attaining a high body temperature, allowing greater mobility and aiding digestion.

BASKING RANGE    The temperature range within which basking reptiles are mostly inactive whilst still remaining watchful. At the top of this range is the VOLUNTARY MAXIMUM temperature, or the thermal point at which the reptile becomes either uncomfortable and seeks shade or sufficiently warmed to carry out its normal activities. At the lower end of the range is the VOLUNTARY MINIMUM, the point where the reptile either seeks direct sunlight and more warmth or retires below ground in order to hibernate, for example.

BATRACHIAN   An archaic term for any amphibian, especially a toad or frog; of the class Batrachia.

BEAD   The slender, outwardly directed curve on the front side rim of a rattlesnake RATTLE that is shaped in such a way as to prevent splitting and acts also as a sound-making mechanism as it strikes the segment next to it when the tail is vibrated.

BEAK   The horny covering (RHAMPHOTHECA) of the jaws or the horny beak-like mouthparts of tadpoles.

BELL   An individual segment of a rattlesnake's RATTLE.

BELL GILL   The greatly enlarged gill, which acts as a respiratory-exchange surface, in tadpoles of certain hylid frogs, including *Gastrotheca* and *Cryptobatrachus*, which have a BROOD POUCH on their backs in which they carry their larvae.

BELL, Thomas   1792–1880, English zoologist. Published the definitive *Monograph of the Testudinata* (1836–42) containing plates by Edward Lear and James de Carle Sowerby.

BELLAIRS, Angus d'Albini   1918–90, the father of herpetology in Britain. Taught embryology in the University of London at St Mary's Hospital Medical School and was Honorary Herpetologist to the Zoological Society of London. He produced numerous papers, particularly on the adaptations of vertebrates and their embryos to the problems of their environment. His books include *Reptiles* (1957), *The world of reptiles* (1966), with Richard Carrington, and the two-volume *The life of reptiles* (1969).

BELLY   The abdomen; the entire undersurface, or VENTER.

BEZOAR STONE   A hard mass such as a hairball or stone occurring in the stomach. Formerly greatly prized as a medicine, bezoars were frequently used in the treatment of SNAKE BITE. Goats were once reared especially for these much sought-after stones.

BIBRON, Gabriel   1806–48, French herpetologist. Co-authored, with André Duméril and his son Auguste Duméril, the ten-volume *Erpetologie generale ou Histoire naturelle complete des reptiles.*

BICARINATE   *See* CARINATE.

BICEPHALOUS (DICEPHALOUS)   Having two heads. A phenomenon sometimes seen in reptiles, particularly snakes, where two fully-functional heads are present on the same body.

BICOLOUR (BI)   Literally 'two colour'; usually relating to snake patterns characterized by alternating RINGS or BANDS of dark (generally black) and light (red, yellow or white), usually red as in the coral snake *Micrurus mipartitus*.

BIENNIAL BREEDING CYCLE   The breeding cycle occurring in the females of certain snake species generally in temperate climates where conditions compel some of them to breed every 2 years.

BIFID   Divided into two rounded projections, or lobes, by a deep central cleft.

BIFURCATED   Divided into two branches, or forked, e.g. the tongue of all snakes and some lizards (VARANIDAE).

BINOCELLATE   Having two eye-like spots, as on the rumps of certain leptodactylid frogs, e.g., *Telmatobius praebasalticus* and *Physalaemus nattereri*, which display them to frighten potential enemies.

BINOCULAR VISION   A type of vision in which the eyes are directed forwards so that the image of an individual object can be focused on the retinas of both eyes simultaneously, thus granting perception of distance and depth. Snakes of the genus *Dryophis* have large, prominent eyes giving them acute three-dimensional vision with the ability to detect the slightest movement.

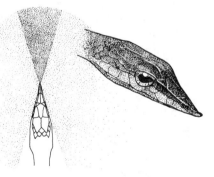

The Asian long-nosed tree snake (*Dryophis nasuta*) has large prominent eyes and a long narrow snout which permit the fields of vision of its eyes to overlap, giving it excellent three-dimensional, binocular vision essential for detecting slight movements and judging distances. The area of dark stippling represents the snake's field of binocular vision.

BINOMIAL NOMENCLATURE   A system for naming animals (and plants) by means of two Latin names, the first indicating the GENUS and the second the SPECIES to which a particular organism belongs, as in *Elaphe guttata* (the corn snake).

BIOGEOGRAPHY   The branch of biology dealing with the geographical distribution of animals and plants, subdivided into animal geography (ZOOGEOGRAPHY) and plant geography, or geobotany.

BIOLOGICAL CLOCK   The ENDOGENOUS mechanism of an organism that produces regular periodic alterations in behaviour or body functions that are synchronized with environmental conditions only triggered by outside factors, as in HIBERNATION, when reptiles kept under artificial conditions either stop or reduce their food intake for a while during the months when they would be hibernating in the wild.

BIOME   A major ecological community extending over a large area and generally characterized by a dominant vegetation: SAVANNA, TUNDRA etc.

BIOTOPE   The specific ecological area where an animal, or animals, live, such as a, river bank, gravel pit, sand dune etc.

BIOTYPE   A group of animals within a species, occurring in the wild state, that resemble, but differ physiologically from, other members of that species.

BIPEDAL   Having two feet; a term used to describe lizards that can stand or run on their hind limbs with their forelimbs held off the ground, as in the frilled lizard (*Chlamydosaurus kingii*).

BIPEDIDAE   Two-legged worm lizards. Family of the SQUAMATA, suborder Amphisbaenia, inhabiting western Mexico. Three species in one genera.

BIRTH PLATE   The LAMINA in chelonians that is present on the shell during the period of hatching and which, in certain species, is shed a short while after hatching, whilst in others it survives as an area encircled by GROWTH RINGS.

BISHOP, Sherman C.   1887–1951, American herpetologist. Author of *Handbook of salamanders* (1943).

BLEB   A small blister containing blood or serum, frequently found on the ventral scales of snakes which are housed in conditions which are too damp. Untreated it can soon develop into a BULLA which in turn can lead to secondary, and sometimes fatal, infections of the skin.

BLOOM   *See* IRIDESCENCE.

BOCOURT, Marie-Firmin 1819–1904, French herpetologist. Worked for the Paris Natural History Museum as a field herpetologist in Mexico, Central America and Thailand, and was partly instrumental in compiling the reptile section of *Mission scientifique au Mexique et dans l'Amerique Centrale: Etudes sur les reptiles et les batraciens* (1870–1909), with Brocchi, Mocquard and Duméril.

BODY CAVITY   *See* COELOM.

BODY GROOVE   A lateral fold in the body surface of certain reptiles and amphibians.

BOIDAE   Pythons and boas. Family of the SQUAMATA, central order Henophidia, inhabiting the tropical and subtropical parts of the world. Over 95 species in some 23 genera in seven subfamilies.

BOJANUS, Ludwig Heinrich 1776–1827, Lithuanian zoologist at Vilnius University. Produced the significant monograph *Emys, anatome testudinis Europaeae* (1819).

BOLUS   A small, soft pellet or lump of faecal matter.

BONY STYLE   The presence of OSSIFICATION in the unpaired, central and hindmost section of the PECTORAL GIRDLE.

BOREAL FOREST   A type of vegetation occurring in a climatic zone which has cold, snowy winters and short warm summers, characterized by a flora dominated by hazels and pines.

BOSS   An elevated swelling or rounded area; a knob-like protuberance; in certain toads of the BUFONIDAE, a rounded eminence on the mid-line of the head between the eyes, or on or near the tip of the snout.

BOULENGER, George Albert 1858–1937, Belgian zoologist. Worked in London at the British Museum (Natural History) where he compiled the *Catalogue of the snakes in the British Museum (Natural History)* which was produced in separate volumes (1882–96). Contributed over 600 papers to many scientific journals. Books include *The tailless batrachians of Europe* (1897 & 1898).

BOURRET, Rene 1884–1950, French herpetologist. Author of several works on South-East Asian reptiles, including *La Faune de l'Indochine: reptiles* (1927) and *Les Serpentes de l'Indochine* (1936).

BRACHIAL   Relating to, or located on, the upper or humeral part of the forelimb; a term for any of the scales on the humeral part of a lizard's forelimb, or brachium.

BRACHYCEPHALIDAE   Short-headed toads. Family of the ANURA, inhabiting south-east Brazil. Two species in two genera.

BRACKISH   Describing a body of water that is slightly briny or salty. Brackish water is often necessary for the successful development of certain amphibian larvae, as in the natterjack toad (*Bufo calamita*).

BRANCHIA   The external gill in aquatic animals, e.g., the larvae of amphibians. Branchial, or branchiate, animals are furnished with gills, or branchiae.

BRANCHIAL FISSURE   A single GILL SLIT on the side of the neck in certain aquatic urodeles, such as *Amphiuma*, which are without external gills.

BRAZIL, Vital Mineiro da Campanha   1865–1950, South American herpetologist and medical practitioner, founder of the Butantan Snake Serum Institute in Brazil where antivenins against the bites of many venomous snake species were developed.

BREAKAGE PLANE (AUTOTOMY PLANE, BREAKING POINT, FRACTURE PLANE)   The SEPTUM, or dividing partition of soft tissue that passes through the centre of a tail vertebra and along which separation, or breakage, occurs in AUTOTOMY.

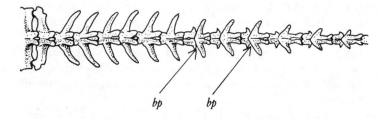

*bp*          *bp*

Breakage or fracture planes (*bp*) in the centre of some vertebrae of a lizard's tail assist separation during the shedding of the tail in autotomy.

BREAKING POINT   *See* BREAKAGE PLANE.

BREATHING PORE   *See* SPIRACLE.

BREHM, Alfred Edmund   1829–84, German zoologist. Director of Hamburg Zoo from 1863 and, in 1869, established the Berlin Aquarium where much importance was placed on the amphibian and reptile collections.

BRIDGE   The part of the shell in chelonians that joins the upper (CARAPACE) and lower (PLASTRON) sections.

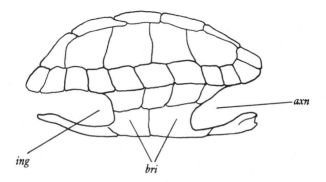

The bridge of a chelonian's shell links the carapace to the plastron: *axn*, axillary notch; *bri*, bridge; *ing*, inguinal notch.

BRILLE   The transparent scale that covers the eye in all snakes and some burrowing lizards. Also called SPECTACLE and, less commonly, WATCHGLASS.

BRISTLE   *See* TACTILE BRISTLE.

BROAD-SPECTRUM LIGHTING   In herpetology, normally used in relation to vivarium lighting equipment that can emit light which is as close as possible to the quality of natural sunlight.

BROAD-SPECTRUM VERMIFUGE   Any one of a number of drugs that are extremely effective in expelling or destroying intestinal worms from different groups and, in many cases, their larval stages.

BROOD   1. To sit on, incubate, or hatch, eggs. Used in reference to snakes of the BOIDAE, subfamily Pythoninae, the females of which coil about their eggs during the period of incubation.   2. To remain with and protectively care for, or cover, eggs. Used in reference to certain lizards and many amphibians, especially salamanders of the PLETHODONTIDAE family.

BROOD CARE   The attention given to eggs and young. The different types of brood care seen in reptiles and amphibians are wide and varied and range from the travelling of hundreds of kilometres to find a particular nesting site, as in the marine turtles, and the brooding of the egg clutch, as seen in some python species, to the protection of the nest and eggs, and even assistance in the hatching of the young, in certain crocodilians.

**BROOD POUCH**   Any pouch, cavity or sac in an animal's body in which eggs can be placed and remain whilst they develop until they hatch. The female Surinam toad (*Pipa pipa*) has many such brood pouches on her back into which her eggs are embedded. In the females of certain hylid frogs, such as *Gastrotheca*, the brood pouch takes the form of one enlarged sac into which the whole clutch of eggs is placed.

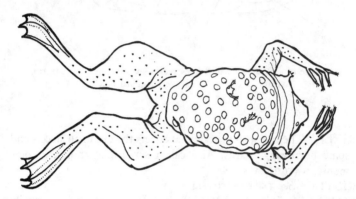

The female Surinam toad (*Pipa pipa*) deposits her eggs in numerous cells, or brood pouches, on her back where they remain throughout their development until they emerge as tiny replicas of their parents.

**BRUMMATION**   A condition of torpor during extended periods of low temperatures; a state of inactivity during which the metabolic processes are greatly reduced but without actual HIBERNATION.

**BUCCAL**   Of, or relating to, the cheek or mouth.

**BUFONIDAE**   True toads. Family of the ANURA, inhabiting most parts of the world except Madagascar, the Arctic and Antarctic regions and New Zealand, as well as many Pacific islands. Introduced into Australia and New Guinea (*B.marinus*). Over 200 species in 20 genera.

**BUFOTOXIN**   One of several TOXINS occurring in secretions from the PAROTOID and many other glands of toads, particularly those of the genus *Bufo*, which act as extremely effective defence mechanisms.

**BULL**   Male; the masculine name for many animals and, in herpetology, used for an adult male crocodilian or chelonian.

BULLA   A large blister, normally greater than 20 mm in diameter, typically containing serum or blood. *See also* BLEB.

BUSHMASTER   *Lachesis muta*, a PIT VIPER of the family VIPER-IDAE, subfamily Crotalinae, inhabiting the tropical rainforests of southern parts of Central America, the southern half of the South American mainland and Trinidad. Although very dangerous it occurs away from human habitation. MONOTYPIC.

BUTTOCK TUBERCLE   The enlarged, conical scale, or SPUR, located on the rear upper part of the leg of some chelonians, e.g., *Testudo graeca*.

BUTTON   1. The first and smallest permanent rattle segment acquired by a JUVENILE rattlesnake. As the snake matures the button usually breaks off. At birth, rattlesnakes possess a 'prebutton' which is lost when they have their first shedding, exposing the button.   2. The bony OSTEODERM present in the scales of many crocodilians. Those crocodiles and alligators that have osteoderms are characterized by having single buttons, one osteoderm button per scale, while all caimans have double buttons, two osteoderms per scale.

# C

CABLE   The jelly-like flexible string in which certain plethodontid salamanders affix their eggs to submerged objects.

CADUCIBRANCHIATE   Possessing transitory gills; said of an amphibian having gills which are lost as it changes from LARVA to ADULT at METAMORPHOSIS.

CAECILIIDAE   Caecilians. Family of the Amphibia, order APODA (or Gymnophiona), inhabiting the tropics, with the exception of Australia and Madagascar. Over 100 species in 26 genera.

CAESARIAN DELIVERY   A term used in herpetology in reference to the manual opening of an egg and removal of the embryo, executed only when the safety of the embryo is thought to be at risk, as for example when the embryo of a post-term egg is suspected of being too weak to hatch without assistance.

CAIMAN   Any one of a group of tropical American crocodilians of the genera *Paleosuchus*, *Caiman* and *Melanosuchus*, belonging to the family ALLIGATORIDAE. Similar to alligators but having a more heavily armoured belly.

CALCANEUM, CALCANEUS   The largest tarsal bone in vertebrates, corresponding to the heel in man. The elongated calcaneum of anurans is joined at both ends to the astragalus, forming the additional segment in the hind limb.

CALCIUM   A soft silvery-white metallic element that is an essential constituent for all living organisms, being necessary for normal growth and development. Calcium is an important component of teeth and bones and is present in the blood, where it is required for muscle contraction and other metabolic processes.

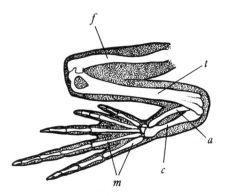

A simplified section of an anuran's left hind limb showing the position of the calcaneum: *a*, astragalus; *c*, calcaneum; *f*, femur; *m*, metatarsal; *t*, tibiofibula.

CALCIUM CYCLE  Reproductively active female day geckos of the genus *Phelsuma* go through a calcium cycle which involves the storing of calcium in the endolymphatic sacs, noticeable as whitish swellings on either side of the neck, and its subsequent deposition as egg shell.

CALCULE  Any one of a number of small, outward–curving, smooth scales occurring on the back of the Chinese crocodile lizard (*Shinisaurus*).

CALIPASH  The greenish glutinous part of the marine turtle found beneath the CARAPACE and considered a delicacy.

CALIPEE  The yellow glutinous part of the marine turtle found beneath the PLASTRON and considered a delicacy.

CALL  The loud trill, whistle, chirp or song of an anuran. In most species it is only the males which call, although the females of a few species also have a certain VOCALIZATION.

CALLUS  A raised area of hard or horny skin; used generally in reference to the lower surfaces of the digits. The TUBERCLE on the foot of an anuran.

CAMBRIAN  The earliest period of the PALAEOZOIC, which occurred from approximately 590 million to 510 million years ago, and was characterized by the appearance of algae and many invertebrates, particularly marine forms such as trilobites.

CANKER (STOMATITIS)  Commonly called 'mouth rot' and occurring in lizards and, more frequently, snakes; an ulceration particularly of the labial region and oral cavity linings.

CANNIBALISM   The act of feeding upon the flesh of the same species. In reptiles and amphibians cannibalism can result from a number of factors, including overpopulation and/or lack of food. In captivity, if two snakes grasp the same food item, the larger will often devour the smaller, although this is usually considered to be accidental; adults also will occasionally look upon their young as prey. Close confinement in vivaria which are too small may encourage such behaviour. A special type of cannibalism is to be found in the tadpoles of certain species of anuran, such as *Hoplophryne*, in which, because they live in water having only a limited supply of food, the majority are devoured by those which are larger and stronger.

CANTHAL   Any one, or all, of the scales located along the upper surface of the CANTHAL RIDGE. The canthals lie behind the level of the PRENASAL and POSTNASAL suture and in front of the SUPRAOCULAR. When the canthals are large and in contact along the mid-line, they are referred to as PREFRONTALS.

CANTHAL RIDGE (CANTHUS ROSTRALIS)   A ridge separating the side of the snout from the top of the head along the line from the tip of the snout to the eye. It may be sharply angular or gently rounded.

CANTHUS ROSTRALIS   *See* CANTHAL RIDGE.

CANTIL   Mexican moccasin (*Agkistrodon bilineatus*), a PIT VIPER of the family VIPERIDAE, subfamily Crotalinae, inhabiting swamps, lowland forests and cane fields from southern Mexico southwards through Guatemala, El Salvador, Nicaragua, Honduras and Belize.

CAPTIVE BREEDING   The breeding and rearing of one or more species under controlled conditions.

CAPTIVE DISTURBANCE   Psychological and physical disturbances of captive reptiles and amphibians can be directly attributed to specific conditions within their vivaria, or to events experienced by the animals during capture and/or transportation, as when psychological shock or physical damage results in newly caught animals refusing to feed. Incorrect captive conditions can also result in other disturbances, such as vitamin deficiency deformations and stunted growth.

CARAPACE   In reptiles of the order Chelonia (turtles, terrapins, tortoises), the domed dorsal part of the shell composed of platelike bones covered on the outside by horny plates, or SCUTES. In some turtles, such as the soft-shelled (TRIONYCHIDAE), it is completely bony with a layer of skin covering it. The thoracic vertebrae and ribs are included in the carapace, but the girdles of the limbs are separate and situated inside the carapace. The flatter underpart of the shell is termed the PLASTRON.

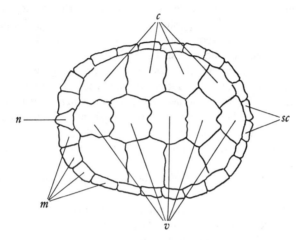

The dorsal view of a chelonian carapace showing a typical arrangement of the horny laminae or scutes: *c*, costal; *m*, marginal; *n*, nuchal; *sc*, supracaudal; *v*, vertebral.

CARBONIFEROUS   The second most recent period of the PALAEO-ZOIC, from approximately 350 million to 280 million years ago, characterized by the appearance on swampy land of amphibians, several primitive reptiles and giant ferns.

CARETTOCHELYIDAE   Fly River turtle. Family of the CHELO-NIA, suborder Cryptodira, inhabiting southern New Guinea (Fly River), Australia (Daly River). MONOTYPIC.

CARINATE   Having carinas, or keels, as seen in the scales of certain lizards. (Bicarinate: having two keels. Tricarinate: having three keels.)

CARNIVOROUS   Feeding entirely upon the flesh of animals.

CARPAL   1. A bone in the distal region of the forelimb of tetrapods, situated between the RADIUS and/or ULNA and the META-

CARPALS.   2. A scale in reptiles situated on the forefoot between the digits and the wrist joint. To indicate scale position the term is often used with a prefix: 'infra-', 'sub-', 'supra-' etc.

CARR   Woodland growing in waterlogged conditions with characteristic flora and fauna and often home to a variety of reptiles and amphibians.

CARUNCLE   In herpetology, the sharp, horny tubercle on the tip of the snout in baby turtles, crocodilians and rhynchocephalians, used to cut a slit in the egg shell at the time of hatching. The prominence is not a true tooth and differs from the calcified EGG TOOTH found in the hatchlings of snakes and lizards.

CASCABEL, CASCAVEL   *Crotalus durissus*, a tropical rattlesnake of the family VIPERIDAE, subfamily Crotalinae, inhabiting mainland South America from southern Mexico to northern Argentina.

CASQUE   The helmet-like structure consisting of thickened skin and/or bone on the heads of certain lizards (e.g., CHAMAELEONIDAE, IGUANIDAE), and amphibians (e.g., casque-headed tree frog, *Tetraprion*).

CASTING CYCLE   The period between each skin shedding or ECDYSIS.

CASTINGS   The undigested, matted remains (bones, hair, feathers etc.) of prey that are regurgitated occasionally by large reptiles such as crocodilians, monitors (VARANIDAE) and large snakes.

CATADONT   Having teeth only in the lower jaw.

CATERPILLAR MOVEMENT   *See* RECTILINEAR MOVEMENT.

CAUDAL   Pertaining to the tail or region of the tail; any pattern, plate, scale or structure on or near the tail of a reptile or amphibian.

CAUDAL DISC   The large, blunt, wrinkled, flattened, elliptical or circular region on the end of the tail occurring in certain snake species especially those of the UROPELTIDAE.

CAUDAL FIN   A vertically flattened, membranous appendage on the upper and sometimes lower surfaces of the amphibian tail acting as an organ of locomotion and balance when swimming.

CAUDATA   Tailed amphibians, also known as the Urodela, containing the newts, salamanders and related forms. An order of the Amphibia, the tailed amphibians are almost entirely confined to the northern hemisphere.

CAUDO–CEPHALIC WAVE   During courtship between snakes, when the male and female are lying close to each other side by side, a wave-like horizontal undulation begins near the vent and ripples forward towards the head, becoming more pronounced as the male moves over and on top of the female and creating light contacts between their bodies. The wave is normally produced in the male snake only and appears to act as a stimulus to encourage the female to mate.

CEMENT ORGAN An alternative term for ADHESIVE ORGAN.

CENOZOIC The present geological era that began some 70 million years ago. Subdivided into two periods, the TERTIARY and the QUATERNARY, the Cenozoic is characterized by the rise of modern organisms, the flowering plants and mammals in particular.

CENTRAL Used in reference to any one of the row of large laminae (usually five) running unpaired down the centre of the CARAPACE in chelonians.

CENTROLENIDAE Glass frogs. Family of the ANURA, suborder Procoela, inhabiting the cloud and rainforests of Ecuador and Columbia in tropical America. 65 species in three genera.

CEPHALIC PLATE Any one of the enlarged scales on the top of the head in reptiles.

CERVICAL Of, or relating to, the neck or cervix.

CESTODA Tapeworms. Class of flatworms (Platyhelminthes) which are parasitic as adults and larvae in both amphibians and reptiles. They lack a mouth and gut and their bodies are divided into many egg-producing segments.

CHAMAELEONIDAE Chameleons. Family of the SQUAMATA, suborder SAURIA, inhabiting Africa, Madagascar, south Asia and southern Europe. 85 species in two genera. (Occasionally spelt Chamaeleontidae.)

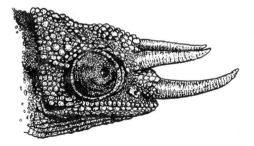

Chameleon: the three-horned chameleon (*Chamaeleo jacksoni*).

**CHECKLIST**   A list of species from a certain area or taxonomic group, or both, sometimes including identification keys, with space provided so they can be marked off as they are seen.

**CHELIDAE**   Side-necked turtles. Family of the CHELONIA, suborder Pleurodira, inhabiting Australia, New Guinea and South America. 40 species in nine genera.

**CHELONIA**   The order of reptiles containing the tortoises, turtles and terrapins. The order is divided into two families: CHELONIIDAE (the sea turtles), and TESTUDINIDAE (the freshwater turtles and land tortoises).

**CHELONIIDAE**   Sea turtles. Family of the CHELONIA, suborder Cryptodira, inhabiting much of the world's oceans from the tips of the southern continents northwards almost to Scandinavia. Eight species in four genera.

**CHELYDRIDAE**   Snapping turtles. Family of the CHELONIA, suborder Cryptodira, inhabiting southern Canada into the eastern USA. Two MONOTYPIC genera.

**CHERNOV**, Sergeï Alexandrovitch   1903–64, Russian herpetologist at the Academy of Science's Zoological Museum in Leningrad. Contributed papers on the Tadzhikistan and Armenian reptiles and amphibians and worked on the amphibian section in *Animal world of the USSR* (1936–1953). With Terent'ev, he co-authored the *Key to the reptiles and amphibians of the USSR* (1949).

**CHICKEN**   The name commonly applied to a juvenile green turtle (*Chelonia mydas*).

**CHINSHIELD**   Any one of the large, paired, elongated scales situated immediately behind the first pair of infralabials on either side of the mid-line on the lower jaw of snakes. Chinshields are always in pairs, with a single pair most often occurring in snakes. In lizards they are the series of paired scales on the mid-line of the lower jaw, behind the MENTAL scales.

**CHOANA**   A funnel-like opening. Used in reference to the hindmost internal openings of the nasal passages in the roof of the mouth.

**CHORIO-ALLANTOIC PLACENTA**   The membrane caused by the uniting of the ALLANTOIS and the CHORION in reptiles having VIVIPARITY. The membrane acts as a form of placenta by allowing a certain amount of exchange between the circulations of the adult and the FOETUS.

**CHORION**   One of the three membranes that are formed during the embryo's development within the egg, and which envelops and protects both yolk sac and embryo.

CHROMATOPHORE A pigment cell of the skin; a specialized body cell that contains the pigment which largely decides the coloration of an animal.

CILIARY The small scales that border the edge of the eyelid in crocodilians and lizards. When describing the upper and lower ciliaries the prefixes 'supra-' and 'infra-' are used respectively.

CIRCADIAN RHYTHM A cycle of behaviour and biological processes that occurs regularly at 24-hour intervals in animals that are normally influenced by internal 'clocks', but which is synchronized to time-related factors from their surroundings. Well defined in many reptiles and amphibians. *See also* PHOTOPERIOD.

CIRCUMNASAL In the CROCODILIA, any one of the row of scales that encircle the nasal protuberance. Also used to describe the enlarged scales, other than the ROSTRAL and LABIAL scales, surrounding the nostril in the geckos (GEKKONIDAE).

CIRRI Projections which descend from the nostrils in the males of some lungless salamanders. The NASOLABIAL GROOVE reaches downward close to the tip of each cirrus.

CLASPING REFLEX The voluntary contractive and spasmodic grasping of any object by a male anuran when touched on the underside of the forelimb or in the region of the chest, during periods of mating activity. The European common toad (*Bufo bufo*), for example, will frequently clasp the fingers of a person if a hand is slowly lowered into the water amongst males awaiting female mates. Not only does it aid the anurans in sex recognition, it also serves to guarantee a male's presence when the female deposits her eggs.

CLASS The category in taxonomy which ranks between the PHYLUM and the ORDER. All reptiles are placed in the class REPTILIA and all amphibians in the class AMPHIBIA.

CLASSIFICATION The cataloguing of living things into systematic groups. *See* TAXONOMY.

CLAVICLE A bone that forms part of the PECTORAL (shoulder) GIRDLE linking the SCAPULA to the STERNUM. The clavicle is generally quite prominent in *Sphenodon*, lizards and anurans, but is frequently much reduced or absent altogether.

CLEIDOIC EGG An egg having a tough, protective shell which allows gaseous exchange but which restricts water loss (although water may be absorbed). Cleidoic eggs are characteristic of reptiles exhibiting OVIPARITY.

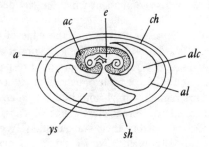

Diagrammatic layout of the various parts of the cleidoic egg: *a*, amnion; *ac*, amniotic cavity; *al*, allantois; *alc*; allantoic cavity; *ch*, chorion; *e*, embryo; *sh*, shell; *ys*, yolk sac.

CLINE   A continuous and gradual change of a variable characteristic between members of a species over a given ecological or geographical range.

CLITORIS   In certain reptiles, an erectile rod of tissue that is the female equivalent of the male penis.

CLOACA, pl. CLOACAE   The common chamber into which the genital, urinary and digestive canals release their contents, and which opens to the exterior through the anus or VENT.

CLOACAL BONES   A pair of small bones, each of which lies in a cavity directly behind the VENT, on either side of the tail, in geckos and snake lizards (GEKKONIDAE and PYGOPODIDAE).

CLOACAL CAPSULE   The thickened cloacal wall in females of certain snake species in which the male HEMIPENIS is densely covered with spines. The cloacal capsule can be felt under gentle finger pressure as a small, firm lump and is therefore useful in determining the sex of an individual.

CLOACAL GAPING   The sexual activity occurring in the females of certain snake species consisting of raising the tail and everting the cloaca indicating receptivity to males.

CLOACAL GLAND   1. The MUSK GLAND of crocodilians and certain chelonians   2. Part of a large, cylindrically-shaped gland surrounding the opening to the anus in male urodeles. The gland discharges into the CLOACA via PAPILLAE lining the cloacal wall.

CLOACAL POPPING   A form of defensive action employed by a few North American snakes (e.g., the western hooknosed snake, *Ficimia cana,* and the coral snakes, *Micruroides euryxanthus* and *Micrurus fulvius*) in which the CLOACA is rapidly extruded and withdrawn, resulting in an audible bubbling or popping sound whilst the writhing tail is held aloft.

CLOACAL PROBE   Any tapered, blunt, smooth instrument inserted caudally, after lubrication with a non-spermicidal fluid such as tap water or sterile saline, into the CLOACA of a snake in order to determine its sex.

The sex of a snake can often only be determined with any certainty by inserting a cloacal probe into either of the two lumina at the base of the tail. Such probes are generally made of stainless steel and should be lubricated before insertion.

CLOACAL SPUR   *See* ANAL SPUR.

CLOACAL SWELLING   In urodeles, the swollen region around the vent, especially noticeable in breeding adults.

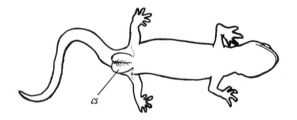

The cloaca in many urodeles (newts and salamanders) often swells noticeably in sexually mature adults, especially males: *cs,* cloacal swelling.

**CLOUD FOREST**   A montane forest characterized by frequent heavy mists, high humidity, cool temperatures and dense, luxurious plant life, normally occurring on the windward slopes of tropical mountains and usually at heights above 1000 m.

**CLUTCH**   Collective noun for the full complement of eggs laid by a single female at one time.

**CNEMIAL**   In crocodilians, any one of the large and sometimes flap-like scales that project on the hindmost fringe of the fore- and hind limbs.

**COCCIDIOSIS**   A protozoan disease that affects cells of the alimentary canal and the blood, most often in juveniles, particularly those of chameleons and snakes; caused by parasitic organisms of the order Coccidia.

**COCCYGEAL STRIPE**   A stripe running longitudinally across the centre of the rump in some frogs and normally referring to a stripe that only crosses that area of the vertebral column to the rear of the SACRUM.

**COCHLEA**   Part of the inner ear of certain reptiles that converts sound waves into nerve impulses.

**COCHRAN, Doris M.**   1898–1968, American herpetologist, Curator of the Division of Reptiles and Amphibians of the United States National Museum, Smithsonian Institution in Washington DC. Published some 80 scientific and popular articles and described five new genera and 90 new reptile and amphibian species. Other publications include *Poisonous reptiles of the world: A wartime handbook* (1943), *Living amphibians of the world* (1961), and *The new field book of reptiles and amphibians* (1970).

**COELOM**   Snakes, lacking a diaphragm, have no abdomen but instead possess a fluid-filled abdominal cavity, or coelom. The presence of a coelom allows separation of the gut from the body wall, providing greater mobility and specialization, and requiring the development of a blood-vascular system. It contains the digestive tract and visceral organs.

**COITUS**   A technical term for copulation, or sexual union.

**COLD-BLOODED**   At one time used to describe all amphibians and reptiles and, although still used today, the term is now generally considered to be unsuitable, particularly for reptiles, many of which may sometimes have body temperatures far above that of so-called 'warm-blooded' animals inhabiting the same region. *See also* HOMOIOTHERM, POIKILOTHERM.

COLLAR 1. A transverse fold of skin on the undersurface of the neck in certain lizards, normally covered with enlarged scales. *See* GULAR FOLD. 2. A band of colour across the nape of the neck, as in the North American collared lizard (*Crotaphytus collaris*).

COLORATION Fixed chiefly by chromatophores in the skin. Reptiles and amphibians generally possess only yellow, red and brown-black colour pigments. Varying shades of blue and green are caused via layering, refraction and scattering of light. Animal coloration often acts as camouflage by softening and breaking up the hard outline of the contours of the body, and gives a certain degree of protection against ultraviolet rays from the sun. Striking and bright colours are frequently found in many poisonous amphibians and venomous reptiles.

COLUBRID Any snake of the family COLUBRIDAE. Although the majority are harmless to man, many species possess enlarged teeth on the rear of the MAXILLA, or upper jaw, and a few species produce venom which is strong enough to cause death in man. *See* OPISTOGLYPH.

COLUBRIDAE Typical snakes. Family of the SQUAMATA, central order Caenophidia, inhabiting every geographical region. Over 2000 species in some 320 genera.

COMB 1. In desert lizards, a fringe consisting of numerous slender, elongated scales on the lateral border of the toes. 2. A term given to the FEMORAL PORES of male lizards in breeding condition, which may exude a wax-like substance and which, when viewed from below, give the appearance of teeth on a comb.

COMPENSATION MOVEMENT The condition, seen in amphibians and reptiles, in which the head faces an imaginary, fixed point as the body of the animal is moved. A toad, if placed upon a slowly revolving turntable, will move its head in the opposite direction to which it is being revolved. As the strain on its neck becomes too much, it will shift its position, enabling it continually to fix its gaze on the same point.

CONCAVE Curving inwards like the inside of a sphere; hollow. In herpetology, used in reference to the PLASTRON of certain male chelonians. Compare CONVEX.

CONCEALED SURFACE Any body surface which is normally hidden when an animal is at rest. These surfaces are frequently marked with striking colours which are suddenly revealed when the animal is alarmed or aroused, thus startling the intruder.

CONCERTINA MOVEMENT   A type of locomotion occurring in snakes in which the animal progresses via a series of alternate contractions and extensions of the body, giving it an accordion-like appearance as it moves across a surface. The movement is similar to that of a looper caterpillar (family Geometridae), but the folding of the body takes place in the horizontal plane rather than the vertical.

CONGENERIC   Of the same genus. Species placed in a particular genus are called 'congeners'.

CONGENITAL   Present at birth. The term describes, or relates to, any defect, deformity or abnormal condition existing at birth. The occurrence of some congenital abnormalities, such as cleft palate, is determined by environmental as well as hereditary factors.

CONICAL   Descriptive of an elevated scale or LAMINA that narrows to a pointed centre.

CONJUNCTIVITIS   An infection of the conjunctiva of the eyes but, in herpetology, normally used to specify a more generalized eye infection, often revealed by an eye discharge.

CONSPECIFIC   Pertaining to individuals or populations of animals belonging to the same species.

CONSTRICTION   The method employed by some snakes to kill their prey in which the victim is squeezed and suffocated.

CONSTRICTOR   In general, any of the giant snakes, such as the pythons and boas, but used to describe any snake which squeezes its prey to subdue or kill it.

CONVERGENCE   The state in which two unrelated species or groups, in the course of evolution, have developed a superficial resemblance to each other or similar adaptations to their environment, even though they are not closely related and may be widely separated geographically. The situation (convergent evolution) occurs when the conditions in which the animals live are similar.

CONVEX   Curving outwards like the outside of a sphere. Used, in herpetology, when referring to the shells of chelonians. *See* CONCAVE.

COPE, Edward Drinker   1840–97, American herpetologist, prolific author of over 1260 publications including *The Batrachia of North America* (1889), *Classification of the Ophidia* (1895), and *The crocodilians, lizards and snakes of North America* (1900). The American Society of Ichthyologists and Herpetologists named their journal *Copeia* in honour of his important work.

COPULATION   The act of sexual union, also called 'coition', which leads to the fertilization of the egg by male sperm.

CORACOID   Either one of the pair of cartilage bones that, in reptiles, form the ventral side of the PECTORAL GIRDLE and which, with both scapulae, form the articulation surfaces for the forelimbs.

CORDON   A term for an individual string of eggs in toads of the genus *Bufo*.

Bufonid toads lay eggs in a string, or cordon (left), whilst typical frogs lay eggs in clumps.

CORDYLIDAE   Girdle-tailed lizards, plated lizards and related species. Family of the SQUAMATA, suborder SAURIA, inhabiting Africa and Madagascar. Approximately 60 species in ten genera.

CORIACEOUS   Of, or resembling, leather and often used as a descriptive of the eggs of many reptiles and the skin of soft-shelled turtles (TRIONYCHIDAE).

CORNEAL LAYER   *See* STRATUM CORNEUM.

CORNUATE   Said of an animal having one or more horns or horn-like structures. Lizards of the genus *Phrynosoma* (the horned 'toads') are cornuate.

Cornuate reptiles have one or more horn-like projections on their heads or bodies. The North American *Phrynosoma* lizards are excellent examples.

CORONOID   A bone in the lower jaw of some reptiles.

CORYPHODONT   Having teeth that increase in length from the front of the mouth to the rear.

COSMOPOLITAN   Distributed throughout every ZOOGEOGRAPH-ICAL REGION of the world.

COSTAL   A plate on the CARAPACE of a chelonian situated between the VERTEBRAL and MARGINAL laminae and covering the PLEURAL bones.

COSTAL GROOVE   Any one of several grooves on the flanks of many urodeles. The area of skin between each groove is called the costal fold.

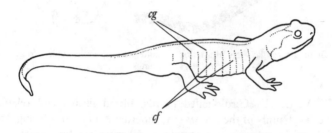

Diagram of a salamander showing the position of the costal grooves (*cg*) and costal folds (*cf*).

COUNTERSUNK   Sunk below the margins of; e.g., the lower jaw of many burrowing snakes which fits securely within the margins of the upper jaw.

COURTSHIP   The establishment of pair-bonding, accomplished by various types of display and largely genetically fixed behaviour, which serve to break down aggression between the sexes and encourage sexual interest. Courtship in amphibians and reptiles is extremely varied and contains specific and ritualistic displays associated with both special coloration and body decoration, as well as with stimulation from touch, smell and sound.

COW   A sexually mature female terrapin.

COWL   A hood, particularly a loose-fitting one, like that of a monk's habit. Used in some literature for the hood of a cobra.

CRANIAL   Of, or relating to, the skull.

CRANIAL CREST    A raised ridge on the top of the head of certain toads, between the eyes (interorbital) or behind the eyes (postorbital). In the toad *Bufo terrestris*, the cranial crest is enlarged and swollen and called the cranial 'club'.

The size, shape and position of the cranial crests situated on the top of the head of certain toad species can be an important feature in their identification.

CRANIUM    The bony part of the skull which encloses the brain.

CREPUSCULAR    Active at dusk and/or just before dawn.

CREST    Any elevated, flexible, cutaneous ridge or fold on the tails and/or backs of many lizards, and which, in the breeding season, develops on the tails and/or backs of male urodeles.

CRESTAL    Any one of a number of enlarged, convex and sharply keeled scales which shape the dorsal crests of the Chinese crocodile lizard (*Shinisaurus*).

CRETACEOUS    The final and most recent period of the MESO-ZOIC, from 135 million to 65 million years ago, marked by the continued domination of both land and sea by the dinosaurs until their rapid and widespread extinction at the end of that period. Aquatic and flying reptiles also became extinct during the later part of the Cretaceous.

CROAK    The low, hoarse, raucous sound made by male anurans. The sound is normally made with the mouth closed whilst air is forced in and out of the lungs and into the VOCAL SAC or sacs.

CROAK REFLEX    A particular response in male anurans when grasped by other males, in which the one grasped utters a low warbling croak which causes the sides of the body to quiver rapidly, making the other release its hold. If the individual grasped is a female, no croak is uttered, the hold is continued and spawning takes place.

CROCODILIA   The order of reptiles containing the crocodiles, caimans, alligators and gharials.

CROCODILIDAE   Family of the CROCODILIA inhabiting the tropics and found in every continent except Europe. 13 species in three genera.

CROSSBAND   Used to describe an area of colour crossing the body from side to side across the back and reaching down to the VENTER but, unlike a RING, not actually joining.

CRUS   That section of the hind limb between the knee and the ankle containing the FIBULA and TIBIA.

CRYPTIC COLORATION   The coloration of an animal that blends with the surroundings, providing it with camouflage and enabling it to remain hidden amongst the vegetation or upon the ground on which it rests.

Many reptiles and amphibians exhibit cryptic coloration which helps them to merge with their background. The strikingly coloured gaboon viper (*Bitis gabonica*) is very obvious against a plain background but amongst the leaves and debris of the forest floor becomes 'invisible'.

CRYPTOBRANCHIDAE   Hellbenders, giant salamanders. Family of the CAUDATA, inhabiting the south-eastern Palaearctic and eastern Nearctic. Three species in two genera.

CRYPTODIROUS   Descriptive of chelonians that are able to retract the head into the CARAPACE by means of an S-shaped bend in the vertebral column and pertaining to any member of the suborder Cryptodira.

CRYPTOSPORIDIOSIS   An important protozoal disease occurring in lizards and snakes, caused by an internal parasite of the genus *Cryptosporidium*. The parasite, a type of coccidian, has a direct life cycle and can pass directly from one host to another. Symptoms include weight loss and mucus–covered regurgitated food. Untreated, death usually follows in a matter of months.

CRYPTOZOIC  Inhabiting secluded and/or dark places, beneath stones, logs and other debris, or in holes and caves.

CUIRASS  The hard, outer protective armour of bony shields and plates in crocodilians.

CUSP  A toothlike projection, as on the jaw of a chelonian.

CUTANEOUS  Pertaining to the cutis, or skin. *See* INTEGUMENT.

CYANOMORPH  A colour phase (MORPH) in which the dominant colour is blue.

CYCLOID  Descriptive of a reptile scale possessing an evenly curved, free border.

Reptilian scales come in many shapes and sizes. Those which possess a free, rounded edge are termed 'cycloid' and are characteristic of many skinks and burrowing forms, such as the blind snakes of the family Typhlopidae.

CYCLOPIA  A birth defect in which only one eye is present, often situated in an abnormal position.

CYCLOTREME  Having a rounded anal orifice, a characteristic of crocodilians and chelonians.

CYST  Usually, any abnormal membranous sac or blisterlike pouch containing semi–solid matter or fluid, but also sometimes referring to the thick–walled protective membrane enclosing an organism or cell larvae, e.g., the larvae of some molluscs encyst in tadpoles.

# D

**DAGGER** An enlarged, sharp, spinelike projection on the inside of the forefoot of certain anurans. It is essentially a long pointed bone, situated where the thumb (absent in most anurans) should be and covered only by skin. In the frog *Babina holsti*, the daggers serve as effective weapons and are capable of drawing blood from a human hand if the animal is handled carelessly. The structure is also found in the genus *Petropedates* and, besides defence, may also assist the male to grasp a female at the time of mating.

**DAMAGE FIGHT** In contrast to RITUAL COMBAT, a fight resulting in severe to fatal injuries to one, or sometimes both animals. In a community of captive lizards such damage fights can occur over the establishment and/or defence of an individual's territory within the vivarium, or during courtship.

**DANCE** In reference to snake-charming, the swaying, side-to-side movements of an alert cobra in which the head and front part of the body is raised from the ground and the hood spread. The cobra 'dances' in response to the charmer's rhythmical body movements and not the music, as is often supposed by onlookers.

**DAUDIN, Francois Marie** 1774–1804, French herpetologist who collaborated with Lacépède and Buffon on the *Histoire naturelle des reptiles* (1802).

**DEATH FEINT** A defensive reflex action in many amphibians and reptiles in which a position similar to that of a dead specimen is adopted. The action is displayed very well in the hognosed snake (genus *Heterodon*) which, when excited or disturbed, rolls onto its back and remains motionless with mouth agape and tongue protruding, recovering its normal posture once the disturbance has ceased. In some species, the feint is evoked by touch whilst in others it is assumed without any external stimuli.

DEFENCE–FIGHT REACTION  A method of intimidation in some toads, directed towards a predator, in which the limbs are extended, raising the inflated body off the ground, and the head thrust forward in the direction of the threat.

DEFENCE REACTION  When most anurans are provoked or suddenly disturbed, a defence reaction is evoked in which the lungs are filled with air, inflating the body, and the head bowed low.

DEGLUTITION  The act of swallowing.

DELAYED FERTILIZATION  *See* AMPHIGONIA RETARDA.

DENDROBATIDAE  Arrow- or dart-poison frogs. Family of the ANURA, inhabiting Central America and tropical South America. 116 species in three genera.

DENTARY  One of the major bones of the lower jaw. The dentary is found in all reptiles and amphibians and, in the snakes, lizards and crocodilians, bears the teeth (lacking in anurans and chelonians) of the lower jaw.

DENTARY PSEUDO-TEETH  Tooth-like structures at the tip of the lower jaw in some anurans. In the tusked frogs (genus *Adelotus*), these structures form two canine-like projections (tusks) on the lower jaws of the males.

DENTICULATE  Very finely toothed; anything having toothlike or sawlike projections.

DENTITION  The number, type, arrangement and physiology of teeth in a particular species. In reptiles and amphibians, the arrangement of teeth may be ACRODONT, PLEURODONT or THECODONT and, in snakes, may be aglyphic, OPISTHOGLYPHIC, proteroglyphic, SOLENOGLYPHIC etc.

DERMAL LAYER  The layer of skin beneath the EPIDERMIS that contains the blood vessels, nerve endings etc. of the skin.

DERMAL PLATE  Any one of the LAMINA on a chelonian shell.

DERMAL TUMOUR  *See* POX.

DERMATEMYDIDAE  Central American river turtle. Family of the CHELONIA, suborder Cryptodira, inhabiting Central America from Mexico to Honduras. MONOTYPIC.

DERMATITIS  In the captive husbandry of reptiles, a condition in which the skin becomes inflamed and which is usually caused by keeping animals in incorrect conditions, e.g., substrate too damp, humidity too high etc. In NECROTIC dermatitis the skin, particularly that of the belly (VENTER), blisters and later sloughs away. *See also* THERMAL BURN.

DERMOCHELYIDAE   Leatherback turtle. Family of the CHELONIA, suborder Cryptodira, inhabiting waters from around New Zealand to within the Arctic Circle. MONOTYPIC.

DEROTREMATOUS   Descriptive of urodeles which, when they become adults, lose their gills whilst retaining the gill slits.

DESERT   A region that is completely, or almost, lacking any vegetation due largely to extremely low rainfall. True deserts have a very sparse fauna, although they are inhabited by several reptiles and anurans.

DETOGLOSSAL   Having part of the border of the tongue fastened to a certain part of the lower jaw and therefore not free as in ADETOGLOSSAL salamanders. Most amphibians are detoglossal.

DEVONIAN   The geological period which began some 405 million years ago in the PALAEOZOIC era, between the SILURIAN and the CARBONIFEROUS periods, and was characterized by a tremendous variety and number of fish, most of which have become extinct. The Devonian period lasted until about 355 million years ago and saw the appearance of the first amphibians.

DEWLAP   A pendulous fold or flap of skin under the throat of some lizards and usually referring to the often extensible dewlap occurring in members of the IGUANIDAE which can, in some genera, be raised or lowered by the action of the HYOID BONE (well-developed in *Anolis*) during various behavioural displays.

DIAPSID   Descriptive of a skull in which there are two TEMPORAL openings. Found in all modern reptiles except the CHELONIA.

DIBAMIDAE   Blind lizards. Family of the SQUAMATA, suborder SAURIA, inhabiting north-eastern Mexico (one species) and South-East Asia, from Indo-China and the Malayan peninsula, Indonesia, and the Philippines to New Guinea. Some 10 species in two genera.

DICEPHALOUS   Possessing two heads. *See also* BICEPHALOUS.

DICHROMATIC   A species having two different colour varieties that are independent of both age and sex.

DIDACTYL   Having two digits, fingers or toes, on a foot, as in the South African lizard *Chamaesaura anguina*, for example.

DIGGER   The enlarged TUBERCLE on the hind foot of toads of the PELOBATIDAE; the SPADE of spadefoot toads.

Certain lizards such as the green iguana (*Iguana iguana*) have prominent
skin folds, or dewlaps, beneath their chins and on their throats, which
are frequently used in display.

DIGIT   A finger or toe. Characteristically, there are five digits in
the basic limb structure of terrestrial vertebrates, each made up of
a series of small bones (phalanges). There are however, some modifications to this plan and in many species the number of digits is
reduced. Some lizards, for example, may only have two or three digits on each foot, and crocodilians have five on their forefeet and
only four on the hind feet.

DIGITAL   Any scale on the digits of both the fore- and hind feet,
situated between the palm or sole and the claw. To show the rel-
evant position of a scale on a digit, the term is supplemented with
a prefix such as 'pre-' or 'post-' etc.

DIGITAL EXPANSION   In lizards of the GEKKONIDAE, that section of the toes, and fingers, that is more or less clearly larger or
wider.

**DIGITAL FRINGE**   The enlarged, free-edged scales along the lateral margins of the longer digits of certain desert-dwelling lizards giving a toothlike aspect to the toe border.

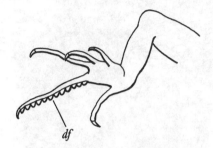

A number of desert-dwelling lizard species have a digital fringe (*df*) of large scales on the side of one or more of the longer toes, enabling them to travel over loose sand.

**DIGITAL PAD**   Either of the paired fleshy structures located on the upper surface of the tips of the digits in certain dendrobatid and ranid frogs and in bufonid toads.

**DIGITAL TREMOR**   The extremely rapid toe vibration which occurs in toads (*Bufo*) when watching or chasing a prey item. Male toads also vibrate the toe of their hind foot against that of the female's during AMPLEXUS.

**DIGITAL WEB**   The membrane connecting the digits, as in the hind feet of crocodilians and anurans and in the fore- and hind feet of marine and freshwater turtles etc.

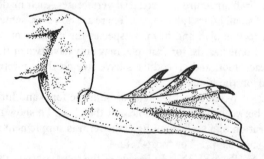

The majority of aquatic reptiles and amphibians have full or partial digital webs linking several or all of the toes, aiding rapid movement through the water.

DIMORPHISM   *See* SEXUAL DIMORPHISM.

DINOSAUR   Any of the large, extinct terrestrial reptiles that were abundant during the MESOZOIC era and which were the dominant land animals for 140 million years.

DIPHYCERCAL TAIL   The type of tail occurring in the larvae of such amphibians as frogs and toads, in which the vertebral column extends to the tip with symmetrical caudal fins above and below it.

DIRECT DEVELOPMENT   The absence of a larval stage, occuring in certain amphibians, which eliminates the many dangers of an aquatic development. Found in various frog and salamander genera throughout the world, the eggs hatch into tiny replicas of their parents, each with adult form and features.

DISC   The circular, flat and enlarged adhesion surface on the tips of the digits in many arboreal lizards and amphibians, enabling them to grip smooth vertical surfaces.

DISCHARGE ORIFICE   The opening near the tip of the fang of a venomous snake through which the venom from the VENOM DUCT is injected into the tissues of a bitten animal.

DISCOGLOSSIDAE   Midwife toads, fire-bellied toads and related forms. Family of the ANURA, inhabiting the PALAEARCTIC, the Philippines and Borneo. There are 11 species in four genera.

DISPERSAL   The distribution, for various reasons (e.g., territorial, climatic), of individual members, pairs or groups of species through a given area. Dispersal in many reptiles and amphibians occurs at the end of the breeding season when territory is forsaken and they move outwards from the breeding place either in a clearly defined direction or at random.

DISPLAY   The obvious, showy and usually ritualized behaviour pattern, seen in courtship and territorial defence etc., that can affect the behaviour of other animals at which the display is directed. Display in reptiles is often enhanced by the aid of various body structures: the hood in cobras (*Naja*); dewlap in iguanas (*Iguana*); the tongue in blue-tongued skinks (*Tiliqua*).

DISRUPTIVE COLORATION   Colours which confuse the eye by disrupting the shape or outline of an animal against its surroundings; camouflage; CRYPTIC COLORATION. An example is well displayed by the gaboon viper (*Bitis gabonica*), the striking colours of which cause it to 'disappear' when lying on the forest floor.

DISRUPTIVE OUTLINE   A particular shape which confuses the eye by disrupting the shape or outline of an animal when seen against its surroundings. An example is well displayed by the Asian horned frog (*Megophrys*), the shape of which helps to conceal it as it sits amongst the leaves of the forest floor.

An Asian horned frog (*Megophrys monticola*) displaying its disruptive outline as it sits amongst the leaves on the forest floor.

DISTAL   Describing the part of a limb, organ or appendage etc. that is located farthest from the centre, median line, or point of attachment or origin. Compare PROXIMAL.

DISTENSION   Swelling, inflation or expansion, as occurs in the throats of male anurans when making their CALL, or in the throats of many snakes when swallowing large food items.

DISTRIBUTION   The location, or occurrence, of a species, also known as its 'range', and usually referring to the pattern formed when plotted on a map.

DISTRIBUTIONAL BARRIER   Referring to an ecological or geographical obstacle or barrier that, for particular animal groups, cannot be overcome, thereby preventing their DISPERSAL and the subsequent extension of their range. Deserts, mountain ranges, oceans and large lakes are distributional barriers.

DITMARS, Raymond Lee   1876–1942, American herpetologist. Worked as Curator of Mammals and Reptiles at New York's Bronx Zoo. Undertook many expeditions and successfully bred many of the animals he collected. One of the first to popularize herpetology in North America, his publications include *Snakes of the world* (1931), *Snake-hunters' holiday* (1935, with W. Bridges), *The reptiles of North America* (1936), *Field book of North American snakes* (1939).

DIURNAL   Active during the daylight hours.

DIURNAL RHYTHM   Any activity cycle in an organism that is related to biological processes which occur regularly at 24-hourly intervals. *See also* BIOLOGICAL CLOCK; CIRCADIAN RHYTHM.

DIVERGENT EVOLUTION   The gradual development, through evolution, of a number of different varieties or species of animals (or plants) from a common ancestor, each adapting to new habitats and different sources of food. *See also* ADAPTIVE RADIATION.

DIVERSITY   *See* SPECIES DIVERSITY.

DOME   The term given to the attitude adopted by female fence lizards (genus *Sceloporus*), which is usually stimulated by the appearance of males and in which the body is raised off the ground on stiffened legs, bending the back into a hump, or 'dome', frequently supplemented with short, jerky jumps.

DOMINANCE   The community hierarchy between and within species (the peck order) and referring to the social standing of an individual within a group. A dominant lizard, for example, is one that is allowed priority in access to food, mates etc. by other members of its species as a result of its size, strength or success in previous aggressive encounters.

DORSAL   Relating to the upper surfaces; the back or spinal part of the body.   1. Any one of the enlarged scales on the upper surface of the body of crocodilians.   2. Any one of the scales on the backs of lizards.   3. Any one of the scales on the upper surface of the body of most snakes (i.e., all scales except the VENTRALS).

DORSOLATERAL   Referring to markings, colours, scales, appendages etc., which are not directly down the centre of the back, nor on the side of the body, but more or less between the two.

DORSOLATERAL FOLD   In certain anurans, a longitudinal, glandular ridge located between the centre of the back and the side of the body.

DORSUM   Of, or relating to, the upper surface of an animal; e.g., the dorsum of the neck is the NAPE.

DOUBLE-CLUTCHING   Said of many reptiles that produce two clutches of eggs or young in the same season (i.e., within one year).

DRACO   The flying lizards, genus of the AGAMIDAE, inhabiting the Indo-Australian Archipelago, South-East Asia and the Philippines, in some 20 species. Identified by the characteristic skin folds (WINGS) on each side of the body which, when spread, form gliding membranes enabling the lizards to glide for distances of over 20 m between trees.

DRAW   To extract the fangs from a venomous snake. Snake-charmers in many parts of the world sometimes render their animals temporarily harmless by drawing their fangs prior to a display.

DUCT   Any bodily tube, channel or passage through which a fluid, especially a secretion or excretion, moves, e.g., VENOM DUCT.

DUD   The term for an unlaid egg in which embryonic development has ceased for one reason or another, causing it to shrivel and harden within the OVIDUCT.

DUGITE   *Pseudonaja affinis*, an extremely dangerous and aggressive snake of the family ELAPIDAE, inhabiting the south-western corner of Western Australia and extending eastwards along a narrow strip of coast to the South Australian border.

DUMÉRIL, André Marie Constant   1764–1860, French herpetologist and anatomist. Published the first comprehensive and systematic work on the reptiles and amphibians in the form of the impressive ten-volume *Erpetologie generale ou Histoire naturelle complete des reptiles*, in co-operation with Gabriel Bibron and, in part, his son, Auguste H.A. Duméril.

DUMÉRIL, Auguste H.A.   1812–70, son of the distinguished herpetologist, André M.C. Duméril. Compiled, in collaboration with Brocchi, Mocquard and Bocourt, the 17-volume systematic work entitled *Mission scientifique au Mexique et dans l'Amerique Centrale: Etudes sur les reptiles et les batraciens* (1870–1909), which became the foundation for Latin-American herpetology thereafter.

DUNN, Emmet Reid   1894–1956, American herpetologist. Publications include *Salamanders of the family Plethodontidae* (1926), *American frogs of the family Pipidae* (1948).

DUPLICATION   Referring to the copying or multiplication of different parts of the body as a result of genetic interferences. Duplication in several forms has occurred in amphibians, urodeles in particular, examples of which include an individual with two heads, two individuals with one head, and specimens with extra limbs.

DUVERNOY'S GLAND   The venom-producing gland of rear-fanged colubrid snakes, usually situated between the eye and the angle of the mouth; named after the French anatomist, D.M. Duvernoy.

DYSTOCIA   Difficulty in giving birth to young or laying eggs. In the case of the latter, the animal is said to be suffering from EGG-BINDING.

# E

EARDRUM  *See* TYMPANUM.

EAR FLAP  Either one of the large upper or small lower skin folds situated at the outer opening of the auditory canal of crocodilians. When the reptile is submerged the flaps are kept tightly shut, preventing water from entering the hearing organs. On land, the upper flap is lifted, revealing a narrow transverse opening which admits sound.

EARTHWORM MOVEMENT  Alternative term for the CONCERTINA MOVEMENT of snakes.

ECARINATE  Descriptive of scales or laminae which do not bear a keel and are therefore entirely smooth.

ECDYSIS  The act of periodically shedding the outer layer of dead, keratinous skin, the STRATUM CORNEUM, to permit further growth in both reptiles and amphibians.

ECOLOGICAL FACTOR  Referring to any one of a number of environmental elements important in the lives of reptiles and amphibians, such as competitors, enemies and parasites, as well as food, water, humidity, temperature etc.

ECOLOGY  The study of animals and plants in relation to their environment and to each other.

ECOSYSTEM  The system involving the entire environment in which an animal lives and the interactions between the living community of plants and animals with the non-living entities and the elements.

ECOTONE  The transition zone between two ecological communities. A woodland edge, for example, is an ecotone separating an open heathland habitat from a forest habitat, along with the particular reptile and amphibian communities which they support.

ECTOGLYPH 1. A venomous snake possessing fangs which are located at the front of the mouth, with channelled grooves down which venom flows into the tissues of the victim. 2. A snake possessing teeth which are located at the rear of the mouth, with channelled grooves.

ECTOPARASITE Any parasite, such as a tick or mite (order Acarina), which attaches itself to the outer part of the body of its host in order to extract nourishment from blood vessels.

ECTOPARASITOSIS Symptoms of disease resulting from infestation with an ECTOPARASITE, which can be a VECTOR of a number of diseases affecting reptiles.

ECTOTHERM (COLD-BLOODED, POIKILOTHERM) An animal having a constant self-regulated body temperature and dependent entirely upon outside heat sources.

EDAPHIC Of, or related to, the ground. The chemical and physical composition of the soil, together with other factors, such as its temperature and water content, play a significant role in the lives of reptiles and amphibians, from egg deposition in, or upon, the soil, to hibernation below ground.

EDENTULOUS Without teeth, referring in particular to the condition of having lost teeth which were once present.

EFT An antiquated, dialectal, or local name for any of the various small semi-aquatic urodele amphibians, e.g., the European smooth newt (*Triturus vulgaris*), and, in many regions, particularly their immature larvae.

EGG-BINDING A condition occurring in reptiles in which eggs fail to be laid and are retained within the oviduct. Causes include physical abnormality or damage and incorrect environmental conditions.

EGG CALLUS *See* EGG TOOTH.

EGG ENVELOPE The jelly-like membrane that surrounds the egg in amphibians.

EGG MASS The whole amount of eggs deposited, in a clump or string, by a single amphibian female. *See* SPAWN.

EGG-RETENTION *See* EGG-BINDING.

EGG SAC The protective membrane which adheres to the eggs of certain urodeles, e.g., *Ambystoma*, *Salamandrella*, as they pass through the oviduct.

EGG TOOTH   The forward-pointing, foetal tooth located on the end of the premaxillary bone in snakes and lizards, used in breaking through the egg shell at birth. The egg tooth is deciduous and falls off shortly after hatching.

ELAPID   Any snake of the mainly tropical family ELAPIDAE possessing fixed venom–conducting fangs at the front of the upper jaw. The family includes the mambas, cobras and coral snakes.

ELAPIDAE   Cobras and their allies. Family of the SQUAMATA, suborder Caenophidia, inhabiting most regions of the world except the HOLARCTIC. Over 160 species in over 50 genera.

ELECTRO-EJACULATION   The collection of sperm from a male reptile by means of a mild electric current, and for use in ARTIFICIAL INSEMINATION.

ELLIPTICAL   Of, or having the form of, an ellipse (a closed curve in the form of a flattened circle), and used to describe the VERTICAL pupils in many reptiles and amphibians.

EMACIATION   The condition seen in some captive, or recently imported, reptiles and amphibians indicative of inadequate metabolism or hastened energy loss and dehydration, as a result of incorrect husbandry, injury or shock, or a combination of these factors.

EMARGINATE   Pertaining to a border that is notched or scalloped in outline and used, in herpetology, to describe an arrangement where the edge of a scale cuts into the otherwise smooth border of a larger one.

EMBRACE   *See* AMPLEXUS.

EMBRYONIC DEVELOPMENT   The progress of the early stages of an animal (embryo), beginning with fertilization of the egg cell and ending at birth or hatching.

EMYDIDAE   Freshwater turtles. Family of the CHELONIA, suborder Cryptodira, inhabiting all continents except Australia. 136 species in some 30 genera.

ENCAPSULATED   Enclosed in a capsule, or membrane, such as the embryo of an amphibian.

END-BODY   *See* MATRIX.

ENDEMIC   Descriptive of an animal (or plant) that is restricted to a biogeographic region, or part of it, and, in some cases, originating there.

ENDOCRINE GLAND   Any one of the glands in an animal that produce hormones and secrete them directly into the bloodstream, including the PITUITARY GLAND, TESTIS and OVARY etc., and collectively form the 'endocrine system'.

ENDOGENOUS Internally; coming from, or developing from, within the animal. Growth rhythms which are not regulated by various environmental stimuli are called 'endogenous rhythms'. Compare EXOGENOUS.

ENDOGLYPH 1. A venomous snake possessing fangs which are located at the front of the mouth, with closed grooves through which venom flows into the tissues of the victim. 2. A snake possessing teeth, located at the front of the mouth, with closed grooves.

ENDOPARASITE Any parasite, e.g., a FLUKE or TAPEWORM, that extracts nourishment from the internal parts of the body of its host.

ENDOPARASITOSIS Symptoms of disease resulting from an infestation with an ENDOPARASITE which can affect the internal organs of reptiles and amphibians.

ENDOSKELETON The internal skeleton of an animal, e.g., the bony or cartilaginous skeleton of vertebrates, which supports the body, protects the vital organs, and provides a system of levers on which muscles can act and produce movement. The endoskeleton consists of a skull, vertebral column, pectoral and pelvic girdles, ribs, and limb elements, and permits growth in the animal.

ENDOTHERM An animal that maintains a constant body temperature via inherent, internal heat sources; a warm-blooded animal or HOMOIOTHERM.

ENDYSIS A term used occasionally to describe the formation of a new epidermal layer. Compare ECDYSIS.

ENEMY REACTION A particular response, in defensive or flight behaviour, evoked by stimuli from a predator or rival, or other threat to the safety of an animal. Examples of enemy reaction among reptiles and amphibians include the DEATH FEINT, hoodspreading in cobras, and the assuming of the BALL POSITION in many snakes, among others.

ENTAMOEBIASIS *See* AMOEBIASIS.

ENTERIC Of, or in, the intestinal cavity. Many parasites are enteric in reptiles and amphibians.

ENTEROLITH A stone or concretion found in the intestine. *See* BEZOAR STONE.

ENTOPLASTRON The only single, centrally located bone in the

PLASTRON of most chelonians. Diamond-shaped, it occurs between and surrounded by the paired EPIPLASTRON and HYOPLASTRON bones.

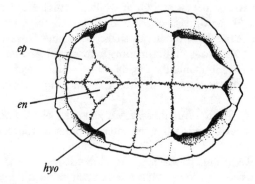

A ventral view of the shell of a chelonian showing the position of the bony entoplastron: *en*, entoplastron; *ep*, epiplastron; *hyo*, hyoplastron.

**ENVENOMATION**   Having VENOM injected into the tissues of the body, as in a case of a venomous SNAKE BITE.

**ENVIRONMENT**   The entire surroundings and range of conditions in which an animal or plant lives, including biological, chemical and physical factors, such as light, temperature, humidity and the availability of water, food etc., which more or less influence its behaviour and development.

**ENZOOTIC**   Pertaining to diseases which affect animals within a limited region. Compare EPIZOOTIC.

**EOCENE**   The second oldest geological epoch of the TERTIARY period, this lasted for some 20 million years, from 55 million to 38 million years ago, and was characterized by the predominance of early hoofed mammals (the ungulates), although many others, including early horses, rodents, carnivores and whales, were also making an appearance.

**EPANODONT**   Having teeth on the lower jaw only, the upper jaw bones being EDENTULOUS.

**EPICORACOID CARTILAGE**   A rear component of the CORACOID cartilage bones in the PECTORAL GIRDLE.

**EPIDEMIOLOGY**   The branch of science that deals with the incidence, transmission, distribution and control of epidemic diseases in a population.

EPIDERMIS   The outermost protective layer of cells of the body of an animal. In vertebrates it consists of several layers of cells and forms the external layer of skin, protecting the underlying tissues and ensuring that the body is waterproof. As it is worn away at the surface it is continuously replaced, in the MALPIGHIAN LAYER immediately beneath, by the growth of new cells (ECDYSIS and ENDYSIS, in reptiles and amphibians).

EPIDIDYMIS   The long narrow coiled tube, derived from part of the embryonic kidney, attached to the surface of the TESTIS in male reptiles, which serves as a temporary storage organ for spermatozoa until their release to the exterior, via the VAS DEFERENS, during mating.

EPIPLASTRON, pl. EPIPLASTRA   Either one of the foremost pair of bones of the PLASTRON of a chelonian. (In the plastron of soft-shelled turtles (TRIONYCHIDAE), the bone is not paired and is generally referred to as the ENTOPLASTRON.

EPIPODIAL   Referring to any one of the bones of the lower forelimb (forearm) or the lower hind limb (lower leg), i.e., the RADIUS and ULNA (forelimb); FIBULA and TIBIA (hind limb).

EPIPTERYGOID BONE   Either one of two vertical struts that support the bones of the palate in lizards.

EPIPYGAL   *See* SUPRAPYGAL.

EPIZOIC   Growing or living on the exterior of a living animal. Ticks and mites, of the order Acarina, are epizoites, living on reptiles.

EPIZOOTIC   Pertaining to a disease that suddenly and temporarily affects a large number of animals. Compare ENZOOTIC.

EREMIAL   Any region in which the predominant weather conditions, particularly low rainfall and adverse winds, prevent the growth of scrub and tree cover. For example, rocky deserts, heathlands, prairies etc. are eremial regions and all are good habitats for many reptile species and certain amphibians.

ERYTHRISM   An excess of reddish pigment in an individual or population compared with its normal species coloration. An erythristic individual is a colour phase in which the dominant colour is red, giving it an ABERRANT appearance.

ESCUTCHEON   In the males of certain gekkonids (*Eublepharis*), an area of ventral scales, directly in front of the VENT and on the undersurfaces of the hind limbs, that are specialized, thick and frequently sharply contrasting in colour to the other VENTRAL scales. It is less noticeable in females.

ETHIOPIAN REGION   One of the six zoogeographical regions of the world, contrived in conformity with land-animal distribution. The Ethiopian region is made up of Africa south of the Sahara and the Malagasy subregion, which consists of Madagascar, the Mascarenes, Seychelle Islands and the southern tip of the Arabian Peninsula. Reptiles and amphibians are well represented in the region in widely distributed and diverse forms and almost all of the CHA-MAELEONIDAE occur in it.

ETHOGRAM   A detailed record and description of every aspect of behaviour within a particular species, observed in the field or in captivity, which, when published, can help greatly to extend present knowledge of an animal's behavioural characteristics.

ETHOLOGY   The study of the behaviour of reptiles and amphibians (and other animal species) in their natural environment.

EUBLEPHARID   Referring to any one of a group of gekkonid lizards which possess prominent movable eyelids, digits which have claws but no LAMELLAE, and a slow stalking gait. Together they form the Eublepharinae, a subfamily of the GEKKONIDAE.

EUPLEURODONT   The term given to PLEURODONT reptiles in which new teeth lie in a vertical row at the base of functioning teeth, moving into empty sockets as and when others are lost (a process termed 'vertical replacement'). Compare SUBPLEURODONT.

EURYAPSID   Describing a skull that has a single upper temporal opening. Found in some fossil saurians of the extinct subclass Euryapsida.

EURYTHERMAL   Said of any animal able to endure a wide variation in temperatures. For example, the leopard gecko (*Eublepharis macularius*) thrives in temperatures which may be as high as 38°C during the day and as low as 15°C at night. Compare STENOTHERM-AL.

EUSTACHIAN TUBE   The tube connecting the middle ear to the back of the throat in vertebrates. Normally closed, it opens during the acts of swallowing and yawning to allow air into the middle ear, thus maintaining atmospheric pressure on each side of the eardrum (tympanum). The tube was named after Bartolomeo Eustachio, the Italian anatomist.

EUTHANASIA   The act of putting to death in a humane manner.

Reptiles and amphibians are euthanased in order to relieve suffering from an incurable disease or mortal wound. Also called mercy-killing.

EXANAL   Referring to any of the scales located around the lateral margins of the anus in the sunbeam snake (*Xenopeltis unicolor*).

EXCITEMENT COLOUR REACTION (ECR)   An immediate or swift alteration in pigmentation of the skin as a direct response to various external stimuli.

EXCITEMENT SECRETION REACTION (ESR)   In certain amphibians, the comparatively swift and liberal production of skin mucus as a direct response to various external stimuli.

EXCRESCENCE   Any natural projection or protuberance and, in particular, an epidermal outgrowth from an organ or part of the body. Frequently used, in herpetology, for many of the various structures occurring on the bodies and limbs of reptiles and amphibians, e.g., the anuran NUPTIAL PAD.

EXCRETION   The removal of harmful waste products, created by metabolic activities, from the blood by the kidneys in the form of urine, which is evacuated with the faeces through the CLOACA.

EXCRETORY ORGAN   Any one of a system of specialized organs, the function of which is to eliminate metabolic waste products, nitrogenous compounds, carbon dioxide, water, salts etc., from the body. Examples of excretory organs in vertebrates are: the kidneys (for nitrogenous compounds, e.g., UREA, and water), the lungs (for water and carbon dioxide), the urinary ducts and the urinary bladder. In chelonians and anurans, the urinary bladder has a secondary function, acting as a water-storage organ. In all snakes, amphisbaenids, varanids and crocodilians, it is entirely absent.

EXFOLIATION   The act of moulting; the peeling off of skin in layers, flakes, scales or plates.

EXOGENOUS   Externally; developing or originating outside an animal. External factors that, in some way, influence an animal, e.g., temperature, humidity and light, are exogenous.

EXOPTHALMOS,   EXOPTHALMUS,   EXOPTHALMIA   The abnormal protrusion of the eyeball. Can occur in both reptiles and amphibians and is usually related to a disease of the thyroid gland.

EXOSKELETON   The protective or supporting structure which covers the outside of the body of some vertebrates and provides protection for internal organs and attachment for muscles. In reptiles, the exoskeleton manifests itself in the form of scales and laminae and, in chelonians, as the shell.

EXOTIC   Not INDIGENOUS to a particular area. Many exotic amphibians and reptiles are now found living in the wild in various parts of the world to which they are alien because of introduction, either accidental or intentional, by man.

EXSANGUINATION   Severing the blood vessels of an animal and allowing it to bleed to death. A method of humane killing of reptiles and amphibians (which are preferably already unconscious); a form of EUTHANASIA.

EXTENSILE   Capable of being stretched or extended.

EXTERNAL EAR OPENING   The part of the ear, consisting of the auricle and the auditory canal, that leads to the outside of an animal's head.

EXTERNAL GILL   In amphibian larvae, the structures of respiration, located on the side of the neck, which, at METAMORPHOSIS, are resorbed in most groups although in some, such as the mudpuppies, *Necturus* etc., they remain permanently throughout adulthood.

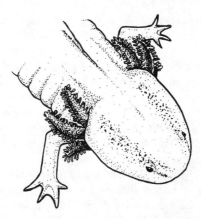

The feathery external gills of the aquatic Mexican axolotl (*Ambystoma mexicanum*).

EXTINCT   No longer existing in a particular area. With so many threats to the environment, many reptile and amphibian species are facing worldwide extinction.

EXUDATE   Any discharged, or exuded, substance, such as cellular debris, from skin pores or wounds etc.

EXUVIAL GLAND   A skin gland in reptiles that releases an oily secretion between the outer epidermal layer and the next layer prior to skin shedding, serving to free it and thus assist its removal. The secretion causes the eyes of snakes to become opaque and take on a cloudy bluish hue. Such snakes are said to be MILKED UP.

EXUVIATION   The act of shedding, moulting or sloughing the skin or similar external covering. In reptiles and amphibians, the exuviae sloughed during ECDYSIS consist of the scales and outer epidermal layers which covered their bodies, including, in chelonians, the laminae on their shells.

EYE SPOT   1. Any one of the rounded, often brightly coloured spots occurring in the skin patterns of some reptiles, especially lizards.   2. Rounded glandular areas of striking and contrasting colour, occurring in pairs, on the rumps of a number of South American leptodactylids, including *Telmatobius praebasalticus*, *Physalaemus nattereri* and some *Pleurodema* species. These eye-like spots, or OCELLI, are displayed in defence behaviour as an intimidation to enemies. Eye spots, in various forms, also occur in many other anurans.

EYE STRIPE   A line that passes 'through' the eye of many reptiles and amphibians, as seen, for example, in the European smooth snake (*Coronella austriaca*).

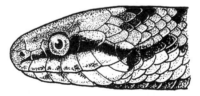

A lateral view of the head of the European smooth snake (*Coronella austriaca*), showing the prominent eye stripe.

# F

**FACE-OFF POSTURE** The position assumed by the males and less frequently, females of many lizard species, in which two individuals present their flanks to one another, usually whilst facing opposite directions and often accompanied by the inflation or compression of the body. The face-off posture is used during the defence of territory or food, or during fights over females etc., and can be seen particularly well in lizards of the genus *Tiliqua*.

**FAECAL ANALYSIS** Examination of the waste products of reptiles and amphibians to determine the presence of disease or parasitic worms etc.

**FAECES** The solid or semi-solid material that is eliminated from the digestive tract through the anus, and consists of indigestible food residues, bacteria, bile, mucus and dead cells from the gut lining.

**FAMILY** The taxonomic category used in the classification of organisms that consists of one or several similar or closely related genera, and ranking between ORDER and GENUS. The scientific name of an amphibian or reptile family always ends in 'idae', e.g., Bufonidae (toads) and Varanidae (monitor lizards), and is derived from a type genus (*Bufo* and *Varanus* in the examples above) that is characteristic of the whole family.

**FAN** The prominent elevated and laterally compressed helmet-like crest on the back of the head in lizards of the *Basiliscus* genus.

**FANG** Any of the recurved, lengthened, hollow or grooved teeth located on the MAXILLA of the upper jaw in snakes. It is usually longer than the other teeth and serves to conduct VENOM.

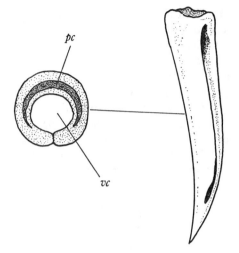

An example of a typical grooved fang and, on the left, a section taken
from its centre: *pc*, pulp cavity; *vc*, venom canal.

FAT BODY   In amphibians and reptiles, one of a pair of organs in
the abdominal cavity attached to the kidneys or near the rectum,
each a mass of fatty (adipose) tissue serving as an energy store for
use during hibernation or periods when food is in short supply.
Also used during breeding, in the formation of sexual products,
they become greatly enlarged prior to mating.

FAT CYCLE   The process in which fat bodies are formed and increase in size, followed by their reduction, as the yolking of the
eggs progresses, to small structures mainly made up of connective
tissue.

FAUNA   All the animal life of a given time, locality or region. The
reptile and amphibian component of the fauna is termed the 'herpetofauna'.

FAUNAL ELEMENT   Used in reference to an animal species that
has evolved within one of the world's six ZOOGEOGRAPHICAL RE-
GIONS and has subsequently become a distinguishing feature of that
region. The tuatara (*Sphenodon*) is, for example, a faunal element of
the AUSTRALASIAN REGION.

FAUNISTICS   The classification of organisms with regard to animals only. A branch of taxonomy.

**FECUNDITY** Fruitfulness; fertility; having the capability of producing eggs or young.

**FEMORAL** 1. Referring to any of the scales on the upper part (thigh) of the hind limb of lizards. 2. Either one of the second rearmost pair of plates (laminae) situated between the ABDOMINAL and ANAL plates on the PLASTRON of chelonians.

**FEMORAL PORES** Small, but comparatively deep, openings in the centres of certain enlarged scales on the undersides of the thighs in some lizards. The pores contain a wax-like material consisting of cellular debris which may, in breeding males, project from the scales' surface, forming a COMB.

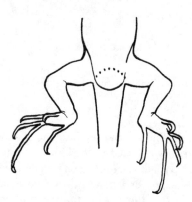

A ventral view of the hind limbs of a lizard showing the femoral pores on the thighs.

**FEMUR** The main long bone forming the upper or thigh bone of the hind limb, extending from the knee to the pelvis.

**FER DE LANCE** *Bothrops lanceolatus,* a PIT VIPER of the family VIPERIDAE, subfamily Crotalinae, found exclusively on the island of Martinique in the West Indies.

**FIBULA** The outer and smaller of the two long bones of the lower hind limb, extending from the knee to the ankle.

**FILARIA** Any parasitic, thread-like nematode worm of the family Filariidae, a few of which are to be found in reptiles, especially certain lizards and crocodilians. Transmitted through the bites of insects, they live in the blood and tissues and spread throughout the body, heavy infestations almost always resulting in death.

FIN   Any laterally flattened, membranous organ on the body and tail of aquatic vertebrates, such as amphibian larvae, used for balance and locomotion when swimming.

FIRMISTERNAL   Descriptive of the pectoral girdle in anurans, in which the epicoracoids are united in the mid-line of the sternum.

FITZINGER, Leopold   1802–84, Austrian herpetologist at Vienna's Imperial Natural History Museum and author of numerous taxa. His work and publications contributed greatly to herpetological knowledge and included *Neuen Classification der Reptilien und ihren Natuerlichen Verwandschaften* (1826), and the much-admired *Bilder-Atlas* (1850).

FITZSIMONS, Fredrick William   1870–1951, South African herpetologist and son of V. F. M. FitzSimons. A noted authority on South African snakes, his many publications included *Snakes of southern Africa* (1919), *Pythons and their ways* (1930), and *Snakes and treatment of snakebite* (1932).

FITZSIMONS, Vivian Frederick Maynard   1905–75, South African zoologist and Director of Pretoria's Transvaal Museum. His publications included *The lizards of southern Africa* (1943), *The snakes of southern Africa* (1962), and *A field guide to the snakes of southern Africa* (1970) which contained a number of line drawings by his brother, D. C. FitzSimons.

FLAGELLUM, pl. FLAGELLA   A long whip-like outgrowth on micro-organisms, spores, gametes etc., that serves as an organ of locomotion and a term used, in herpetology, for the slender filament on the end of the tail of certain anuran larvae.

FLASH COLORATION   Referring to the very striking and con-

During various behavioural displays, the *Anolis* lizards will suddenly erect a brightly coloured dewlap on their throat in order to startle an aggressor or rival. The use of vivid colours in this way is known as 'flash coloration'.

trasting colour on a normally CONCEALED SURFACE of many amphibians and reptiles, examples of which include the black and orange markings on the thighs and flanks of the otherwise green Ecuadorian leaf-folding frog (*Phyllomedusa tomopterna*) and the yellow, orange or red DEWLAP of *Anolis* lizards.

FLATWORM   Any free-living or parasitic invertebrate of the phylum Platyhelminthes, which contains tapeworms and flukes. Their flattened bodies possess only one opening to the intestine and they are without a circulatory system. Many forms occur in both reptiles and amphibians.

FLICKING   A particular activity seen in the aquatic *Xenopus*, in which both of the forelimbs are suddenly thrust forward together and then withdrawn a number of times in quick succession, and occurring whilst the amphibian is either suspended in the water or resting on the bottom. It serves to locate food, in the form of aquatic invertebrates, which, when touched by the forelimbs, are quickly grasped and drawn into the mouth.

FLIPPER   1. Any one of the small, irregular-shaped pieces of skin cut from the legs of crocodilians in the commercial skin trade.   2. The flat, broad limb of sea turtles (family CHELONIIDAE), specialized for swimming.

FLUKE   Any parasitic flatworm of the class TREMATODA, which can occur in various internal organs of reptiles and amphibians.

FLUORESCENT LIGHTING   A form of lighting often used to illuminate vivaria and emitted from a tube, coated with a thin layer of phosphor on its inner surface, in which an electrical gas discharge is maintained. In the husbandry of reptiles, the gas is usually mercury vapour and emits ULTRAVIOLET RADIATION which causes the phosphor to fluoresce.

FLUVIAL   Of, relating to, or occurring in, rivers and streams.

FOAM NEST   A structure built by a number of different frog species, e.g., *Leptodactylus*, *Physalaemus*, in which to house their eggs and developing larvae. The nests of certain *Limnodynastes* species are built actually on the water's surface, whilst others, such as those of *Physalaemus* species, are constructed over small pools of water, suspended on a leaf. In American leptodactylids the JELLY is whipped into a frothy mass of foam by kicking movements of the hind legs of the female and/or male, whereas in Australasian myobatrachids it is created from bubbles produced by paddling movements of the female's front legs.

FOETAL WASTAGE   In herpetology, used in reference to the loss of apparently viable eggs or FOETUS.

FOETUS   The embryo in the later stages of development when its external features resemble those of the animal after birth. A term still used in herpetology but in its correct sense should be limited to embryos possessing an umbilical cord (i.e., mammals).

FOLD   *See* DORSOLATERAL FOLD.

FOLIFORM   Used to describe reptile scales that have an extensive free edge.

FOLLICLE   A sac or small cavity occurring within a tissue or organ and having an excretory, secretory or protective function. Follicles within the ovary, for example, contain developing egg cells (ova).

FOLLICLE GLAND   A pit-like structure located near the hindmost border of the VENTRAL scales of all crocodiles and gharials.

FOLLICULAR MATURATION   The formation, in the GERMINAL tissues, and maturation of ovarian follicles, culminating in the release of ova which then enter the oviduct where they are fertilized if copulation occurs. The process of follicular maturation is closely linked to the FAT CYCLE.

FOOD CHAIN   The sequence of organisms, existing in a natural community, through which food energy is transferred, and expressed as feeding relationships in linear form. Each organism, or link in the chain, obtains energy by eating the one below it and is eaten, in turn, by the one above it. For example, if a locust feeding upon a leaf is eaten by a frog, which is in turn eaten by a snake, which is then eaten by a buzzard, the resulting food chain would be: plant–herbivore–insectivore–carnivore–carnivore. The buzzard, in this example, is the top predator, or tertiary consumer. Because many animals have more than one food source, the idea of a 'food web' is perhaps more acceptable.

FOOT STAGE   The point in the development of anuran larvae, immediately following the PADDLE STAGE, in which the characteristic features of the foot become evident.

FOOT STAMP   A particular form of behaviour occurring in certain lizards, in which the loser of a fight flattens its body to the ground and stamps its feet. This action indicates submission to its rival which then ceases its attack, allowing the loser to take flight.

FORAMEN   Any small orifice, passage or perforation, such as that found in a bone through which blood vessels and nerves pass.

FORAMEN MAGNUM   The large opening at the base of the

skull which allows the connection between the spinal cord and the brain.

FORAMEN PANIZZAE  An opening or partition (septum) near the base of the aorta of the heart in crocodilians, providing a passage between the left and right aortic arches enabling oxygen-rich blood to mix with blood poor in oxygen.

FORCE-FEEDING  In the husbandry of captive reptiles, the act of forcing a snake or lizard to swallow or eat food when the health and well-being of the particular animal is at risk, due to its continued reluctance to feed voluntarily for one reason or another.

FORM  1. Shape or size as distinct from texture, colour etc.  2. A vague term used in classification when the correct taxonomic rank is not clear.  3. Any distinct variety or MORPH occurring within a species.  4. A hollow or scrape in soil or amongst vegetation made by a terrestrial chelonian in which to sleep.

FOSSA  An anatomical depression, shallow cavity or hollow area.

FOSSORIAL  Burrowing; describing species that live largely below the soil or beneath ground vegetation, or their skeletons and limbs which are adapted for digging and burrowing.

FOVEA  The shallow depression on the retina of the eye, opposite the lens, present in reptiles (also in many mammals and birds) and characterized by numerous, slender and densely packed cones, giving greater image definition and better perception of colour.

FOVEAL  Any one of the small scales bordering the LOREAL PIT of viperid snakes, which usually lie outside of the LACUNAL scales, over the SUPRALABIAL scales, beneath the LOREAL and directly in front of the eye. *See also* POSTFOVEAL, PREFOVEAL.

FRACTURE PLANE  *See* BREAKAGE PLANE.

FREEZE  To become fixed, rigid or motionless; to remain in a fixed position for a length of time, especially through fear. Many reptiles and amphibians may freeze when suddenly disturbed or threatened.

FREEZE-DRYING  A process for preserving various organisms and substances, consisting of rapid freezing followed by desiccation in a vacuum. A technique used for preserving snake VENOM.

FRENOCULAR  Commonly used for a scale situated between the LOREAL and the PREOCULAR scales, or, in snakes, between the loreal and the eye.

FREQUENCY MODULATION  In VOCALIZATION, the variation in pitch, over a length of time, of the CALL of a frog or toad.

FRICTION DISC  *See* ADHESIVE PAD.

FRIGHT CRY  The distress call of many anurans when grasped suddenly, in which a loud scream is emitted through an opened mouth and readily distinguished from the typical anuran breeding call emitted with a closed mouth. The fright cry may well be successful in intimidating or startling some attackers but its use as a defence against snakes, which are unable to hear air-borne sounds, is doubtful.

FRILL  The enormous, free-edged fold of skin, covered with large keeled scales, located below and at either side of the head in the agamid frilled lizard (*Chlamydosaurus kingii*) of Australia and New Guinea. Normally folded back against the body, the frill is erectible, by means of a row of cartilaginous extensions ('ribs') of the hyoid apparatus, and extended during threat and courtship displays. The frill of an adult male may attain 300 mm in diameter.

FRINGE  Any row of scales or spines extending from the body of reptiles but commonly used for the broad edging of scales on the digits of certain lizards (e.g., the genera *Acanthodactylus, Uma*) that enlarges the surface of the foot, aiding locomotion in loose sand.

FROG MALARIA  The mosquito-transmitted disease known as 'amphibian malaria', caused by a protozoan, *Plasmodium bufonis*, which parasitizes frogs and toads.

FROG TOXIN  Any one of a number of poisonous substances, collectively known as batrachotoxins, secreted from the skins of many anurans (e.g., the families RANIDAE, HYLIDAE, DENDROBATIDAE and BUFONIDAE). In sufficiently high concentrations, frog toxins may prove fatal should they enter the bloodstream.

FRONTAL  1. Pertaining to the scale, scales, or the space occupied by them (frontal area), on the top of the head situated between the SUPRAOCULAR scales, in chelonians, most lizards and snakes. 2. A bone, narrow and prominent, on the outer surface of the skull roof, located between the eye sockets (ORBITS), usually separate from, but sometimes joined to, other bones such as the PARIETAL.

FRONTAL ORGAN  *See* PARIETAL EYE.

FRONT-FANGED  *See* ENDOGLYPH.

FRONTONASAL  The scale, or scales, lying between the INTERNASAL, LOREAL and PREFRONTAL scales on the head in many lizards and chelonians, but rare in snakes. In snakes of the TYPHLOPIDAE family, the frontonasal is one of a pair of scales lying above the NASAL and posterior to the ROSTRAL.

**FRONTOPARIETAL 1.** The enlarged, either single or paired scale on the top of the head in chelonians, situated between the FRONTAL and the PARIETAL scales. **2.** In lizards, any one of the PLATES on the top of the head between the frontal and the parietal scales. **3.** In anurans, the bone resulting from the union of the frontal and the parietal bones.

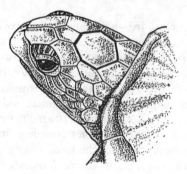

The head of a green turtle (*Chelonia mydas*), with the frontoparietal scale outlined.

**FRONTOPARIETAL FORAMEN** In certain anurans, the large opening in the skull separating the paired FRONTOPARIETAL bones.

**FRONTOSQUAMOSAL ARCH** In certain urodeles, the bony arch which unites the FRONTAL and SQUAMOSAL bones.

**FUZZY** A newborn mouse or rat that has just started to grow its fur.

# G

GAIT   The manner of walking or running. For example, the leopard gecko (*Eublepharis macularius*) has a slow, stalking gait.

GALL BLADDER   A small, pouch-like extension of the bile duct, occurring in most vertebrates, lying between the liver lobes and serving as a store for bile, which is produced in the liver and released in reaction to food entering the duodenum.

GALLERY FOREST   Any forest along the banks of a watercourse in a region mostly free of other tree growth, and reliant upon the water table more than upon the climate as a whole.

GALLIWASP   In the family ANGUIDAE, any lizard of the genus *Diploglossus*, inhabiting Central and northern South America.

GAMETE   A mature, reproductive cell capable of uniting with another to form a new individual (ZYGOTE). Ova and spermatozoa are gametes.

GAPING   The condition, most frequently witnessed in snakes, in which the mouth is constantly opened, often for several minutes at a time, and often with the head and neck raised off the ground. The cause of gaping is almost always a respiratory infection in which the air passages become partially or totally blocked, making breathing difficult.

GARIAL   An alternative spelling of GHARIAL.

GASTRALIA   Bony, rib-like rods located in the dermal layer of the skin of the abdomen, in crocodilians and the tuatara (*Sphenodon*). Gastralia, or 'abdominal ribs', are not connected to the vertebral column and lie outside the true ribs in the area between the pectoral and pelvic girdle.

**GASTROENTERITIS**  An important and serious disease in reptiles, especially snakes, caused by parasitic protozoans of the genus *Entamoeba* and affecting the blood vessels and mucous membrane of the intestine. Unless treated early, it can spread throughout the infected reptile's body via the bloodstream with death resulting soon after.

**GASTROLITH**  Any of the stones occurring in the stomachs of crocodilians, deliberately swallowed to grind up food in the absence of the ability to chew.

**GASTROSTEGE**  Any one of the wide VENTRAL plates on the undersurface of most snakes.

**GAVIAL**  An alternative name for GHARIAL.

**GAVIALIDAE**  Gharials. Family of the CROCODILIA, inhabiting deep rivers of the Orient, especially the Ganges, Indus and Irrawaddy. MONOTYPIC.

**GEKKONIDAE**  Geckos. Family of the SQUAMATA, suborder SAURIA, inhabiting the tropical, subtropical, and warmer temperate regions of the world. Over 800 species in some 80 or more genera.

**GENE**  A unit of heredity, composed of DNA, carried in the chromosome transmitted from generation to generation by the GAMETES and governing the development and characteristic features of an individual. In the captive breeding of reptiles and amphibians, it is necessary to periodically replenish the GENE POOL to avoid INBREEDING depression.

**GENE FIXATION**  The establishment of a GENE once it becomes present in every individual of a given population.

**GENE POOL**  The total number and variety of the genes of a given breeding population or species existing at a given time.

**GENERATION TIME**  The amount of time necessary for a generation of hatchlings or newborn (NEONATES) to become sexually mature and produce their own young. The generation time for young blue-tongued skinks (*Tiliqua gigas*), for example, is 12 months under correct conditions.

**GENETIC**  Of, or relating to, heredity or the features and traits acquired by the offspring from their parents. The blueprints of inherited characteristics are passed on to the young in GENES, a particular genetic arrangement being termed a GENOTYPE.

**GENIAL**  A term frequently used by early authors for the CHINSHIELD in snakes and lizards.

**GENIOLABIAL**  A scale, in alligator lizards (genus *Gerrhonotus*), situated between the INFRALABIAL and CHINSHIELD scales.

GENOTYPE   The genetic composition of an organism, or a group of organisms all having the same genetic composition.

GENTAMYCIN   An antibiotic useful in reptile husbandry for the treatment of a wide range of bacterial diseases and particularly successful against GRAM-NEGATIVE BACTERIA.

GENUS, pl. GENERA   A taxonomic category used in the classification of organisms, consisting of a group of species having similar structural characteristics and ranking below FAMILY and above SPECIES. The common name of an organism is sometimes identical or similar to that of the genus, e.g., viper, *Vipera*; chameleon, *Chamaeleo*.

GERMINAL   Of, or relating to, a germ or a germ cell, or relating to the embryonic stage of development.

GERMINAL EPITHELIUM   Embryonic tissue consisting of one or more sheets of closely packed cells that cover the internal and external surface of the body in the earliest state of growth.

GESTATION   The period of development, or carrying of embryos, by the female of an animal exhibiting VIVIPARITY, from the fertilization of the egg to the birth of the young (PARTURITION).

GHARA   The prominent, fleshy hump that appears on the tip of the snout of mature male gharials, and which develops to form a lid covering the nostrils. During the male's territorial patrols, or when courting, the lid flaps as the reptile exhales, producing a loud buzzing noise that serves as a warning to competitors. This cartilaginous nose-knob is named 'ghara' from the Hindi term for 'mud pot', and it is this feature that gives the species its common name, GHARIAL.

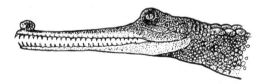

Mature male gharials develop a large fleshy knob, known as a ghara, on the tip of their snouts, which serves as a noise-producing chamber.

**GHARIAL, GARIAL, GAVIAL** A large, monotypic, fish-eating Indian crocodilian (*Gavialis gangeticus*) with a very long slender snout.

**GILL** A respiratory organ used by aquatic animals to effect the exchange of respiratory gases between the animal's blood or body fluids and the water in which it lives. Located in the region of the neck, gills may be feathery, as in urodele and young anuran larvae, or enclosed, as in older anuran larvae. *See also* ALLANTOIC GILL, EXTERNAL GILL, INTERNAL GILL, OPERCULAR GILL.

**GILL ARCH** Any one of the curved cartilaginous or bony bars situated one behind the other and extending dorsoventrally on each side of the pharynx, supporting the amphibian gills.

**GILL RAKER** Any one of the cartilaginous or bony filaments on the inside of a GILL ARCH in amphibian larvae, which serve as filters and prevent solid substances from being carried through the gill slits.

**GILL SLIT** In certain amphibians and amphibian larvae, any one of the series of paired, narrow openings at the base of the external gills through which water can flow from the sides of the pharynx to the outside.

**GIRARD, Charles Frederic** 1822–95, a Swiss zoologist who worked at the Smithsonian Institution, Washington DC, with Spencer Fullerton Baird, with whom he co-authored many publications, including the *Catalogue of North American reptiles* (1853).

**GIRDLE** 1. The ring of bones situated anteriorly (PECTORAL GIRDLE) and posteriorly (PELVIC GIRDLE) in the trunk of the TETRAPOD body, supporting the arms (forelimbs) and legs (hind limbs) respectively. 2. In the commercial crocodilian skin trade, the term given to any of the pieces skinned from the belly and thighs directly in front of the vent and most frequently taken from large caimans, e.g., *Melanosuchus*.

**GIRTH** The measurement around a reptile or amphibian, usually at the abdomen or, in snakes, at mid-body. Frequently incorrectly given as the diameter but the true girth of an animal is its circumference.

**GIZZARD** The thickened, muscular stomach of crocodilians, often found to contain GASTROLITHS which aid in digestion.

**GLAND** Any one of a number of cells, occurring either within special organs or individually in the epithelium, that synthesize chemical substances and secrete or excrete them directly into the bloodstream or through a duct, e.g., oil, wax, saliva, venom etc.

GLANDULAR SCALE   The modified, secretory scale in certain lizards, situated anterior to the CLOACA or on the thigh.

GLIDE   The method of unpropelled movement through the air used by certain arboreal reptiles (e.g., flying lizards of the genus *Draco*) and amphibians (e.g., flying frogs of the genus *Rhacophorus*) in their progress from one tree to another or to the ground, in which the body or appendages are flattened or spread and act as a gliding surface.

Certain species of arboreal frogs have developed skin flaps on parts of
their limbs and bodies which, together with the webs on their feet,
provide them with a surface which enables them to glide through the air.

GLOTTIS   The opening from the PHARYNX to the TRACHEA (windpipe), the front section of which, in snakes, is protruded during the act of swallowing large prey items and therefore prevents the reptile from suffocating.

GLOVE   An area of densely packed, hook-like processes on the undersurface of each forelimb in male *Xenopus* frogs, used to maintain a firm hold on the females during AMPLEXUS.

GLUED AMPLEXUS   A form of AMPLEXUS in which the males in certain anuran species attach themselves to the backs of females by means of a sticky secretion produced in abdominal glands. Occurs in a number of plump, short-limbed species, including members of the genera *Breviceps*, *Gastrophryne* and *Kaloula*.

GLYPHODONT   Having teeth, which are grooved, through which VENOM flows into the tissues of a bitten animal; having FANGS.

GOITRE   A disturbance in the development, growth and function of the thyroid gland caused, usually, by an iodine-related reduction in hormone secretion. Amphibian larvae with thyroid disease frequently double or even treble in size, fail to metamorphose and die. In reptiles, a goitre often results in an enlargement of the thyroid gland, appearing as a hard, fibrous growth in the region of the throat.

GONAD   One of the usually paired reproductive organs responsible for the production of GAMETES, such as the male TESTIS (producing spermatozoa) and the female OVARY (producing egg cells, or ova).

GONADAL RECRUDESCENCE   The formation of spermatozoa in male testes after a period of dormancy. In many reptiles, especially temperate species, it occurs after or during a period of warming which has been preceded by a period of cooling (HIBERNATION).

GONADAL SUPPRESSION   The failure of spermatozoa to develop in the GONADS which, in reptiles, is usually due to prolonged exposure to temperatures below the lower limit of their optimal thermal range, resulting in infertile matings.

GOUT   A condition, sometimes affecting reptiles, in which urates normally expelled from the body via the kidneys accumulate in the tissues, joints (uratic arthritis) or internal organs (visceral gout). The deposition of urate crystals destroys the internal organs so that they can no longer function correctly and, untreated, can result in death.

GRAB-STICK   Any instrument used to grasp and restrain snakes and lizards, particularly aggressive or venomous species. Such sticks usually consist of a strong pole or rod with a grasp arrangement at one end and a trigger for opening and closing the grasp at the other.

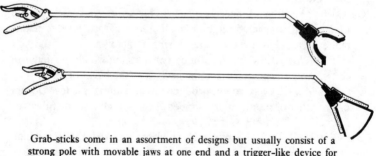

Grab-sticks come in an assortment of designs but usually consist of a strong pole with movable jaws at one end and a trigger-like device for moving the jaws at the other.

**GRAM-NEGATIVE BACTERIA** One of two major groups of bacteria commonly found in reptiles and amphibians and including those of the *Aeromonas* and *Pseudomonas* genera. *See* AEROMONAS INFECTION, PSEUDOMONAD INFECTION.

**GRANULAR GLAND** One of several glands occurring in the skin of amphibians, producing a toxic secretion that can cause much irritation and damage to mucus membranes and which, in some species of *Bufo*, can be squirted some distance. Granular glands are frequently enlarged and arranged close together, e.g., the PAROTOID in members of the BUFONIDAE family of toads.

**GRAVID** The term used, in herpetology, to describe the condition of a female carrying eggs or young, from fertilization to the moment of birth or, in species exhibiting OVOVIPARITY, from fertilization to the birth of the young still enclosed in their egg membranes.

**GRAY, John Edward** 1800–75, British zoologist at the British Museum (Natural History), London, he produced a number of catalogues, among them the *Catalogue of shield reptiles* (1855 & 1870), relating to the collections held at the BM(NH), which included many descriptions of new taxa.

**GROIN** The slight depression or hollow at the point where the hind limbs join the abdomen.

**GROOVE** A long, narrow channel or furrow on a bodily structure or part, e.g., the COSTAL FOLD in urodeles, and the groove in the teeth of many reptiles, linked with the conduction of venom.

**GROUND COLOUR** The usually plain-coloured background on which other colours, patterns or markings are overlaid.

**GROWTH RING** (ANNUAL RING) Any one of the number of con-

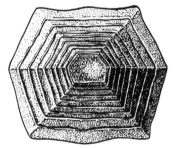

Growth rings on the laminae of many chelonians indicate the amount of growth attained during the reptile's life, with each ring representing one season.

centric, ring-like areas (annuli) occurring on the laminae of many chelonians, most obvious in juveniles, and each one corresponding to one season's growth.

GUANOPHORE   A pigment cell of the skin containing white or blue crystals of guanine, a substance related to uric acid.

GÜNTHER, Albert Carl   1830–1914, German herpetologist and ichthyologist at the British Museum (Natural History), London. As well as contributing several publications on fish, his many herpetological contributions included catalogues of the collections held at the BM(NH), including the tailless amphibians (1858), colubrine snakes (1858) and the giant land tortoises (1877). He wrote the classic *Reptiles of British India* (1864), which provided the basis for all modern research on the reptiles and amphibians of that region, and the reptile and amphibian section of the *Biologica Centrali-Americana* (1885–1902), which is considered one of the most significant works on the herpetology of Central America.

GULAR   On, or pertaining to, the region of the throat. Also used for the foremost laminae (paired or single) on the PLASTRON of most chelonians.

GULAR DISC   A distinct, circular area of skin in the centre of the throat of many male anurans. Thicker than the skin surrounding it, the gular disc, which overlies the VOCAL SAC, is expanded as the throat inflates when the amphibians CALL.

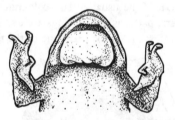

The underside of an anuran showing the gular disc on the throat, which expands during calling.

GULAR FAN   An alternative term for DEWLAP.

GULAR FOLD   A transverse fold of skin across the rear of the throat directly in front of the point where the forelegs join the abdomen. The fold is well developed in many urodeles and in some lizards, where its presence or absence, and the scales upon it, is taxonomically significant.

The gular fold is well developed in many lizards, transversing the underside of the throat and usually edged by enlarged scales.

GULAR SAC   An area of expandable skin on the throat of many male anurans, which inflates like a balloon when the animal calls; the VOCAL SAC of frogs and toads.

GULAR TENTACLE   An alternative term for BARBEL, one of the fleshy projections occurring on the chins and throats of some chelonians.

GYMNOPHIONA   The limbless amphibians – CAECILIIDAE, or APODA, an order of tropical worm-like animals of the class Amphibia.

# H

**HABITAT** The particular region, characterized by certain features such as vegetation, climate and topography etc., where an animal or plant lives.

**HABU** Any one of the Asiatic PIT VIPERS of the genus *Trimeresurus*, the largest of which is the Okinawa habu (*T. flavouridis*) of the Ryukyu Islands, which reaches some 2000 mm in length. Others are the Chinese habu (*T. mucrosquamatus*), the Sakishima habu (*T. elegans*) and the himehabu (*T. okinovensis*).

**HAEMATOCRYAL** An alternative description for a POIKILO-THERM.

**HAEMOTOXIC** Describing the effects of certain snake-venom components which destroy blood vessels and prevent the blood from functioning. Compare NEUROTOXIC.

**HAEMOTOXIN** Any constituent of snake venom that results in a breakdown of the blood cells, causing internal haemorrhaging and localized bruising.

**HALLUX** The first (innermost) digit on the hind foot of most four-limbed reptiles, and amphibians (and other tetrapods).

**HALTERE** *See* STABILIZER.

**HAMADRYAD** The king cobra (*Ophiophagus hannah*), the longest venomous snake in the world, inhabiting India and South-East Asia.

**HARDERIAN GLAND** In reptiles, one of the two large glands connected with each eye which produce the 'tears' which help to keep the eye moist. Associated with the NICTITATING MEMBRANE in crocodilians, chelonians and lizards. *See also* LACRIMAL GLAND.

HARDUN  *Agama stellio*, a lizard of the family AGAMIDAE, occurring in rocky habitats in north-eastern Africa to south-western Asia and parts of Greece.

HEAD–BODY LENGTH  The length of a caecilian, anuran, crocodilian, snake or lizard, measured along the centre of the body from the tip of the snout to the vent; the SNOUT–VENT LENGTH.

HEAD CAP  The area of black coloration that covers the top of the snout in coral snakes (*Micrurus* and *Micruroides*), extending backwards frequently to spread over most or all of the PARIETAL scales on the top of the head.

HEADSLAP  The action performed by mature crocodilians, in which the head is lifted above the water so that the lower jaw is just visible. This position is frequently held for several minutes before the reptile rapidly opens and closes its jaws as if biting at the water, creating a sudden audible 'pop', followed by a tremendous splash. The display, consisting of the headslap, JAWCLAP and related behaviour, serves to attract females during courtship and acts also as a deterrent to rival males.

HEATH  A lowland area, with a sandy, acid and infertile soil, dominated by heather (*Calluna vulgaris*), with scattered trees and bushes, notably gorse (*Ulex europaeus*). Good examples are the sandy heaths of southern and western England, many of which contain interesting and, in some cases rare, reptiles and amphibians.

HEAT SENSORS  *See* LABIAL PIT; LOREAL PIT.

HEDONIC  Having pleasurable sensations and, as used in herpetology, acting as a stimulus to sexual activity.

HEDONIC GLAND  Any gland, situated on various parts of the head and tail in certain urodeles, the secretion of which induces sexual excitement or stimulation in the females when the male rubs it against the female's body.

HEIFER  A subadult female terrapin.

HELEOPHRYNIDAE  Ghost frogs. Family of the ANURA, inhabiting South Africa. Three species in one genus.

HELMET  The bony structure on the top and back of the skull of certain lizards, especially *Basiliscus*.

HELMINTH  Any one of a miscellaneous group of parasitic worms and flukes inhabiting the respiratory, circulatory or digestive system, and found in reptiles and amphibians. Examples are the phylum ACANTHOCEPHALA and classes NEMATODA, TREMATODA and CESTODA.

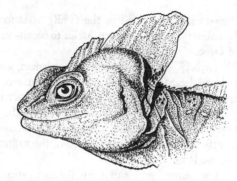

A profile of an adult male plumed basilisk (*Basiliscus plumifrons*), showing the bony helmet on the back of the head.

HELODERMATIDAE   Beaded lizards. Family of the SQUAMATA, suborder SAURIA, inhabiting south-western North America and parts of Central America. The only venomous lizard in the world. Two species in one genus.

HEMIPENIS, pl. HEMIPENES   The copulatory organ of male snakes and lizards, paired and located within the base of the tail behind the cloaca. The surface may be covered with an array of hooks and spines which help to hold the organ securely in place in the female's cloaca during copulation.

The paired hemipenes of male snakes are often covered with small spines which help to secure them within the female's cloaca during mating.

HERBIVORE   An animal that feeds upon grass and plant matter. Many terrestrial chelonians are herbivorous.

HERMAPHRODITE   An animal that possesses both male and female organs of reproduction.

HERP   An abbreviation for herpetology, but used frequently for any individual amphibian or reptile.

HERPES   A highly contagious disease, commonly known as 'grey spot', occurring mainly in freshwater chelonians, especially juveniles. Herpes viruses are also found in marine turtles, iguanid lizards and many snakes.

HERPETOFAUNA   The term used to embrace all the reptile and amphibian populations of a particular area, region or country.

HERPETOLOGY   The study of reptiles and amphibians, including their anatomy and classification (taxonomy), history and behaviour, and embracing ecology, biochemistry, immunology, zoogeography, toxicology and computer science.

HERPTILE   Any individual amphibian or reptile. Considered by some to be slang and therefore inappropriate in academic literature, the term is used widely nevertheless by both amateur and professional authors.

HERPTILIARY   An outside, open-air enclosure used to house amphibians and/or reptiles in near natural conditions.

HETERODONT   Having teeth of several types, such as molars and canines, for different purposes, such as crushing, grinding, tearing and cutting etc. Contrast with HOMODONT.

HETEROGENEOUS   Lacking pure genes for a characteristic feature. For example, a reptile or amphibian that is heterogeneous for albinism has the characteristic coloration typical of its species, but carries one gene for albinism.

HETEROMORPHOUS   Differing in some way, e.g., size, shape, function etc., from that which is usually considered normal for a particular species.

HIBERNACULUM, pl. HIBERNACULA   The winter retreat of a hibernating animal. The location in which an amphibian or reptile hibernates, or remains inert during the colder part of the year. The hibernaculum may be a disused rodent burrow, a mine shaft, in mud, beneath the roots of trees, or under decomposing debris etc., where humidity and temperature remain relatively constant.

HIBERNATION   An extended period of rest, torpor or inertness during the winter months, in which metabolism is greatly slowed down. Hibernation occurs in most temperate reptiles and amphibians and is frequently very prolonged in the most northerly species.

HIERARCHY   The dominance–submission interrelationship (peck order), between each successive grade or rank established within a population of animals, with the most dominant member holding its position over the lower, more submissive grades by periodic combat or threat displays and allowed priority in access to females, food etc. by subordinates. Such a hierarchy has to be carefully planned and observed in a mixed-sex community of lizards if serious injuries, and even fatalities, are to be avoided amongst captive animals.

HINGE   The broad, flexible joint in the shell of certain chelonians that allows the front or rear of the shell to close, enabling the reptile to seal itself within when threatened. Examples of the hinge occur in the mud turtle (*Kinosternon*) in the PLASTRON, and in the hingeback tortoise (*Kinixys*) in the CARAPACE, amongst others.

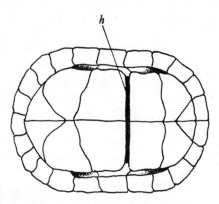

The hinge (*h*) on part of the shell of certain chelonians enables the reptile to seal itself in when threatened. The illustration shows a hinge in the plastron of a mud turtle (*Kinosternon*).

HOLARCTIC   The largest zoogeographical region comprising the PALAEARCTIC (Old World) and NEARCTIC (New World) regions, and covering most of the northern hemisphere. Faunal groups from these two regions are basically similar.

HOLBROOK, John Edward   1794–1871, American medical practitioner and herpetologist whose *North American herpetology* became the basis of American herpetology when it was published as a five-volume, second edition in 1842. The first edition was produced in three volumes between 1836 and 1838.

HOLOCENE   Pertaining to the second and most recent epoch of the Quaternary period. *See* RECENT.

HOMEOSTASIS   The regulation of a metabolic balance within an animal, such as the maintenance of body temperature. It enables cells to function more efficiently and any factor that disrupts, or threatens to disrupt, homeostasis is known as a 'stressor'. STRESS, in captive reptiles or amphibians, is any disruption of the normal physiological processes of the animals' internal environment, or homeostasis.

HOME RANGE   The area or areas which an individual animal occupies during its life, including both permanent and seasonal territories, together with the tracks and corridors through which it moves. Not to be confused with the DISTRIBUTION of the SPECIES as a whole.

HOMING   Pertaining to an animal's ability to return home, frequently after having travelled great distances. Particularly prevalent in many amphibians, the homing instinct enables them to return to breed in the same waters where they themselves were spawned.

HOMODONT   Having teeth which are all of a single type, and occurring, for example, in anurans in which all the teeth are correspondingly small, conical prominences on the MAXILLA, PREMAXILLA, and VOMER bones of the upper jaw. Contrast with HETERODONT.

HOMOGENEOUS   Of the same kind; uniform, and used in herpetology to describe the state in which scales on a reptile correspond in shape and size.

HOMOIOTHERM   Warm-blooded; an animal e.g., a bird or mammal, that maintains its internal body temperature at a constant level by using metabolic processes to override fluctuations in the temperature of the environment. The extinct pterosaurian reptiles are thought to have been homoiothermic, but all RECENT reptiles and amphibians are cold-blooded, or POIKILOTHERM.

HOMOLOGOUS   Used in comparative anatomy to refer to features having the same evolutionary origin but not necessarily the same function. The forelimbs and hind limbs of all terrestrial vertebrates are built on the same five-digit (PENTADACTYL) arrangement and are said, therefore, to be homologous.

HOOD   The flattened skin expansion of the back of the neck region in certain erect cobras.

**HOODIE**   Herpetologists' slang for any of the cobras which spread a HOOD when alarmed.

**HOPPER**   The name given to individual subadult mice, on account of their habit of leaping in the air when pursued.

**HORN**   Used in herpetology for any, usually pointed, epidermal projection on the head of an amphibian or reptile, such as the enlarged, elongated scales on the snout of the African vipers (*Bitis gabonica* and *B. nasicornis*) and above the eyes in *Cerastes cerastes*. In amphibians, examples include the fleshy excrescences above the eyes in the frogs *Ceratophrys cornuta* and *Megophrys nasuta*.

**HORNBACK**   In the commercial skin trade, the rough, dorsal skin of a crocodilian, in the centre of which are the large, bony dorsal scales, normally possessing raised keels, and bordered on both sides by the smoother, squarish scales of the ventral surface.

**HOST**   The organism in, or on, which another organism (the PARASITE) lives and derives nourishment. If a snake is parasitized by a tapeworm, for example, the snake is the host.

**HOT-ROCK**   An artificial stone, containing a heating element which emits a gentle heat, for use in a vivarium as a supplementary source of heat.

**HUMERAL**   The second foremost pair of laminae, situated between the GULAR and the PECTORAL laminae on the plastron of chelonians.

**HUMERUS**   The long bone of the upper forelimb in all tetrapod vertebrates. Its upper, rounded head articulates with the SCAPULA, and the lower end with the RADIUS and ULNA, at the elbow.

**HUMIDITY**   Relating to dampness, or the measure of the moisture content in the air. Humidity is an important factor in the successful keeping and breeding of reptiles and amphibians, with some species requiring almost none at all, and others depending on it completely for their survival.

**HUMP**   The natural, rounded protuberance on the lower back in anurans, where the vertebral column joins with the pelvic girdle.

**HUSBANDRY**   Every aspect of the care and management of both domestic and captive wild animals.

**HYBRID**   The often sterile offspring resulting from the pairing of a male of a certain species, genus or race etc. with the female of another.

**HYBRIDIZATION** (INTERGRADE)   Interbreeding between individuals of different species that differ genetically in at least one characteristic, the product of such a cross being called a HYBRID. Only species that are related can hybridize, the offspring from such unions being either similar in appearance to one of the parents or intermediate to both, depending on whether a particular inherited characteristic is dominant or recessive.

HYDRIC   Used in reference to areas or regions that are wet or swampy etc.

HYDROPHIIDAE   Sea snakes. Family of the SQUAMATA, central order Caenophidia, inhabiting the Indo-Pacific and neighbouring tropical and subtropical seas. 46 species in 16 genera.

HYDROPS   In anurans, a condition in which excess fluid collects in one or more of the lymph sacs lying beneath the skin. Captive anurans seem particularly susceptible to hydrops, as do the larvae of females which have had oviposition induced artificially.

HYDROTAXIS   The movement of an organism in response to the stimulus of water, an example of which occurs in hatchling marine turtles which make straight for the sea on emerging from the sand, even though they may not be able to see it.

HYGROSCOPIC   Able to absorb moisture readily from the air, as do many reptile eggs which absorb moisture throughout their incubation and must therefore be deposited in a humid environment.

HYLIDAE   Tree frogs. Family of the ANURA, suborder Procoela, inhabiting most tropical and subtropical parts of the world except Africa. Approximately 600 species in over 27 genera.

HYOBRANCHIAL APPARATUS   Group of muscles and bones which, in urodeles, enables the tongue to protrude from the mouth.

HYOID BONE   A horseshoe-shaped bone which supports the tongue in tetrapod vertebrates. In some lizard species, such as *Anolis*, the bone is movable and used to extend and strengthen the throat pouch during courtship and territorial displays.

HYOPLASTRON, pl. HYOPLASTRA   Either one of the second foremost pair of bones in the PLASTRON skeleton of a chelonian.

HYPAPOPHYSIS   A usually single, spine-like process on the vertebrae in some snakes and lizards. In egg-eating snakes (genus *Dasypeltis*), the tips of the hypapophyses in the oesophagus are used to break the shells of eggs as they are swallowed.

HYPEROLIIDAE   Family of the ANURA, inhabiting Africa and Madagascar, with the exception of one species (*Tachycnemis seychellensis*) which occurs on the Seychelle Islands. 193 species in 14 genera.

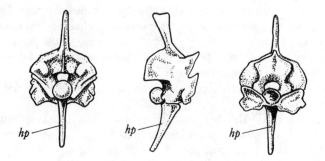

A front, side and rear view of a snake vertebra showing the
downward-pointing, spine-like hypapophysis (*hp*).

HYPERTHERMIA   A condition in which the body temperature is
dangerously high. Reptiles and amphibians will die if exposed to
temperatures above their VOLUNTARY MAXIMUM, which varies from
one species to another but lies only a few degrees above the upper
limit of their normal activity range.

HYPERVITAMINOSIS   A nutritional disorder found mostly in
captive reptiles and caused by an excess of vitamins in their diet.
Too much vitamin D3, for example, can cause metabolic disturbances of the bones.

HYPNOTIC REFLEX   An alternative term for DEATH FEINT.

HYPOCALCEMIA   A deficiency of body calcium.

HYPOPLASTRON, pl. HYPOPLASTRA   Either one of the second hindmost pair of bones in the PLASTRON skeleton of a chelonian.

HYPOTHENAR TUBERCLE   The small, knob-like projection
situated beneath the base of the outermost (fourth) digit of an anuran forefoot.

HYPOTHERMIA   A condition in which the body temperature is
dangerously low. Reptiles and amphibians will become torpid as
the ambient temperature is lowered and if it continues to fall below
their VOLUNTARY MINIMUM death will follow.

HYPOVITAMINOSIS (AVITAMINOSIS) A nutritional disorder
that can develop in captive reptiles and amphibians, resulting from
a failure to provide sufficient or correct vitamins in their diets.

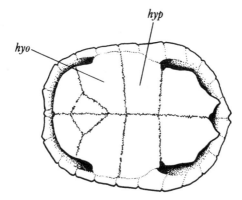

A ventral view of a chelonian shell in which the position of the
hypoplastron bone is shown in relation to the hyoplastron: *hyo*,
hyoplastron; *hyp*, hypoplastron.

Swollen eyes and lack of appetite in chelonians due to a lack of vitamin A, and convulsions in certain fish-eating snakes due to a lack
of vitamin B1, are both examples of hypovitaminosis.

# I

**ICHTHYOPHIIDAE**   Caecilians. Family of the GYMNOPHIONA, inhabiting tropical South America, South-East Asia and the Indo-Australian islands. 43 species in 4 genera.

**IGUANIDAE**   Iguanas, anoles and allied forms. Family of the SAURIA, inhabiting North and South America including the West Indies, Galapagos Islands, Madagascar, Fiji and Tonga. Over 680 species in more than 50 genera.

**ILIUM**   The largest, widest and uppermost of the three bones that constitute each half of the PELVIC GIRDLE in tetrapod vertebrates.

**IMAGO**   An entomological term for an adult insect, but occasionally used in herpetology for the stage in the life cycle of an amphibian following METAMORPHOSIS.

**IMBRICATE**   The term used to describe body scales that overlap in a way similar to the slates on a roof. Contrast with JUXTAPOSED.

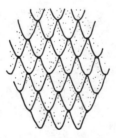

Reptile scales that overlap each other in a uniform way are termed 'imbricate'.

IMMUNITY   The ability of an organism to resist disease or toxins. The science concerned with the occurrence and causes of immunity is called immunology.

IMPACTION   The condition in which hard faeces, undigested food items, or ingested stones, sand grains etc., have gathered and formed an impassable blockage in the alimentary canal.

INBREEDING   Breeding between individuals that are closely related to each other, e.g., between parents and offspring or between SIBLINGS. Contrast with OUTBREEDING.

INCUBATION   The period of development of eggs, especially in an incubator, where heat and humidity are important factors.

INCUBATION PERIOD   The length of time necessary for an egg, or eggs, to develop, and varying from species to species. Generally expressed in days, the incubation period can be as short as 56 days in some snakes and lizards or as long as 340 days in certain chelonians.

INCUBATOR   A box-like apparatus in which reptile eggs can be artificially hatched under constant and sterile conditions.

INDIGENOUS   Occurring, or living naturally, in a particular place or region, but not restricted to that place or region. The European common frog (*Rana temporaria*), for example, is indigenous to the British Isles, whereas the marsh frog (*Rana ridibunda*) is not, having been introduced there by man.

IN EGG   In reptiles exhibiting OVIPARITY, said of a female carrying eggs.

INFRACEPHALIC   Pertaining to the VENTRAL, or undersurface, of the head.

INFRALABIAL   The lower labial; any one of the enlarged LABIAL scales bordering the lip of the lower jaw.

INFRAMARGINAL   A lamina situated between the PECTORAL and ABDOMINAL laminae of the plastron and the MARGINAL laminae of the carapace in most chelonians. *See* AXILLARY, INGUINAL.

INFRAMARGINAL GLAND   In some chelonians, a musk gland situated at the point where the carapace joins the plastron.

INFRAMAXILLARY   An alternative term for the CHINSHIELD of snakes.

INFRA-RED   Of, pertaining to, or made up of, radiation occurring within the part of the electromagnetic spectrum with a wavelength shorter than radio waves but longer than light. Situated below or beyond the red in the spectrum of ordinary light.

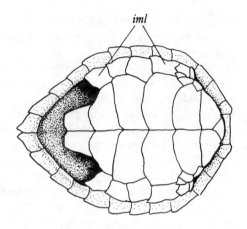

A ventral view of a chelonian shell showing the position of the
inframarginal laminae (*iml*).

INFRASOUND   In crocodilians, a form of acoustic communication
caused by subaudible body vibrations from rapidly contracted
trunk muscles as the reptiles lie just below the water's surface.
Barely perceptible by man, the sound waves radiating from a crocodilian's body have a very low frequency (1–10 hertz) and, under-
water, can travel long distances. Used by a number of species
during courtship, infrasound is frequently accompanied by a HEAD-
SLAP and JAWCLAP.

INFRATYMPANIC   The term for any one of the scales in crocodilians that occupy the lower margin of the opening to the ear.

INGUINAL   1. Of, or relating to, the area directly in front of the
point where the hind limb joins the body; the groin.   2. In chelonians, the lamina on the rear border of the BRIDGE, between the
CARAPACE and PLASTRON.

INGUINAL AMPLEXUS   A form of AMPLEXUS in which the
males of certain anuran species grasp the females directly in front
of the hind limbs, bending their bodies during spawning in order
to bring their cloacae as close as possible to those of the females.

INGUINAL LAMINA   In chelonians, any one of the INFRAMAR-
GINAL laminae situated directly in front and to the side of the IN-
GUINAL NOTCH.

INGUINAL NOTCH   Either one of the two U-shaped notches

In inguinal amplexus the male anuran grasps the female tightly about
her body just in front of her hind legs.

situated at either side of the rear of the chelonian shell through
which the hind limbs protrude.

INNOMINATE BONE   The body of bone in reptiles that makes
up each half of the pelvic girdle, resulting from the union of the
ISCHIUM, ILIUM and PUBIS.

INSECTIVORE   An animal that feeds on insects. Many lizards and
most anurans are insectivorous.

INSTINCT   The innate ability of animals to behave in a particular
genetically fixed way in response to external stimuli. Instinctive reactions are performed involuntarily, e.g., an anuran's insect-catch-
ing tongue-flick is always executed in the same way, whether prey
is caught or not, and young marine turtles always make straight for
the sea on hatching from their eggs, even though they have never
seen it before and may not be able to see it from their nest.

INSULAR   Of, or relating to, islands.

INTEGUMENT   One or more tissues forming the outermost body
layer of an animal, serving to protect and insulate the body from its
external environment.

INTERANAL   A single LAMINA situated between the ANAL laminae
of the PLASTRON and occurring exclusively in the marine turtles
(CHELONIIDAE).

INTERCALARY CARTILAGE   In hylid frogs, an additional cartilaginous component situated between the penultimate and last
bones of the digits.

INTERCALARY REPLACEMENT   Tooth replacement, characteristic of amphisbaenids and certain lizards, in which new teeth lie

at an angle at the base of, and in between, the functioning teeth, moving obliquely into empty sockets as and when the others are lost.

**INTERCANTHAL** In rattlesnakes, any one of the many small scales on top of the snout between the CANTHAL scales where, in other snake species, the larger, regular head scales, or plates, are situated.

**INTERCHINSHIELD** Any one of the scales situated between the elongated and paired CHINSHIELDS in certain snakes, e.g., several rattlesnake species.

**INTERDIGITAL MEMBRANE** The WEB that joins the digits of many amphibians and reptiles.

**INTERFEMORAL** Any one of the scales occupying the area between the hind legs on the undersurface of lizards.

**INTERFEMORAL SEAM** The narrow line running between the FEMORAL laminae in the chelonian PLASTRON.

**INTERGENIAL** In snakes, any one of the scales situated between the large, paired CHINSHIELDS.

**INTERGRADE** Crossbreed; HYBRID, or the interbreeding of closely related species or subspecies in the wild (e.g., *Vipera aspis* × *Vipera berus*) or in captivity (e.g., *Python sebae* × *Python molurus bivittatus*).

**INTERGULAR** A single lamina situated between the GULAR laminae of the plastron in the suborder Pleurodira (side-neck turtles).

**INTERHUMERAL SEAM** The narrow line running between the HUMERAL laminae in the chelonian plastron.

**INTERNAL FERTILIZATION** The vital process of sexual reproduction occurring within the female's body and usually an adaptation to life in a terrestrial environment. Internal fertilization occurs in all reptiles and in a few amphibians, e.g., certain species of *Ascaphus, Nectophrynoides* and *Eleutherodactylus.*

**INTERNAL GILL** The organ of respiration, developed in most fishes, formed as outgrowths from the wall of the pharynx and situated in gill slits. It is ventilated as water, drawn in through the mouth, is forced from the pharynx, past the gills and out through the gill slits. The larvae of amphibians have EXTERNAL GILLS which project from the body so that water passes over them as the animal moves.

**INTERNARIAL DISTANCE** The space between the NARES, or nostrils, the measurement of which can aid identification.

INTERNASAL   Any one of the enlarged scales, or plates, in lizards and snakes on the dorsum of the head at the front of the snout between the NASAL and directly behind the ROSTRAL scales. Usually paired in snakes.

INTERNASAL SPACE   In amphibians, the area of skin on the head between the external nostrils.

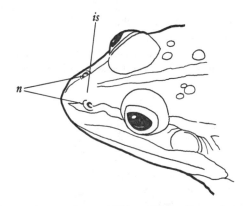

The internasal space of an amphibian refers to the area between the nares or external nostrils: *is*, internasal space; *n*, nares.

INTEROCCIPITAL   1. In crocodiles, a small, centrally situated scale on the rear of the head between the OCCIPITAL scales.   2. In certain lizards, a centrally situated enlarged scale, or plate, on the back of the head, situated directly behind the INTERPARIETAL.

INTEROCUFRONTAL   In the VIPERIDAE, any one of the scales on the head that occupy the area between the FRONTAL and SUPRAOCULAR scales.

INTEROCULABIAL   Any one of the scales situated below the eye and between the SUBOCULAR and SUPRALABIAL scales in some snake species, e.g., rattlesnakes.

INTEROCULAR   Used in reference to the area on top of the head between the outer margins of the eyelids. For example, any pale or dark narrow stripe on the top of the head between the eyes is termed an 'interocular bar'.

INTERORBITAL   In certain snakes and lizards, any one of the small, irregular scales occupying the area, between the ORBITS, on the back of the head, as seen in many boids for example.

INTERPARIETAL   In many lizards, a median scale situated between the PARIETAL scales on the top of the head and the site of the external opening of the PARIETAL EYE in some species.

**INTERPECTORAL SEAM** The narrow line running between the PECTORAL laminae in the chelonian PLASTRON.

**INTERPREOCULAR** In rattlesnakes, any small scale inserted between the upper and lower PREOCULAR scales.

**INTERRUGAL SPACE** In lizards of the genus *Anolis*, the slightly sunken surface occupying the space between the ridges, or rugae, on the top of the head.

**INTERSCALAR** (INTERSTITIAL SKIN) Of, or pertaining to, the usually thin skin lying between the scales of reptiles.

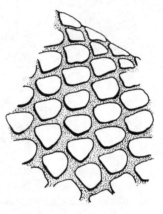

The thin skin that lies between the scales of reptiles is known as 'interscalar' tissue and is represented here by the stippled area.

**INTERSPACE** The area of pigmentation separating one pattern element from another on the backs of snakes and lizards.

**INTERSPECIFIC** Between two or more species.

**INTERSTITIAL SKIN** *See* INTERSCALAR.

**INTERSUPRAOCULAR** Any one of the often irregularly placed scales on top of the head, situated between the SUPRAOCULAR scales.

**INTERXIPHIPLASTRAL NOTCH** In chelonians, the notch situated posterior to the point where the paired XIPHIPLASTRON plates meet on the anal part of the PLASTRON.

**INTRASPECIFIC** Within a single species.

**INTRODUCED** Referring to any individual animal or species brought from an area where it occurs naturally to an area where it is not INDIGENOUS; also termed 'naturalization'. Such introductions are termed 'aliens' or 'exotics', e.g., the cane toad (*Bufo marinus*) is an alien to Australia where it has been introduced by man.

INTROGRESSION   The introduction of genes from one species into the GENE POOL of another by HYBRIDIZATION.

INTROMISSION   The alignment of the cloacae and insertion of the male's HEMIPENIS (in snakes and lizards) or PENIS (in chelonians, crocodilians and caecilians) into the cloaca of the female.

INTROMITTENT ORGAN   The male copulatory organ in animals which reproduce by INTERNAL FERTILIZATION, e.g., the HEMIPENIS of lizards and snakes, the PENIS of crocodilians, caecilians and chelonians, and the TAIL in frogs of the ASCAPHIDAE.

INVERTEBRATE   Any animal lacking a vertebral column, and including such diverse forms as worms, arthropods (including insects) and molluscs.

INVOLUTION   The regression and eventual disappearance of an organ.

IN YOUNG   In reptiles exhibiting OVOVIVIPARITY or VIVIPARITY, said of a female carrying unborn young.

IONIDES, Constantine Philip   1901–68, naturalist, game-ranger and herpetologist with a worldwide reputation. During his numerous safaris, in which he visited every country of Central Africa, he contributed greatly to herpetological knowledge, discovering several new forms and devising new methods of catching and handling the more dangerous species. In addition he played a very important role in the development of the National Museum in Nairobi, personally collecting many of its rarer animals.

IRIDESCENCE   The rainbow lustre in reptiles, resulting from the arrangement and structure of the scales and occurring usually as a purple, green or bluish sheen which changes colour with a change in the angle of view. Iridescence is particularly noticeable in the sunbeam snake (*Xenopeltis unicolor*). In many species of snakes, certain lizards and several amphibians, it is considered, by herpetologists, to be a sign of good health.

IRIDOPHORE   A type of CHROMATOPHORE containing purines, which, unlike the MELANOPHORE and xanthophore, does not produce colours but diffracts light, which results in various iridescent effects, such as the green colour of many anurans which takes on a bluish hue when seen in a different light.

IRIS   The often brightly coloured, circular area of muscular tissue in the front of the eye, serving as a diaphragm to control the size of the PUPIL and thereby regulating the amount of light entering the eye.

ISCHIUM   The rearmost of the three bones that constitute each half of the pelvic girdle in tetrapod vertebrates.

ISODONT   Having teeth that are comparatively regular in both appearance and size, as in most lizards and non-venomous snakes.

# J

JACARE  A Brazilian name for the CAIMAN. Examples include jacare-tinga, the spectacled caiman (*Caiman crocodilus*); jacare-curua, the broad-snouted caiman (*C. latirostris*); and jacare-acu, the black caiman (*Melanosuchus niger*).

JACKSON'S METHOD  An old method of treatment once used for the bites of VENOMOUS snakes. Developed by Dr Dudley Jackson, it involved cutting across and around the fang punctures with cross-shaped incisions. As the swelling at the site of the bite increased, so the incisions were lengthened, whilst suction was applied to them.

JACKSON'S RATIO  Formulated by Dr Oliphant Jackson, an eminent veterinary surgeon who did much important work on reptile health and husbandry. His ratio is one of the criteria that can be used to show the state of health of spur-thighed and Hermann's tortoises (*Testudo graeca* and *T. hermanni*) when they are maintained in captivity. By comparing the length of the CARAPACE with the weight of a particular tortoise, the resulting point, plotted on a graph, can indicate whether or not that tortoise is in good health.

JACOBSON'S GLAND  A GLAND located within the snout of *Salamandra*. Once assumed to be part of JACOBSON'S ORGAN, the majority of anatomists today consider that urodeles lack that organ, although the name for the gland still persists.

JACOBSON'S ORGAN  A modified part of the nasal sac forming the major sense organ in many reptiles, it consists of a pair of pouch-like structures embedded in the frontal region of the palate and lined with sensory tissue. In an active snake, the tongue is constantly protruded and withdrawn. Upon withdrawal, the forked tips are thrust into these spiral, blind-sac openings and any particles that have been picked up from surrounding objects or the air are conveyed to the sensory lining of Jacobson's organ for analysis by the brain, via a special branch of the OLFACTORY nerve. The organ is absent in adult crocodilians.

JACURA   The northern tegu (*Tupinambis nigropunctatus*) of the TEIIDAE family, inhabiting central and northern South America.

JAN, George   1791–1866, Italian zoologist. Compiled *Iconographie generale des ophidiens*, a three-volume work, illustrated by Sordelli, describing all the snakes then known.

JARARACA   Probably the most abundant PIT VIPER in the world, *Bothrops jararaca*, of the family VIPERIDAE, subfamily Crotalinae, inhabiting Brazil, Paraguay and northern Argentina.

JARARACUSSU   *Bothrops jararacussu*, a PIT VIPER of the family VIPERIDAE, subfamily Crotalinae, inhabiting Brazil, Paraguay and northern Argentina.

JAWCLAP   An acoustic and subsonic signal employed by most crocodilian species especially during courtship. The opened jaws are suddenly and sharply clapped shut either on or below the water surface, an action frequently accompanied by a HEADSLAP. The jawclap appears to act as a deterrent to rival males and as an attraction to females, which sometimes respond with their own jawclap.

JELLY   Gelatinous material exuded partly from glands in the walls of the oviducts and partly from glands in the CLOACA in amphibians. Affixed to the eggs as they pass through, the jelly may be set down in concentric layers, or as jelly envelopes, the number of which varies with the species, or it may form an uninterrupted tube without any noticeable layering, as in the JELLY STRAND of members of the BUFONIDAE.

JELLY FLOAT   In eggs of the frog *Kaloula*, a wide, marginal structure, formed soon after ovulation in the exterior jelly envelope of each egg, enabling the CLUTCH to float at the water's surface.

JELLY STRAND   The often considerably lengthy string of JELLY that coats the eggs of toads of the genus *Bufo*. Bufonid jelly is made up of four layers: the two central ones envelop each individual egg and the two outer ones are common to the whole CLUTCH.

JIZZ   Originally a term used by birdwatchers which has recently found its way into herpetology; the combination of delicate and indefinable characteristics that is frequently the simplest method of recognizing and isolating species that are closely related. The successful use of jizz relies largely upon the observer having some experience of the animals concerned.

JORDAN'S RULE   The closest-related individuals of a particular species do not occur in the same region, or in a distant one, but in an adjoining area, either partly or completely separated by an obstacle or boundary.

JUBAL   In lizards of the genus *Eumeces*, the greatly enlarged scale, or scales, located directly behind the head.

JUGAL   1. Used by some authors to describe a scale situated below the eye in crocodiles, with 'first jugals' being the row of scales on the margin of the lower eyelids and 'second jugals' the row below those.   2. In reptiles and certain amphibians, particularly caecilians, a dermal bone in the BUCCAL area, ventrally bordering the eye and extending behind the upper jaw bone (MAXILLA) forming part of the lipline.

JUGULAR   Of, or relating to, the neck and/or throat. In snakes, any one of the scales situated between the CHINSHIELD and lower LABIAL scales.

JURASSIC   The middle period of the MESOZOIC era, from 195 million to 135 million years ago. Reptiles were large and plentiful, dominating the vertebrates, and the pterosaurs, the first flying reptiles, occurred. Fossils of the earliest-known primitive bird (*Archaeopteryx*) and of the first mammals are found in Jurassic rocks.

JUVENILE (juv.)   A very young, newly hatched or newborn individual, often displaying proportions and colorations differing from those of the ADULT.

JUXTAPOSED   Term used to describe body scales that do not overlap but are disposed in a side-by-side fashion. Compare with IMBRICATE.

# K

**KEEL** 1. Any ridge running from front to back on the CARAPACE or PLASTRON of a chelonian. 2. The slightly raised line, or ridge, on the middle of a single scale in some species of snakes, the distribution, presence (or absence) and definition of which are all important in CLASSIFICATION. 3. The elevated border along the upper surface of the tail in some urodeles, which can sometimes extend onto the body. The dorsal fin on anuran tadpoles is also termed a keel.

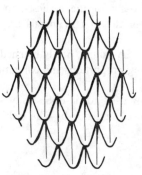

Keeled scales: the keels on the scales of reptiles or the shells of chelonians are features useful in the identification of these animals.

**KERATIN** A tough, fibrous, sulphur-containing protein that occurs in the outer layer of the skin (EPIDERMIS) of both amphibians and reptiles, and which furnishes the rudimentary constituent for the formation of scales, spines, claws and horns etc.

KERATITIS   Inflammation of the cornea; most common in chelonian genera.

KERATOPHAGY   The eating of KERATIN or keratinous materials. The majority of amphibians and some reptiles (mainly lizards of the family GEKKONIDAE) devour all or part of their skins during the act of sloughing, or ECDYSIS. The dead, cornified cells in the sloughed EPIDERMIS are an important supply of protein too valuable to waste.

KIDNEY DISEASE   Any one of several infectious (nephritis) or non-infectious (nephrosis) diseases of the urinary organs, of which GOUT is the most significant in reptiles. Causes of kidney disease in reptiles include vitamin deficiency, parasite infestations and *Pseudomonas* infections.

KINK   The sharp bend occurring in a digit of the frog genus *Rhacophorus*, brought about by an extra cartilaginous component, the INTERCALARY CARTILAGE.

KINOSTERNIDAE   Mud and musk turtles. Family of the CHELONIA, suborder Cryptodira, inhabiting eastern Canada and extending into South America. Approximately 20 species in two genera.

KLAUBER, Laurence Monroe   1883–1968, American herpetologist who carried out intensive and widespread studies of rattlesnakes (CROTALIDAE), culminating in the two-volume *Rattlesnakes; their habits, life histories and influences on mankind* (1956). He also produced many papers on other reptile taxa of the south-western USA.

KNOB   A rounded projection, lump, stud or boss and used in reference to the enlarged keels on scales located near the anus in some species of snakes, termed 'knobbed anal keels'.

KUFI   Levantine or blunt-nosed viper (*Vipera lebetina*). Member of the VIPERIDAE family of the SQUAMATA, subfamily Viperinae, inhabiting Middle East, north Africa, north-west Pakistan and the Cyclades. A bold and dangerous species attaining 1200 mm in length.

KYPHOSIS   Hunchback; the backward curvature of the spine resulting either from injury or disease, or may be CONGENITAL in origin. Occurs predominantly in chelonians where it manifests itself as an abnormality in the CARAPACE.

# L

LABIAL   Of, or pertaining to, the upper or lower lip (labium) in
reptiles; any one of the row of scales bordering the mouths of
snakes and lizards on the upper and lower lips and termed upper
labial and lower labial respectively.

LABIAL GLAND   In the genus *Salamandra*, a glandulous area in
the skin of the lips and chin.

LABIAL PIT   Any one of a number of cavities, varying in size and
disposition from one genus to another, each set in an individual
upper or lower LABIAL scale; found in many snakes of the BOIDAE
family and in one or two other species, and serving as highly sensitive thermoceptors able to detect temperature differences as low
as 0.025°C. The labial pit also enables the snake to seek and find
warm-blooded prey in complete darkness and is similar in both
structure and function to the PIT of the Crotalinae, or PIT VIPERS.

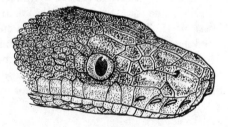

Labial pits, each situated in an individual labial scale, on the upper or
lower lips of certain snakes, are highly sensitive to temperature
fluctuations and help the reptiles to detect their prey at night.

LABIAL TEETH   Small, horny cusps situated, in transverse rows like the rasps on a file, on the lips (labia) of anuran larvae.

LABIUM, pl. LABIA   A lip, or any lip-like structure.

LACÉPÈDE, Bernard   1756–1825, French zoologist. Described many new reptile and amphibian species, and his four-volume *Natural history of oviparous quadrupeds and serpents* (1789), was the first comprehensive world summary of reptiles and amphibians.

LACERTIDAE   'Typical' lizards. Family of the SQUAMATA, suborder SAURIA, inhabiting most of Europe, Asia and Africa (except Madagascar). Over 200 species in some 20 genera.

LACERTILIA   An alternative term, preferred by some authors, for the SAURIA (lizards), the suborder of SQUAMATA.

LACRIMAL   In rattlesnakes, the enlarged scale situated between the PREOCULAR and POSTOCULAR scales and bordering the lower frontal area of the ORBIT.

LACRIMAL GLAND   In reptiles, one of the two large glands connected with each eye, that produce the 'tears' that help to keep the eye moist. It is situated towards the back of the eye, its secretions emptying into the conjunctival space under the eyelid where they lubricate and cleanse the exposed eye surface. Closely associated with the NICTITATING MEMBRANE of chelonians, crocodilians and lizards. *See also* HARDERIAN GLAND.

LACRYMAL   An alternative spelling for LACRIMAL, used in earlier literature.

LACUNAL   Any one of the enlarged and outward curving scales forming the inner and part of the outer borders of the PIT in crotaline snakes.

LACUNOLABIAL   A large, single scale in certain crotaline snakes, resulting from the union of the prelacunal and the second (or occasionally, the third) supralabial scales.

LAEVOGYRINID   A term given to most anuran larvae which possess a single SPIRACLE on the left side of their bodies.

LAMELLA, pl. LAMELLAE   In herpetology, used most frequently for the series of thin, either single or divided, transverse plates extending across the underside of the digits in many lizard species.

LAMINA, pl. LAMINAE   Any one of the horny, epidermal scutes covering the bony plates in the skeleton of the CARAPACE and PLASTRON of many chelonians. The term is used less frequently today, many authors preferring the word 'scute'.

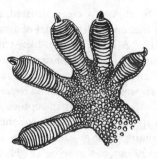

A ventral view of the foot of a gecko showing the broad transverse lamellae on the digits which enable the lizard to grip smooth surfaces.

**LAMINAR NUCLEUS**   The slightly off-centre, JUVENILE area (AREOLA) of the lamina in many chelonians.

**LANTHONOTIDAE**   Earless monitor. Family of the SQUAMATA, suborder SAURIA, inhabiting Borneo. MONOTYPIC.

**LARGE-SCALE HIDE**   A term used in the commercial skin trade for soft-bellied species of crocodilians that have 20–25 transverse ventral scale rows. *See also* SMALL-SCALE HIDE, TRANSVERSE VENTRAL SCALE ROWS.

**LARVA**   The stage in the life of many animals, e.g., many invertebrates, most amphibians and certain fishes, that follows the embryo and precedes the adult stage. A larva very often bears little or no resemblance to its parents and must undergo a METAMORPHOSIS before it assumes the characteristic features of the adult.

**LARYNX**   The upper portion of the TRACHEA (windpipe) of tetrapod vertebrates which, in reptiles and amphibians (and mammals), contains the vocal cords.

**LATASTE, Fernand**   1847–1934, French herpetologist and professor of medicine. His work in herpetology was involved principally with the amphibians of north-western and western Europe.

**LATERAL**   Pertaining to, or situated on, the sides; any one of the scales on the side of a lizard's body that are neither DORSAL nor VENTRAL scales.

**LATERAL DERMAL FOLD**   An alternative term for the DORSO-LATERAL FOLD on the sides of the body in some amphibians and occurring in a number of lizard species also. Frequently shortened to dermal fold.

LATERAL LAMINA   An alternative term for the COSTAL lamina in many chelonians.

LATERAL LINE SYSTEM   A series of sense organs (NEURO-MASTS) disposed on the head and along the body in aquatic amphibians, responsible for the detection of sounds and changes in pressure, in water.

A simplified diagram of a clawed frog (*Xenopus laevis*), showing the row of slightly raised sense organs on the back of the head and along the sides of the body which form the lateral line system serving to detect vibrations in water.

LATERAL UNDULATION   *See* SERPENTINE LOCOMOTION.

LD50   The median lethal dose (LD) of a substance that will kill half (50%) of a group of experimental animals to which it is exposed. It is frequently used as a standard measure of snake-venom toxicity.

LEECH   Any freshwater or terrestrial annelid worm of the class Hirudinea. Leeches are either carnivorous predators or blood-sucking parasites, feeding upon the blood or tissues of other animals. Chelonians and crocodilians are frequently parasitized by leeches of the genus *Haementeria*, due mainly to the fact that both the leeches and the reptiles lead aquatic or semi-aquatic existences and share the same habitats.

LEIOPELMATIDAE   Family of the ANURA, inhabiting the north-western USA and New Zealand. Four species in two genera.

LENTIC   Of, inhabiting, or relating to, still waters.

LEPIDOSIS   The pattern and disposition of scales.

LEPTODACTYLIDAE   Family of the ANURA, inhabiting Central and South America. Over 700 species in 52 genera.

Leeches have been found on a number of aquatic and semi-aquatic
amphibians, and reptiles such as crocodilians and freshwater chelonians,
with which they share the same habitats.

LEPTOTYPHLOPIDAE   Thread snakes. Family of the SQUAM-
ATA, suborder OPHIDIA, inhabiting tropical America, Africa and extending into western Asia. 50 species in 2 genera.

LETHAL DOSE   *See* LD50.

LEUCISTIC   Descriptive of an animal having a body that is partially or completely white, or colourless, but with eyes that retain
their usual pigmentation (eye pigment is lacking in a true ALBINO).
Such leucistic animals are sometimes termed 'dilute albinos'.

LID OEDEMA   A disease of the HARDERIAN GLAND, usually associated with an abnormal accumulation of fluid causing swelling and
resulting in protrusion of the eyelids, occurring in a number of
chelonian genera.

LIMB BUD STAGE   The phase in the life of larval anurans when
the limbs are nothing more than plain bud-like outgrowths lacking
any recognizable external features.

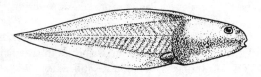

Limb bud stage: the period of development in a tadpole when the limbs
have yet to assume recognisable features.

LINGUAL   Of, or relating to, the tongue.

LINGUAL FOSSA   In snakes, the small, V-shaped indentation in the underside of the ROSTRAL scale, through which the tongue can protrude while the mouth remains shut.

The lingual fossa, or indentation in the underside of the rostral scale, through which the tongue can protrude through an otherwise closed mouth.

LINGUATULID   A modified, worm-like ARACHNID, occurring almost exclusively in reptiles as an ENDOPARASITE.

LINNAEUS or VON LINNÉ, Carl (L. or Linn.)  1707–78, Swedish naturalist, botanist and physician. Established the Stockholm Academy of Sciences and exerted an influence in his fields of natural history and botany that has had few parallels in the history of science. Famous for formulating the basic principles for classification, and for founding modern systematic botany in 1753. Three years later he presented, for the first time, in the tenth edition of his work, *Systema Naturae*, a binomial (two–name) system of NOMENCLATURE, in which each species received two names: the first one for the genus; the second for the particular species. He immediately received acclaim from scientists throughout the world and the system, named after him, is in universal use today. In 1788, the Linnéan Society was founded in England in his honour, publishing transactions and journals on matters of natural history.

LIPOPHORE   A pigment cell of the skin associated with red and yellow coloration.

LIQUID INTAKE   Most reptiles satisfy their liquid requirements by drinking fresh water. Snakes and chelonians immerse the tips of their snouts in water and swallow using muscular movements of their throats, and lizards lap up water droplets with their tongues. Many desert species rarely drink water, receiving most, if not all, of the liquid they require from the food they eat. In aquatic amphibians, liquid absorption takes place through the whole surface of the body, including the CLOACA, while they are submerged in water; other species obtain any moisture they may need from their prey.

LITTORAL   Of, relating to, or inhabiting, the shallow waters or shores of a sea, ocean (marine littoral) or lake (freshwater littoral).

LIZARDLET   A term used very occasionally for a newborn or hatchling lizard.

LIZARD POX   *See* POX.

LOBE   Any rounded or curved projection that forms part of a larger structure. Used in herpetology for: **1.** The area on a chelonian PLASTRON directly in front and to the rear of the BRIDGE and termed 'anterior lobe' and 'posterior lobe' respectively. **2.** Any one of the enlarged areas on any one of the horny rings that constitute the rattle in *Crotalus* and *Sistrurus*.

LOCOMOTION   The power, ability, or act of moving from one place to another. Locomotion in reptiles and amphibians takes many forms, from the lateral movements of the body and tail in aquatic urodeles and amphibian larvae to the trot and gallop in certain lizards and crocodilians. Limb reduction, present in varying degrees in many lizard families, amphisbaenids, caecilians, several urodeles and, ultimately, snakes, has resulted in the development of particular forms of locomotion to suit their different modes of life and adapted to the variable habitats in which they live. These include CONCERTINA, RECTILINEAR, SERPENTINE and SIDEWINDING MOVEMENT.

LONGEVITY   Literally, 'long life', but used generally for the period in an organism's life from its hatching or birth to its natural death. The longevity, or life span, of reptiles and amphibians can vary from as little as one or two years in some of the smaller species to well over 150 years in larger species, e.g., the Aldabran giant tortoise (*Geochelone gigantea*).

LONGITUDINAL   Of, or relating to, length; located or running along the length.

LONGITUDINAL TYPE (RECTIFORM)   Used in reference to a particular arrangement, common to most snakes, in the scalation. See SCALE ROW.

LORA   The parrot snake (*Leptophis ahaetulla*) of the family COLUBRIDAE, subfamily Colubrinae, inhabiting the dry forest areas of Mexico through to Argentina.

LORE   The space, usually in the form of a very shallow depression, on the surface of the head of snakes directly in front of the eye.

LOREAL   A scale situated between those of the nostril (NASAL scales) and those of the eye (PREOCULAR scales), but not touching either, in snakes, which usually have just one, and in lizards, which may have several.

LOREAL PIT   The PIT on the side of the head of crotaline snakes (pit vipers).

LORICA, pl. LORICAE   A hard, outer covering, or CUIRASS; used in herpetology for the protective, bony armour of plates, shields and laminae of crocodilians and chelonians.

LORILABIAL   In lizards, any one of a number of scales situated in a longitudinal row between the LOREAL and SUPRALABIAL scales.

LOWER LABIAL   *See* LABIAL.

LOWER ROSTRAL   The scale situated at the centre of the tip of the lower jaw in snakes and lizards, bordered on either side by the first lower labials.

LUMBAR   In crocodilians and lizards etc., the area of the back directly in front of the hind limbs.

LUMBAR GLAND   In certain anurans, e.g., the leptodactylid *Pleurodema bufonia* and allied species, a distinct, enlarged and glandulous area of the lower back and sides between the pelvis and the abdomen.

LUMEN, pl. LUMINA   The space, cavity or canal enclosed within a duct, tube or similarly-shaped organ, of which the central passage of the digestive tract is an example.

LUMEN EXIT   In venomous snakes, the point where the VENOM DUCT opens at the base of the FANG, allowing venom to flow down or through it.

LUNGWORM   Any one of a number of parasitic NEMATODE worms, especially of the genus *Rhabdias*, occurring in the lungs of many amphibians, snakes and some lizards. Untreated infestations in captive animals often result in death.

LURE   1. The bright, contrastingly-coloured tip of the tail in a number of juvenile snakes, such as certain arboreal species of *Trimeresurus*, that can be elevated and waved around, thereby attracting inquisitive prey to approach within striking distance.   2. The flesh-coloured, motile worm-like projection from the tongue of the alligator snapping turtle (*Macroclemys temmincki*) that serves to attract small fish as the reptile lies submerged with its mouth agape.

# M

**MACROCEPHALY**  The condition of having a grossly enlarged head or skull, occurring occasionally in certain aged individuals of some chelonians.

**MALACHITE GREEN**  A substance often used in the treatment of various fungal infections of the shells of captive aquatic chelonians.

**MALAR**  Of, or relating to, or on, the cheek or cheekbone.

**MALAR SCALE**  An enlarged scale on the lower jaw of *Amphisbaena*.

**MALE RELEASE CALL**  In anurans, a vocal sound uttered by either or both male and female during AMPLEXUS, if and when grasped by one or more other males. The call informs other males that a pairing has already taken place and causes them to release their grasp.

**MALPIGHIAN LAYER**  The innermost layer of dividing cells at the base of the epidermis of vertebrates. The cells contain MELANIN and move gradually upwards through the epidermal layers where they become hardened, forming the STRATUM CORNEUM, replacing those cells which are constantly being sloughed off.

**MAMUSHI**  A Japanese name for the subspecies of Haly's pit viper (*Agkistrodon halys blomhoffi*), which is responsible for many incidents of snake bite in Japan each year, although fatalities are comparatively rare.

**MANDIBLE**  The cartilage and bone (DENTARY) of the lower jaw in vertebrates. Teeth situated on the dentary bone are termed 'mandibular teeth'.

MANGROVE SWAMP   A tidal region typical of many tropical and, occasionally, subtropical sheltered coasts, frequently with freshwater lagoons and river deltas, and characterized by dense thickets of evergreen trees and shrubs of the genus *Rhizophora*, with stiltlike intertwining aerial roots. Mangrove swamps are important habitats for many amphibians and reptiles, including terrestrial, arboreal and sea snakes, certain varanid lizards and several *Crocodylus* species.

MARGINAL   Of, on, in, or forming, a margin or border.   1. Any one of the laminae appearing as a border around the edge of the bony part of the CARAPACE in chelonians.   2. Any one of the scales in the upper of two rows lying laterally directly beneath and adjacent to the DORSAL scales in crocodilians.

MARINE   Of, relating to, or inhabiting, the sea.

MARSH   An area of low, waterlogged land, usually near or on the edge of lakes or rivers etc., and an important habitat for many species of reptile and amphibian, e.g., water snakes (*Natrix*, *Nerodia* etc.) and anurans and urodeles (*Rana*, *Triturus* etc.).

MARSUPIAL POUCH   A sac-like cavity (marsupium) formed from the skin on the back of female marsupial frogs (genus *Gastrotheca*). The pouch opens directly above the CLOACA and receives the fertilized eggs which remain there until they have developed into free-swimming tadpoles (*G. marsupiata*) or completely metamorphosed young frogs (*G. ovifera*).

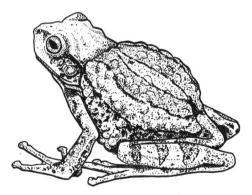

The marsupial pouch of this frog, *Gastrotheca riobambae*, is full of developing eggs which may be over 200 in number.

**MASK**   1. The dark, broad band or stripe, occurring in some anuran species, running laterally from the nostril or the eye to the tympanum and, sometimes, beyond.   2. The face-like markings, or pattern, on the back of the spread HOOD in several species of cobra.

**MASSASAUGA**   *Sistrurus catenatus*, a rattlesnake of the family VIPERIDAE, subfamily Crotalinae, inhabiting a variety of habitats from marshland to rocky desert hillsides, from the Great Lakes of Canada to northern Mexico.

**MATRIX**   The fleshy tail tip in rattlesnakes (*Crotalus, Sistrurus*), from which each successive horny ring, or segment, of the RATTLE develops.

**MAXILLA**   The upper jaw bone of vertebrates, and in reptiles and amphibians either one of two, usually tooth-bearing, bones separated at the front of the jaw by the PREMAXILLA BONES. In viperid snakes the maxilla bears the fangs and in chelonians the teeth are replaced by a horny covering (BEAK).

**MECKEL'S CARTILAGE**   In reptiles and amphibians, the ossified cartilage that forms the articular bone of the lower jaw.

**MEDIAL**   Of, or occurring in, the middle.

**MEDIAN**   Of, or occurring towards, the middle.

**MEDIAN EYE**   The PARIETAL EYE of early vertebrates.

**MEDIAN GULAR**   A scale situated on the throat either between or directly behind the CHINSHIELD scales.

**MEDIOGYRINID**   A term given to anuran larvae which possess a single SPIRACLE in the centre of their bodies, e.g., the LEIOPELMATIDAE and DISCOGLOSSIDAE.

**MEGADONT**   Having teeth that are not regular in either size or appearance.

**MELANIN**   Pigment granules of the skin responsible for dark brown to black coloration in animals.

**MELANISM**   An overproduction of the pigment melanin resulting in animals that are entirely, or nearly, all-black, often as a response to environmental factors. Melanism is not uncommon among certain species of snake and lizard, such dark, or melanistic, individuals sometimes receiving the term 'melanos'.

**MELANO**   *See* MELANISM.

**MELANOPHORE**   A cell of the skin containing the black or dark brown pigment MELANIN.

**MELANOSARCOMA**   *See* TUMOUR.

**MEMBRANE**   A very thin, sheet-like tissue that connects, lines or covers organs and cells of animals (and plants). Examples are the NICTITATING MEMBRANE that covers the eye in many reptiles, and the WEB that connects the digits in many amphibians.

MENTAL   The single MEDIAN scale on the front edge of the lower jaw, directly in front of the CHINSHIELD in lizards, and between the first lower LABIAL scales in snakes.

MENTAL GLAND   A gland situated in the skin of the chin of certain male urodeles, the secretion from which stimulates the females into becoming sexually responsive to mating.

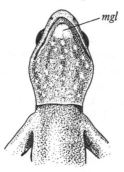

Ventral view of the head of a male salamander showing the position of the mental gland (*mgl*).

MENTAL GROOVE   The medial furrow on the undersurface of the lower jaw between the CHINSHIELD scales in snakes. It allows the jaw, and the skin upon it, to expand during the swallowing of large food items.

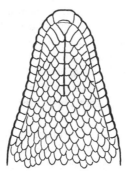

The underside of the head of a boid snake showing the mental groove on the chin which allows the jaw to expand.

**MERCY CRY**   An alternative term for the FRIGHT CRY of anurans.

**MERCY-KILLING**   The humane killing, or EUTHANASIA, of an animal to relieve suffering from disease or injury.

**MERISTIC**   Of, or relating to, the number of parts, organs or other countable structures of an organism, e.g., the scales of snakes.

**MERREM, Blasius**   1761–1824, German zoologist and the first accurately to separate the reptiles and amphibians, in *Versuch eines Systems der Amphibien* (1820). He combined the snakes and lizards in a single order, the SQUAMATA, and also separated the crocodilians from the lizards.

**MERTENS, Robert**   1894–1975, German zoologist and herpetologist, and Director of the Senckenberg Museum in Frankfurt am Main, Germany. His contribution to herpetology was tremendous with over 600 publications to his credit, a number of which he coauthored, including the definitive identification keys and checklists for the recent crocodilians, chelonians and tuataras, which he compiled with Wermuth (1955 & 1961).

**MESIC**   Of, relating to, or inhabiting, areas that are damp but not swampy.

**MESOGLYPH**   Any one of a number of snakes in which the FANG is situated close to the middle of the relatively short maxillary bone of the upper jaw. To the front of the fang lie from two to ten smaller teeth, whilst to the rear of it there are no teeth at all. Examples of mesoglyph snakes are seen in the similar, and closely related, African genera, *Polemon* and *Miodon*.

**MESOPLASTRON**   Either one of the pair of non-adjacent dermal bones situated between the HYOPLASTRON and HYPOPLASTRON bones of the PLASTRON, typical of certain primitive chelonian species but still surviving in the musk turtles (*Sternotherus*) of eastern North America, and the helmeted terrapins (PELOMEDUSIDAE) of Central Africa and Madagascar.

**MESOPTYCHIAL**   Any one of the scales situated on the outer surface of the GULAR FOLD or on the rear, central area of the undersurface of the throat (mesoptychis) directly in front of the PECTORAL GIRDLE in lizards.

**MESOZOIC**   The middle geological era dating from the end of the PALAEOZOIC, approximately 230 million years ago, to the beginning of the CENOZOIC, approximately 70 million years ago. The dinosaurs, ichthyosaurs, pterosaurs etc. were the dominant animals at that time and the Palaeozoic is often termed the 'Age of Reptiles'.

Most of them, however, had become extinct by the end of the era. The Mesozoic era is made up of three main periods: the TRIASSIC, JURASSIC and CRETACEOUS.

METABOLISM   Chemical balance and reactions that occur in cells within the body, resulting in growth, energy production, removal of waste products etc. The rate of metabolism is the speed, higher in a warm-blooded animal (HOMOIOTHERM) than in a cold-blooded animal (POIKILOTHERM), at which the chemical reactions occur.

METACARPAL BONE   Any one of the rod-shaped bones that form the METACARPUS in the forefoot or lower forelimb of tetrapod vertebrates, and articulate proximally with the CARPALS, and distally with the PHALANGES. In a typical pentadactyl (having five digits) limb there are five metacarpals, although there are adaptations to this plan and, in many species, the number is reduced.

METACARPUS   The collection of METACARPAL BONES that forms part of the skeleton of the forefoot or lower forelimb in tetrapod vertebrates.

METAMORPHOSIS   The rapid transformation occurring in an amphibian when the LARVA takes on the physical appearance of the ADULT. In anurans the most obvious sign is the loss of the tail and rapid growth of the legs. In urodeles it is the disappearance of the CAUDAL FIN and feathery gills.

METATARSAL BONE   Any one of the rod-shaped bones that

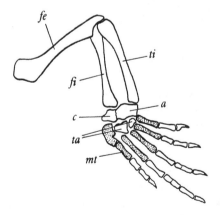

Diagram of the hind limb of a lizard in which the metatarsal bones are shown stippled: *a*, astragalus; *c*, calcaneum; *fe*, femur; *fi*, fibula; *mt*, metatarsal; *ta*, tarsal; *ti*, tibia.

together form the METATARSUS in the hind foot or lower hind limb
of tetrapod vertebrates, and articulate proximally with the TARSAL
bones and distally with the PHALANGES. In a typical pentadactyl
(having five digits) limb there are five metatarsals, although there
are adaptations to this plan and, in many species, the number is reduced.

METATARSAL TUBERCLE   A prominent knob-like projection
present on the hind foot of many anurans and used by certain
species (e.g., *Scaphiopus, Pelobates*) as a SPADE for digging.

METATARSUS   The collection of METATARSAL BONES that forms
part of the skeleton of the hind foot or lower hind limb in tetrapod
vertebrates.

MICROHYLIDAE   Narrow-mouthed toads. Family of the ANURA,
inhabiting New Guinea, Asia, Africa, Madagascar, South America
and North America. 279 species in 59 genera.

MID-BODY SCALE ROW   1. In snakes, the number of scales
lying on an imaginary line running around the centre of the body,
beginning and ending at, but not including, the large, elongated
VENTRAL scales.   2. In lizards, the number of scales lying on an
imaginary line running completely around the centre of the body.

MID-DORSAL   Of, relating to, or on, the centre of the back or
DORSUM.

MID-RIB   The gristly mid-section of the vocal cord in certain anuran species.

MID-VENTRAL   Of, relating to, or on, the centre of the abdomen
or VENTER.

MIGRATION   *See* SEASONAL MOVEMENT.

MILK   To extract the venom from venomous reptiles by skilful and
manual means. Milking a venomous reptile is generally done by
mechanically or electrically stimulating the venom glands to discharge their contents into a vessel over which the reptile has been
persuaded to open its mouth.

MILKED UP   The term commonly used to describe a snake that is
preparing to SLOUGH its skin which, together with the eye, assumes
a pale bluish tinge caused by an oily secretion from the EXUVIAL
GLAND that forms between the old and new skin, moistening the
old one prior to ECDYSIS.

MILK SNAKE   Originally, the harmless North and Central
American colubrid, *Lampropeltis triangulum*, but used today for any
of the tricoloured *L. triangulum* subspecies.

MILT  The spermatozoa and seminal fluid of a male anuran expelled, during AMPLEXUS, as the female simultaneously deposits her eggs which are then fertilized as the milt flows over them.

MIMIC  Referring to any species that closely resembles, or assumes the appearance of, a different, usually distasteful or venomous species. Among reptiles, examples can be seen in the harmless tricoloured MILK SNAKES (*Lampropeltis triangulum* ssp.), which mimic the venomous coral snakes (*Micrurus* and *Micruroides*).

MIOCENE  The fourth epoch of the TERTIARY period, beginning approximately 25 million years ago at the end of the OLIGOCENE, and lasting some 18 million years, when it was superseded by the PLIOCENE.

MITE  A small arthropod of the order Acarina, which also includes the ticks. The snake mite (*Ophionyssus natricus*) is particularly significant in reptile collections as it can act as a VECTOR of disease. Newly imported or freshly caught specimens should receive a period of isolation from the main collection to first ensure that any mite infestations are eradicated.

MOCQUARD, François  1834–1971, French herpetologist. Contributor to the 17-volume *Mission scientifique au Mexique et dans l'Amerique Centrale: Etudes sur les reptiles et les batraciens* (1870–1909), in joint authorship with Brocchi, Duméril (Auguste) and Bocourt.

MOLCHPEST  The feared and little understood disease that occurs, often in epidemic proportions, among captive urodeles, and is characterized by a variety of symptoms, including dermal inflammation and the subsequent development of abscesses which spread rapidly over the body, but, most significantly, by an unusual odour which the diseased amphibian, and the water in which it is housed, emits. Affected specimens invariably fail to respond to treatment and eventually die.

MOLOCH  The thorny devil (*Moloch horridus*), an Australian lizard of the family AGAMIDAE.

MONITOR  Any one of the large, predatory lizards of the family VARANIDAE, inhabiting Africa, southern Asia and Australasia.

MONOCELLATE  Possessing a single eye-like spot or OCELLUS.

MONODACTYL  Possessing a single digit on the fore- or hind foot, as in certain lizard species (e.g., SCINCIDAE).

MONOSPECIFIC  1. Pertaining to a genus that contains a single species only.  2. An alternative term for MONOVALENT.

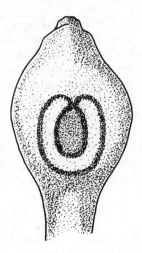

The monocellate spot, or ocellus, on the back of the hood of the
monocled cobra (*Naja naja kaouthia*).

**MONOTYPIC**  Containing a single form (TAXON) only, e.g., a
species in which there is no subspecies. Contrast with POLYTYPIC.

**MONOVALENT**  Possessing antibodies for a single particular organism or substance, and a term used commonly for any antivenom
that acts against the venom of a single snake species only.

**MONSOON FOREST**  A type of deciduous forest of eastern and
south-eastern Asia, that has a more or less well-determined monsoon climate.

**MONTANE**  Of, relating to, or inhabiting, mountains or mountain-
ous regions.

**MONTANE DRY FOREST**  A type of forest, characterized by
low deciduous trees, thick, thorny shrubs, and numerous types of
grasses, occurring mainly between altitudes of 500 and 1500 m.

**MONTANE MOIST FOREST**  A type of forest, occurring
mainly at altitudes above 1000 m, in regions in which the seasons
are well-determined, and receiving rainfall approximately intermediate in amount to that received by montane dry and montane
wet forests.

**MONTANE WET FOREST**  A type of extremely damp forest,
occurring mainly at altitudes over 1500 m and analogous in charac-
ter to the highest parts of the CLOUD FOREST.

MORPH   A form or phase; different from the normal, e.g., the European viper (*Vipera berus*), in which the characteristic zig-zag running from the back of the head to the tail tip is replaced by a straight-edged longitudinal stripe.

MORPHOLOGY   The study of the phases, or forms, of organisms.

MOULT   The act of sloughing, or casting off, the old, transparent outer layer of skin during ECDYSIS.

MOUTH ROT   *See* STOMATITIS.

MUCRONATE   Ending in a sharp point, a term used to describe scales that are overlapping and taper into a spine.

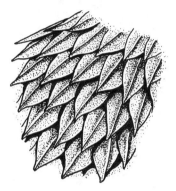

Mucronate scales.

MUCUS   The slimy secretion produced by certain cells in the mucous membranes and glands of animals, the function of which is to lubricate and protect the surface upon which it is secreted. In many amphibians the mucous on the skin may be toxic to a varying degree, and this toxicity is particularly well developed in that of the arrow-poison frogs of the family DENDROBATIDAE which, in some cases, can cause heart failure if it enters the blood stream.

MUDDLE   To 'feel', with either the hands or feet, for aquatic chelonians as they lie hidden in the mud of dark or cloudy waters.

MUGGER   A large, freshwater crocodile, *Crocodylus palustris*, inhabiting rivers, lakes and man-made waterways in the Indian subcontinent from eastern Iran, Pakistan, northern India and Nepal to Bangladesh and south to Sri Lanka. Also called the marsh crocodile.

MULGA   *Pseudechis australis*, a large and formidable snake of the

ELAPIDAE family, also known as the king brown snake, found in a variety of habitats in Australia, with the exception of the extreme south, and New Guinea.

MÜLLER, Lorenz 1868–1953, German herpetologist and contributor of numerous works on reptile and amphibian systematics, including the checklist *Die Amphibien und Reptilien Europas* (1928 and 1940) which he co-authored with Robert Mertens.

MÜLLERIAN DUCT The female OVIDUCT of vertebrates which, although it develops in both sexes and is linked to the WOLFFIAN DUCT, becomes vestigial in the male.

MULTICARINATE Possessing more than one KEEL, as in the carapace of many chelonians.

MULTIVALENT An alternative term for POLYVALENT.

MUSK GLAND A gland secreting a strong-smelling, heady odour, used by male animals to stimulate the females into sexual activity. In crocodilians there are two pairs of musk glands, one pair situated at the corner of the jaw (the ANGULAR GLAND) and the other pair situated in the cloaca (the CLOACAL GLAND). Musk glands are also found in snakes (the ANAL GLAND) and in some chelonians.

MUSSURANA *Clelia clelia*, a rear-fanged snake of the family COLUBRIDAE, subfamily Boiginae, inhabiting Central and South America.

MUZZLE Very occasionally used by some authors for the SNOUT of certain reptiles, with particular reference to crocodilians.

MYCOSIS Any one of a number of infections or diseases caused by parasitic fungi, and affecting the mucous membranes of the internal organs, and skin, of reptiles.

MYOBATRACHIDAE Family of the ANURA, inhabiting Australia. 106 species in 20 genera.

# N

NAIL   The enlarged scale, or scales, forming a sharp, horny spine on the tail tip of certain chelonians, e.g., the European Hermann's tortoise (*Testudo hermanni*).

NAKED   Used in reference to the HEMIPENIS in some snakes, which lacks any surface decoration in the way of hooks or spines.

NAPE   The back of the neck and, in snakes, referring to the dorsal area directly behind the head.

NARES, sing. NARIS   The paired nasal openings, or nostrils, between the NASAL CAVITY and the exterior, consisting of the internal nares (or choanae), which open into the BUCCAL cavity, and the external nares, which open to the outside.

NASAL   A scale, situated on the side of the head, that borders or contains a nostril (or naris). See also POSTNASAL and PRENASAL.

NASAL CAVITY   A paired cavity in the head of all vertebrates, lined with a mucous membrane rich in sensitive OLFACTORY receptors and connected by internal nares to the respiratory system, and by external nares to the outside.

NASAL CLEFT   The NASAL GROOVE in blind snakes of the TYPHLOPIDAE.

NASAL GLAND   A gland occurring in the nostrils of certain terrestrial iguanids (e.g., *Ctenosaura, Sauromalus* and *Dipsosaurus*) and the marine iguana (*Amblyrhynchus cristatus*) that discharges through a duct in the nasal cavity and serves as a means of excreting excess salt from the body. In crocodilians, marine turtles, and many other lizards, excess salt is excreted in the form of 'tears' from the LACRIMAL GLAND.

NASAL GROOVE   In snakes of the family TYPHLOPIDAE, a cleft, or furrow, which in some species may be only partially developed, running from the PREFRONTAL scale, through the nostril, and over the NASAL scale to the lip.

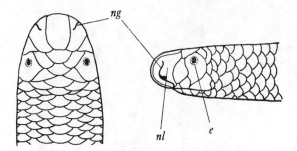

The nasal groove is situated within the nasolabial scale of thread snakes (Leptotyphlopidae) and blind snakes (Typhlopidae): *e*, eye; *ng*, nasal groove; *nl*, nasolabial.

NASOLABIAL   In the thread snakes (LEPTOTYPHLOPIDAE) and blind snakes (TYPHLOPIDAE), the scale on the head containing the nostril, or naris.

NASOLABIAL GLAND   Any one of a group of glands situated within, and serving to irrigate, the NASOLABIAL GROOVE of lungless salamanders (PLETHODONTIDAE).

NASOLABIAL GROOVE   A cleft, or furrow, extending downward from each of the external NARES and across the edge of the upper lip in lungless salamanders (PLETHODONTIDAE).

NASOROSTRAL   The small scale, or scales, situated on the head in certain pit vipers of the *Bothrops* genus, in the space between the ROSTRAL and the NASAL scales.

NATURAL SELECTION   The process, which Darwin called the 'struggle for survival', by which those individual organisms best fitted for their environment survive, whilst those less well fitted do not, thus helping to ensure the survival of the species as a whole, individuals having unfavourable characteristics being 'selected against'. Natural selection, according to Darwinism, results in evolution when acting on a diverse population because it can lead to speciation by favouring a mutant if it displays features particularly advantageous to its mode of life.

NEARCTIC  One of the six zoogeographical regions of the world, part of the HOLARCTIC, and consisting of North America from the Central Mexican Plateau in the south to the Aleutian Islands and Greenland in the north.

NECK BITE  The bite to the NAPE of the neck in many species of snake and lizard and applied by the male to the female during copulation. The neck bite rarely results in any serious injury although, if copulation occurs frequently over a period of days, or weeks, the scales in the neck region may become quite badly marked.

NECROPSY  An autopsy, or post-mortem examination, performed to ascertain the cause of death.

NECROSIS  The death of one or more cells of the body, usually localized, and usually a result of a restricted blood supply to that part.

NECROTIC  Causing death, as in tissue death occurring, for example, in snakes with necrotic dermatitis.

NECROTIC STOMATITIS  *See* STOMATITIS.

NEKTONIC  Pertaining to free-swimming animals that inhabit the middle depths of open water such as a lake or sea. The TADPOLE, or larva, of certain amphibians, that spends its period of development in such bodies of water, is termed a 'nektonic tadpole'.

NEMATODA  The class of both free-living and parasitic animals containing the roundworms and eelworms. Nematode worms occur as ENDOPARASITES in several internal organs, particularly the lung and alimentary canal, of both reptiles and amphibians.

NEOLITHIC  The recent Stone Age, originating in the Middle East approximately 10 000 years ago and lasting until the beginning of the Bronze Age some 7000 years ago.

NEONATE  A newborn, or hatchling, reptile.

NEOTENIC  Describing an organism or species that is sexually mature and capable of reproduction but retaining the appearance, form and habits of the larva. Such an animal is called a 'neotene'.

NEOTENY  The condition in which the larval features are retained in the adult due to the larva's failure to metamorphose. The axolotl (*Ambystoma mexicanum*) is probably the most well-known example of an animal species that engages in neoteny.

NEOTROPICAL  Of, relating to, or inhabiting, any one or more of the tropical regions of the New World, consisting of South America and North America south of the tropic of Cancer. The Neotropical is one of the six main zoogeographical regions of the world.

**NERVOUS SYSTEM** A system of specialized cells and tissues in multicellular animals, in which information is communicated between receptors and effectors, and which allows the regulation and co-ordination of many body functions. In reptiles and amphibians (and in all other vertebrates) it consists of the central nervous system (the brain and spinal cord) and the peripheral nervous system (the cranial and spinal nerves and their branches).

**NEURAL** (DORSAL, VERTEBRAL) Any one of the central row of bones of the CARAPACE, in chelonians, corresponding to the central VERTEBRAL laminae. Anterior to the neurals is the PRONEURAL, posterior is the PYGAL.

**NEUROMAST** One of many groups of cutaneous sensory cells, situated within pits or canals, either scattered or arranged in orderly rows on the body and head of aquatic amphibians (and most fishes). The sensory cells bear minute hairlike projections which are sensitive to changes in pressure, and can detect vibrations in the surrounding water too low to be perceived by the ear. *See also* LATERAL LINE SYSTEM.

**NEUROTOXIC** Describing the effects of certain snake-venom components which are poisonous or destructive to the NERVOUS SYSTEM. Compare HAEMOTOXIC.

**NEUROTOXIN** Any constituent of snake venom that results in a partial or total breakdown of the NERVOUS SYSTEM, acting mainly by paralysis of the motor nerve cells which transmit impulses from the brain or spinal cord to various effector organs, such as glands or muscles etc.

**NEWT** Any one of the various small semi-aquatic urodeles, such as the palmate newt (*Triturus helveticus*) of Europe, which together with the salamanders and related forms constitute the order CAUDATA.

**NEWT PLAGUE** The epidemic-like, fatal disease of urodeles, also known as MOLCHPEST, and occurring frequently in captive animals, apparently through incorrect or inadequate husbandry.

**NEW WORLD** The Americas.

**NICHE** The status or functional role filled by an organism in a particular community, often called its 'ecological niche'. A particular organism's niche is determined by the food it eats, temperature tolerances, enemies etc. No two species can coexist in the same niche, for competition would then occur and one would replace the other by natural selection.

NICTITATING EYELID   The NICTITATING MEMBRANE.

NICTITATING MEMBRANE   The third eyelid, in certain amphibians and reptiles, consisting of a thin, transparent fold of skin situated in the inner corner of the eye, which can be drawn across the cornea, beneath the moveable upper and lower eyelids, to clean and protect the surface without hindering the animal's vision.

NOBLE, Gladwyn Kingsley   1894–1940, American herpetologist and Curator of Herpetology at the American Museum of Natural History in New York. *The biology of the Amphibia*, which he published in 1931, went on to become one of the definitive works on the natural history and biology of amphibians.

NOCTURNAL   Active or occurring after dark.

NOD   The repeated raising and lowering of the head in quick succession, observed in the males of many lizards, particularly iguanids such as *Anolis, Leiocephalis, Sceloporus* etc., when in the immediate proximity of females of the same species, and apparently a way of acknowledging their sex.

NOMENCLATURE   A system of naming organisms, or groups of organisms, with a SCIENTIFIC NAME. In scientific work only one system is used, giving two names to a species, e.g., *Eryx conicus* (rough-scaled sand boa), and three to a subspecies, e.g., *Eryx conicus brevis*.

NOMINATE RACE   The first defined of a species upon which subspecies, if any, are based. For example, in the case of the rainbow boa (*Epicrates cenchria*), the nominate race, or subspecies, is the Amazonian one *E.c. cenchria*, while the one occurring in Bolivia is named *E.c. gaigei*. The name of a subspecies, like that of a species, always begins with a small initial letter. One subspecies under each species has a name that is the same as that of the specific name, and this is known as the nominate race.

NON-POISONOUS   Lacking the effects or qualities of a poison; incapable of killing or inflicting injury.

NOOSING   A method of capturing lizards in which a loop of thread or thin rope is tied, usually with a slipknot, to the end of a pole or cane, and lowered over the head and neck of a basking animal and pulled abruptly upwards resulting in its safe restraint.

NOSE KNOB   The prominent hump, or GHARA, on the tip of the snout of a mature male gharial.

NOSTRIL   Either one of the pair of external openings to the air passages, situated at the end of the snout.

NOTCH   *See* AXILLARY NOTCH, INGUINAL NOTCH.

NOTCHED DIGITAL DISC   Referring to the toe pad of certain arboreal frogs, which is not circular as in most other species but indented around its anterior edge.

NOTOGAEA   The name given to the two combined southern zoogeographical regions of the world, the AUSTRALASIAN and the NEOTROPICAL.

NUCAL   A variant spelling of NUCHAL.

NUCHA, pl. NUCHAE   Pertaining to the back, or NAPE, of the neck, e.g., a scale on the back of the neck of a crocodilian is termed a 'NUCHAL SCALE'.

NUCHAL BONE   The PRONEURAL bone of a chelonian carapace.

NUCHAL CREST   A longitudinal, central series of enlarged scales or fold of skin on the back of the neck in many lizards.

NUCHAL LAMINA   The central front lamina (the precentral) overlying the PRONEURAL bone in a chelonian carapace.

NUCHAL SCALE   1. In crocodilians, any one of the usually two rows of enlarged, osteoderm-reinforced scales on the back of the neck.   2. In certain lizards, any one of the scales situated on the back of the neck directly behind the head.

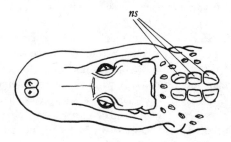

The nuchal scales (*ns*) in crocodilians are usually situated in two rows on the back of the neck.

NUCHAL SHIELD   A single, small lamina, or scute, situated medially between the frontmost pair of MARGINAL laminae on the carapace of a chelonian.

NUCHODORSAL GLAND   Any one of a number of glands situated beneath the skin of the nape region in several Asiatic water snakes (e.g., various Natricinae, *Macropisthodon* and others), the secretion of which is of uncertain function and only released if the skin covering the gland is broken, when it can cause irritation if allowed to come into contact with the mucous membranes.

NUCHOMARGINAL  Any one of the group of small scales arranged around the NUCHAL SCALES on the back of the neck in crocodilians.

NUPTIAL EXCRESCENCE  *See* NUPTIAL PAD.

NUPTIAL PAD (NUPTIAL EXCRESCENCE)  In male anurans, an area of usually roughened and darkly pigmented skin developing prior to and during the breeding season, and usually, but not always, disappearing once breeding has ceased. The nuptial pad is usually evident on certain digits, particularly the thumb, but can also occur on areas of the chin, chest and undersurfaces of the limbs etc., and serves to maintain a firm hold on a female during AMPLEXUS.

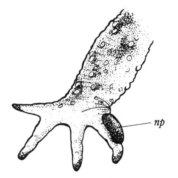

Nuptial pads (*np*) may occur on various parts of the body in anurans but especially on one or more of the digits, the thumb in particular.

NUTRITIONAL  SECONDARY  HYPERPARATHYROID-ISM (NSHP)  A condition arising in captive reptiles as a direct result of an excess of phosphorus in the diet causing the bones to weaken. It can also arise from an incorrect calcium : phosphorus balance, or insufficient calcium in the diet. In juvenile and sub-adult reptiles NSHP is more commonly known as rickets. When the condition occurs in adult animals it is known as osteomalacia.

NYMPH  A term generally referring to the larval form of certain insects, such as the dragonfly, which develops into an adult without going through a pupal stage. In herpetology, it is used occasionally for the immature stage, or TADPOLE, of urodeles.

# O

OAR   The vertically compressed tail of a sea snake.

OBLIQUE TYPE   Used in reference to a particular arrangement in the scalation of snakes. *See* SCALE ROW.

OCCIPITAL   Of, or relating to, or situated on, the occiput, or back of the head or skull.

OCCIPITAL CONDYLE   A single or paired, rounded, bony prominence that protrudes from the back (occiput) of the tetrapod skull and articulates with the first cervical vertebra (the atlas), allowing the raising and lowering of the head. In amphibians there are two and in reptiles just one.

OCCIPITAL SCALE   Occasionally used in reference to the scale containing the vestigial PARIETAL EYE, situated directly behind the PARIETAL scales (and INTERPARIETAL scales if present) in many lizards.

OCCIPUT   The hindmost part of the head or skull of vertebrates, where it joins the vertebral column.

OCEANIC   Of, relating to, or inhabiting, the ocean. The sea snakes of the Hydrophinae, a subfamily of the ELAPIDAE, are true oceanic reptiles, spending the whole of their lives in a marine environment.

OCELLATED   Having eye-like spots, or OCELLI.

OCELLUS pl. OCELLI   Any one of the circular, eye-like spots consisting of two or three concentric light and dark rings around a contrastingly coloured central spot, occurring in the skin patterns of some reptiles, particularly lizards, and certain amphibians.

OCULAR   1. Any one of the scales forming the border of the ORBIT of the eye. The SUPRAOCULAR, SUBOCULAR, PREOCULAR and POST-

OCULAR scales refer respectively to those lying above, below, in front of and behind the eye. In blind snakes (family TYPHLOPIDAE), the ocular scale actually covers the eye which lies, barely visible as a dark spot, beneath it. **2.** An enlarged and irregular scale situated between the SUPRACILIARY and SUPRAOCULAR scales on the head of a crocodilian.

OCULOLABIAL   In blind snakes (TYPHLOPIDAE), the cephalic scale originating from the union of the OCULAR (sense 2) with the LABIAL directly beneath it.

ODONTOID   Resembling a tooth. Odontoid structures occur on various bones in the mouth in certain anurans and, in the aggressive African bullfrog (*Pyxicephalus adspersus*), they are large enough to inflict serious bites.

ODONTOID PEG   *See* ODONTOID PROCESS.

ODONTOID PROCESS   (ODONTOID PEG) The toothlike, upward projection on the second cervical vertebra (the axis) of the vertebral column, which in reptiles (and mammals and birds also) articulates with the first cervical vertebra (the atlas), allowing side-to-side movement of the head.

OESOPHAGEAL TEETH   The highly modified, enamel-coated HYPAPOPHYSIS of egg-eating snakes (Dasypeltinae), used to break the shells of eggs as they are swallowed.

OESOPHAGUS   The muscular tube in the alimentary canal that links the buccal cavity or pharynx with the stomach. The mucous membrane lining is folded, permitting great expansion during the passage of food which is directed down to the stomach by rhythmic, wavelike contractions of circular and longitudinal muscle layers situated along its length.

OKADA, Yaichiro   1892–1976, Japanese ichthyologist and herpetologist, regarded as the father of herpetology in Japan. He published many works on both the fishes and the reptiles and amphibians of that country, including the classic *The tailless batrachians of the Japanese Empire* (1931).

OLD WORLD   The continents of the world known before the discovery of the Americas, comprising Europe, Africa and Asia.

OLFACTORY   1. Of, or relating to, the sense of smell (olfaction). 2. One of a number of nerves or organs (e.g., JACOBSON'S ORGAN) connected with the sense of smell.

OLIGOCENE   The third epoch of the TERTIARY period, beginning about 38 million years ago, after the EOCENE epoch, and lasting for about 13 million years when it was followed by the MIOCENE epoch. It was characterized by the gradual disappearance of earlier mammals and their replacement by more modern groups, such as the first pigs, tapirs and rhinoceroses.

OLIGODONT   Possessing only a few teeth, each one spaced well apart from the other.

OLIGOPHYDONT   Possessing a number of sets of teeth which are shed periodically throughout an animal's life culminating with one full set of permanent teeth. Characteristic of many lizards, and crocodilians.

OMNIVORE   An animal that feeds on both animal and vegetable matter. Omnivorous reptiles are to be found in many lizard and chelonian families. Although the larvae of many amphibians eat plant matter at some stage in their development, the adults are strictly carnivorous, except for one species of South American tree frog (*Hyla truncata*), which besides insects includes the fruits of certain trees in its diet, thus having the distinction of being the only known truly omnivorous amphibian.

ONTOGENESIS, ONTOGENY   The entire course of development of an individual organism, from the fertilized egg through to adulthood. Compare PHYLOGENESIS.

OOCYTE   In the ovary of female animals, any one of a large number of reproductive cells that has the potential to become an OVUM. In snakes, for example, oocytes are being formed continually by germinal tissue cells within the OVARY. The ovarian FOLLICLE then matures and releases OVA which are in turn fertilized by sperm.

OOGENESIS   The formation and growth of ova (egg cells) in the ovary of female animals.

OPERCLE   Technical term given to the EAR FLAP of a crocodilian.

OPERCULAR GILL   In anuran larvae, the GILL enclosed beneath the OPERCULUM. Referred to occasionally, but incorrectly, as the INTERNAL GILL.

OPERCULUM   A lid-like flap, or process, covering an aperture; a cover of skin in anuran larvae (tadpoles) that grows back over the gills, completely enclosing the gill chamber with just a single opening to the exterior, the SPIRACLE.

OPHIDIA   The snakes. A suborder of the SQUAMATA. (Sometimes known as the SERPENTES.)

OPHIOLOGY   The branch of zoology dealing with the study of snakes.

OPHIOPHAGY   The eating of snakes. Any organism that habitually includes snakes in its diet is termed 'ophiophagous'. Many reptiles, and even large anurans, will feed upon snakes if given the opportunity but certain snakes themselves have a preference for snakes over other prey and will even devour their own kind. The king snakes (*Lampropeltis*), king cobra (*Ophiophagus hannah*), indigo snake (*Drymarchon corais*) and kraits (*Bungarus*) are some of the more well-known ophiophagous snake species.

OPHIOTOXICOLOGY   The branch of science concerned with the venoms of snakes, their nature, effects and antidotes.

OPISTHODONT   *See* TEETH.

OPISTHOGLYPH   Any venomous snake in which the venom-conducting teeth are situated towards the rear of the mouth on the upper jaw (MAXILLA). A rear- or back-fanged, snake. A number of workers now use the term ECTOGLYPH (sense 2).

The skull of a typical opisthoglyph snake in which the venom-conducting teeth are located at the rear of the upper jaw.

OPISTHOGLYPHIC TEETH   The venom-conducting fangs of back-fanged colubrid snakes, on which the grooves are situated either anteriorly or posteriorly.

OPTIMUM TEMPERATURE RANGE   The particular limits within which a reptile or amphibian can function normally. In reference to captive husbandry, the most satisfactory range of temperatures, between the VOLUNTARY MINIMUM and VOLUNTARY MAXIMUM, at which a given species should be housed (generally equal to those temperatures experienced by the animal in the wild) in order for it to continue its natural functions and habits.

ORAL DISC   The area around the mouthparts of anuran larvae (tadpoles), consisting of the mandibles (BEAK), lips, or labia, and the arrangement of horny, rasping cusps. The arrangement of these structures varies with the species and is therefore taxonomically significant.

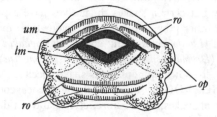

Diagram of the oral disc of an anuran tadpole: *lm*, lower mandible; *op*, oral papillae; *ro*, rasping organ; *um*, upper mandible.

ORAL FESTOON   *See* ORAL PAPILLAE.

ORAL PAPILLAE   In anuran larvae, the numerous, small, nipple-like projections that commonly form a fringe (the oral festoon) encircling the mouth, functioning as tactile, and possibly also chemical, receptors.

ORBIT   The bony socket of the eye; the border of skin around the eye of a reptile or amphibian.

ORBITAL   An alternative term for the OCULAR (sense 1) scale on the border of the eye in reptiles.

ORBITAL APPENDAGE   Used in reference to the fleshy, horn-like structures above the margin of the upper eyelid in certain anuran species, e.g., *Ceratophrys cornuta* and *Megophrys nasuta*.

ORDER   The taxonomic category used in the classification of organisms that consist of one or more similar families. Similar orders form a CLASS and may be separated into suborders. Zoological order names typically end in '-a', as for example, SQUAMATA (snakes, lizards and amphisbaenids) and ANURA (frogs and toads).

ORDOVICIAN   The second oldest geological period of the PALAEOZOIC era, beginning about 510 million years ago at the end of the CAMBRIAN period, and lasting for about 70 million years when it was superseded by the SILURIAN period. It is characterized by being almost completely lacking in vertebrates, with the exception of certain jawless fishes, although marine invertebrates were particularly abundant.

ORGAN   Any distinct part of an organism consisting of a group of different tissues specialized to perform particular vital functions.

Examples in reptiles and amphibians include the INTROMITTENT ORGAN of copulation, the kidney, lung, eye, ear, etc.

ORGANISM   An individual living animal or plant capable of maintaining the processes characteristic of life, especially reproduction.

ORGAN OF LEYDIG   The vestigial third eye (the PARIETAL EYE) of reptiles.

ORGANOGENESIS   The formation and developmental progress of organs within an organism.

ORIENTAL   One of the six zoogeographical regions of the world, including the tropical southern Asian countries of India and Sri Lanka, to Borneo, Java and the Philippines. The boundary between the Oriental and Australasian regions has caused much argument in the past. *See* WALLACE'S LINE.

ORIENTATION   The ability of an animal to determine its exact position with regard to the points of a compass, or its adjustment to its surroundings or other external stimuli. Orientation occurs, for example, as a reptile or amphibian alters the position of all, or part, of its body in response to heat or light.

ORNAMENTATION   Used in reference to all the many varied embellishments or anatomical structures that occur on the limbs and bodies of many reptiles and amphibians, e.g., the CREST, DEWLAP, FIN, HORN, SPINE etc.

OROPEL   A local name, used in parts of Central America, for the yellow colour morph of the eye-lash viper, *Bothriechis* (*Bothrops*) *schlegelii*.

OSMOREGULATION   The process by which animals control the water content and concentration of salts within their bodies. In reptiles, salt excess in the body is excreted via certain SALT GLANDS such as the LACRIMAL and NASAL GLANDS.

OSSICLE   Any small, often irregularly-shaped bone in the body of an animal, especially one of three in the middle ear.

OSSIFICATION   The formation of bone, or the actual process of being converted into bone. The bony abdominal ridges in crocodilians are ossifications of the skin.

OSTEODERM   A bonelike dermal plate or area beneath the epidermal scales in some reptiles, e.g., crocodilians, helodermatid lizards etc., giving added protection and strength to the skin.

OSTEOMALACIA   A disease occurring in captive adult reptiles characterized by a softening of the bones and resulting from a deficiency of calcium and phosphorus or vitamin D, or a combination of all three. See NUTRITIONAL SECONDARY HYPERPARATHYROIDISM.

OUTBREEDING   Breeding between entirely unrelated or only distantly related individual animals of the same species. Crossing between one species and another (HYBRIDIZATION) generally results in sterile offspring and there are, consequently, various behavioural mechanisms to discourage it. Outbreeding increases the number of heterozygous individuals, thereby producing populations with more variation and adaptability towards changes in the environment.

OVARY   The female reproductive organ which produces eggs, or ova.

OVIDUCT (MÜLLERIAN DUCT)   The tube, or duct, that carries the eggs from the OVARY to the CLOACA.

OVIPARITY   Reproduction involving the production of undeveloped eggs, within membranes or shells, that are laid or spawned by the female. The entire development of the embryos, which are nourished in their eggs by large yolk sacs, occurs outside of the mother's body. Reptiles and amphibians reproducing this way are termed 'oviparous'.

OVIPOSITION   The process of depositing eggs.

OVIPOSITOR   The egg-depositing structure situated at the posterior of the abdomen in female insects, and certain fishes, from which eggs are extruded often into, or beneath, otherwise inaccessible places. In herpetology, the term is applied to the extension of the OVIDUCT in a few female anurans, e.g., the Surinam toad (*Pipa pipa*), which is protruded from the body and used to deposit individual eggs in each of the specialized dermal brood pockets on their backs.

OVOTHECA   A widened section of the female anuran OVIDUCT in which the unfertilized eggs are held for a short time prior to AMPLEXUS.

OVOVIVIPARITY   Reproduction involving the production of eggs which have a well-developed membranous covering and a store of yolk for the embryos' nourishment, are retained within the female's body during embryonic development, and hatch immediately before, during, or just after, they are laid. Reptiles and amphibians reproducing this way are termed 'ovoviviparous'. Compare OVIPARITY, VIVIPARITY.

OVULATION   The release of an egg (OVUM) from the OVARY.

OVUM   A mature reproductive cell (GAMETE) of female animals, produced by the ovary and capable of developing into a new individual of the same species when fertilized by sperm from a male.

OXYURIDAE   A family of endoparasitic nematode worms, known commonly as threadworms, containing some 150 species, a number of which infect the intestinal mucous membranes of reptiles, especially chelonians.

# P

PADDLE  The flattened limb of a marine turtle, specialized for swimming.

The modified limb or paddle of a marine turtle.

PADDLE STAGE  The phase in the life of larval anurans in which the limb bud becomes a paddle-like form, culminating in the appearance of recognizable features of the foot.

PAEDOGENESIS  Reproduction by an animal whilst still in the pre-adult, or larval, form. A type of NEOTENY, paedogenesis occurs, for example, in the axolotl (*Ambystoma mexicanum*), a larval form of salamander which, although retaining larval features, such as gills and fins, can breed and produce offspring similar to itself.

PALAEARCTIC REGION One of the six zoogeographical regions of the world, comprising the whole of Europe, the former USSR, Africa north of the Sahara, and most of Asia north of the Himalayas.

PALAEOCENE The oldest geological epoch of the TERTIARY period, beginning some 65 million years ago at the end of the CRETACEOUS period, and lasting for about 11 million years until the beginning of the EOCENE period, and characterized by the absence of many reptiles and the presence of numerous primitive mammals now extinct.

PALAEOZOIC The first and oldest era, in which life forms became diverse and abundant, beginning about 580 million years ago at the end of the PRECAMBRIAN, and lasting for some 350 million years when it was succeeded by the MESOZOIC era. It consists of the Lower Palaeozoic (CAMBRIAN, ORDOVICIAN and SILURIAN periods) and the Upper Palaeozoic (DEVONIAN, CARBONIFEROUS and PERMIAN periods).

PALATAL TEETH The innermost row of teeth situated on the PALATINE and PARASPHENOID dermal bones on either side of the PALATE.

PALATE The roof of the mouth. Skin covering the palate in amphibians is modified as a surface for respiration.

PALATINE Either one of the pair of, in some species, tooth-bearing bones in the roof of the mouth, situated directly behind the VOMER which forms part of the palate.

PALATINE TEETH A term used generally for any teeth situated on any of the bones of the palate, e.g., VOMERINE TEETH, but, in snakes, referring to those teeth situated on the PALATINE bone.

PALMAR Of, or relating to, the palm or ventral surface (face) of the hand or forefoot.

PALMAR TUBERCLE A small, knob-like projection on the ventral surface, or palm, of the hand or forefoot in anurans.

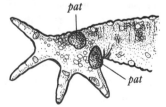

Palmar tubercles (*pat*) on the ventral surface or palm of a toad's hand.

**PALMATE**   Digitate; shaped like an open hand, with parts diverging from a common base, each connected by a web. The European newt (*Triturus helveticus*) is named the 'palmate newt' after the webbing between the digits of the hind feet of the male during the breeding season.

**PALPATION**   A method used to locate either ovarian FOLLICLES or ova in a female snake. The snake is allowed to move slowly over the palms of the hands whilst it is grasped gently but firmly. Follicles or ova, if present, can be felt in the snake's venter as they pass across the palms.

**PALPEBRA**   The eyelid.

**PALPEBRAL**   Of, or relating to, the eyelids, as in 'palpebral membrane' (the transparent eyelid in many anurans), or any of the numerous small scales on the upper eyelids of lizards (the SUPRAOCULAR scales), for example.

**PALPEBRAL APPENDAGE**   The ORBITAL APPENDAGE of certain anurans, e.g., *Ceratophrys cornuta*.

**PALPEBRAL DISC**   The transparent spectacle on the lower eyelid of certain skinks, e.g., *Leiolopisma*, permitting vision when the eyes are closed.

**PALPEBRAL MEMBRANE**   The transparent eyelid in many anuran species, e.g., certain ranids and hylids, serving to protect the eye whilst still permitting vision.

**PALUDARIUM**   Used occasionally in reference to a vivarium in which a tropical rainforest habitat has been re-created, with densely planted epiphytes and bromeliads etc., and, in larger facilities, small trees and shrubs, and also containing an area of water for more aquatic reptiles and fishes.

**PALUSTRAL, PALUSTRINE**   Of, related to, or inhabiting, marshes or swamps.

**PANOPHTHALMITIS**   A slowly progressive disorder in snakes which are kept in suboptimal conditions, occurring either as an isolated condition or supplementing other bacterial diseases. An obstruction of the LACRIMAL DUCT system of the eye, it is caused by GRAM-NEGATIVE BACTERIA spreading up through the lacrimal duct into the area between the BRILLE, or transparent scale covering the eye, and the cornea, resulting in a characteristic inflammation, discoloration, and swelling of the eye, causing blindness and necessitating its surgical removal if the snake is to survive.

**PAPILLA, pl. PAPILLAE**   A thin, small, elongated, and often flexible, fleshy projection, on or in the body of an animal, that may be tactile in function.

**PAPILLOMATA** A form of dermal tumour often seen in the skin of certain lizards. *See* POX.

**PARACHUTE** The free, membranous flaps and frills on the sides of the head, trunk, tail and limbs, and between the toes, of gekkonid lizards of the genus *Ptychozoon*, and the wide webbing between the toes in frogs of the genus *Rhacophorus*, permitting them to slow their descent when leaping or gliding from one tree branch to another or to the ground.

**PARAMYXOVIRUS** A highly contagious viral disease affecting snakes and, in particular, members of the families ELAPIDAE and VIPERIDAE. The characteristic symptoms include gaping, lethargy, refusal to feed and rapid degeneration of muscle tone.

**PARAPINEAL EYE** *See* PARIETAL EYE, PINEAL COMPLEX.

**PARAPINEAL ORGAN** *See* PINEAL COMPLEX.

**PARAPSID** Descriptive of a type of skull found in extinct Ichthyopterygia, characterized by a single, high temporal opening and considered to be a variant of the EURYAPSID skull.

**PARASITE** Any organism that derives its nourishment from another (the HOST). In reptiles and amphibians, such an organism may occur on the skin (an ECTOPARASITE) or in the body (an ENDOPARASITE). Heavy infestations may lead to disease in, and eventual death of, the host.

**PARATOID** A variant spelling of PAROTOID.

**PARAVENTRAL** Any one of the scales making up the series that run longitudinally on either side of the VENTRAL scales in snakes.

**PARAVERTEBRAL** Pertaining to one or both sides of the vertebral, or MID-DORSAL, in reference to scales or markings etc. A stripe, for example, lying on either side of and paralleling the vertebral line of the back is termed a 'paravertebral stripe'.

**PARENTERAL** The method by which drugs are administered other than by mouth. In the case of reptiles, drugs administered parenterally are given subcutaneously.

**PARIETAL** 1. Either one of a pair of large scales situated on the top of the head in snakes, directly behind the FRONTAL and lying over the parietal bones that form the main part of the roof of the skull. 2. Any one of the large scales situated on the top of the head in lizards, behind the FRONTOPARIETAL plates (sense 2). 3. The area of the head in snakes and lizards, occupied by many small scales which replace the large, paired parietal scales in certain species.

PARIETAL EYE (FRONTAL ORGAN, MEDIAN EYE, ORGAN OF LEYDIG, PARAPINEAL EYE, PINEAL EYE, PINEAL ORGAN, THIRD EYE) The vestigial sensory structure, or 'third eye', that develops from an outgrowth of the forebrain of early vertebrates, situated in the centre of the skull between the PARIETAL scales. *See* PINEAL COMPLEX.

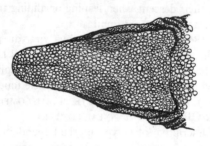

Evidence of the parietal eye can still be seen in certain reptiles, especially monitor lizards (*Varanus*) in which it appears externally as an enlarged scale in the centre of the top of the head.

PARKER, Hampton Wilder 1891–1968, British herpetologist at the British Museum (Natural History), London. Publications include the monograph *Frogs of the family Microhylidae* (1934), and the standard handbook *Snakes: a natural history* (1977) which he co-authored with A.G.C. Grandison.

PAROTID GLAND A comparatively large, serous, salivary gland in many mammals and, in man, lying in front of and below each ear. In certain colubrid snakes the gland has become modified for the production of venom and is often associated with the enlarged grooved teeth of rear-fanged species, in which it is known as DUVERNOY'S GLAND.

PAROTOID GLAND Either one of the pair of large, external, wart-like, toxin-secreting glands situated behind the eye, on the neck, or around the shoulder region, in many anurans and certain urodeles (e.g., *Bufo*, *Salamandra*).

PARTHENOGENESIS Reproduction, without fertilization by a male, in which an unfertilized ovum develops directly into a new

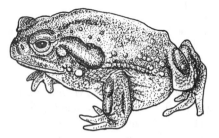

The parotoid glands of this Colorado river toad (*Bufo alvarius*) appear as large, kidney-shaped structures between the eye and the shoulder.

individual; virgin birth. Parthenogenesis occurs in several reptile genera, including the blind snake (*Typhlina bramina*) and has been observed in some forms of the urodele genus *Ambystoma*.

PARTHENOGENIC   Any organism that reproduces without a male element, i.e., that engages in PARTHENOGENESIS.

PARTURITION   The process or act of giving birth or laying eggs.

PATAGIAL RIB   Any one of the five to seven pairs of false ribs, in the flying lizards (genus *Draco*) used to support the fan-like wing, or PATAGIUM.

PATAGIUM   The membranous web of skin between the limbs and body that serves as a wing in gliding animals.

PECK ORDER   *See* DOMINANCE.

PECTINATE   Shaped like the teeth of a comb, as in the feathery gills of the axolotl (*Ambystoma mexicanum*).

PECTORAL   1. Of or relating to, the area of the body where the forelimbs originate; the chest, breast, or thorax.   2. Either one of the third pair of laminae on the PLASTRON of a chelonian.

PECTORAL AMPLEXUS   (AXILLARY AMPLEXUS)   The sexual embrace of anurans in which the male's forelimbs clasp the female from behind in the region of the chest.

PECTORAL FOLD   A skin fold, or groove, crossing the chest area between the forelimbs in some amphibians.

PECTORAL GIRDLE   That part of the vertebrate skeleton to which the front or upper limbs are attached, consisting, in mammals, of two ventral clavicles (collar bones) and two dorsal scapulae (shoulder blades). In reptiles the clavicles are functionally replaced by the CORACOID bones.

PEDICEL   *See* PEDUNCLE.

PEDICLE   *See* PEDUNCLE.

PEDUNCLE (PEDICEL, PEDICLE)   Any small stem, or stalk, such as that produced by certain urodeles to affix their eggs to some secure object.

PELAGIC   Of, relating to, or inhabiting, the upper waters of the open seas. Some sea snakes (genus *Pelamis*) and the marine turtles (CHELONIIDAE) are the only truly pelagic reptiles.

PELOBATIDAE   Spadefoot toads. Family of the ANURA, inhabiting North America, Europe, North Africa, Middle East and parts of Asia. Over 55 species in nine genera.

PELODYTIDAE   Parsley frogs. Family of the ANURA (frequently placed in the PELOBATIDAE), inhabiting south-western Europe, Caucasus. Two species in a single genus.

PELOMEDUSIDAE   Helmeted side-neck turtles. Family of the CHELONIA, suborder Pleurodira, inhabiting South America, Africa and Madagascar. Approximately 17 species in five genera.

PELVIC AMPLEXUS (INGUINAL AMPLEXUS)   The sexual embrace of anurans in which the male's forelimbs clasp the female from behind in the region directly in front of the hind limbs.

PELVIC GIRDLE   That part of the vertebrate skeleton to which the hind or lower limbs are attached. It is absent in the majority of snakes, whilst in others, and in some lizards, it is vestigial.

PELVIC GLAND   Part of an enlarged, tubiform gland situated within the CLOACA in male urodeles and associated with spermatophore production. *See also* CLOACAL GLAND.

PELVIC SPUR (ANAL CLAW, ANAL SPUR)   Either one of the two remnants of hind limbs, visible on either side of the vent in boid snakes and a few other species. In several species the spurs in the male may be noticeably longer than those of the female and can often be useful guides in the sexing of individuals.

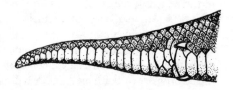

The pelvic spurs of boid snakes, and certain other species, are situated on either side of the vent and are the remnants of ancestral hind limbs.

PENIS   The male copulatory organ of higher vertebrates; the INTRO-MITTENT ORGAN of reproduction in chelonians, crocodilians and caecilians.

PENTADACTYL   Possessing five digits.

PENTADACTYL LIMB   A type of limb characteristic of tetrapod vertebrates, i.e., reptiles, amphibians, mammals and birds, that has evolved from the paired fins of ancestral fishes in association with the transition from water to land. Various modifications to the basic design, consisting of an upper arm (or thigh), forearm (shank), and hand (or foot) with five fingers or toes, have been made for different functions and methods of progression, particularly by the reduction, loss or fusion of the terminal bones as adaptations to running, swimming, burrowing etc.

PERINATAL   Of, relating to, or occurring, directly before, during or after, birth.

PERIPHERAL   Any one of the marginal bones that occur as a border around the edge of the chelonian CARAPACE, each one lying beneath a MARGINAL lamina.

PERISTALSIS   The rhythmic muscular contractions that occur within various bodily tubes, especially the alimentary duct, serving to transport food items and/or waste products through the body. Peristaltic contractions are probably most noticeable in snakes as they engage in swallowing large prey.

PERITONEUM   A thin, translucent membrane that lines the interior of the abdominal cavity and surrounds most of the viscera. Reptiles do not possess a diaphragm and therefore lack a true abdominal cavity, having instead a COELOM. The abdominal cavity, coelomic cavity and peritoneal cavity are, for practical purposes, nevertheless synonymous.

PERITONITIS   An infection of the PERITONEUM which, in reptiles, can result from a number of other conditions, such as an inability to lay eggs or deliver young (DYSTOCIA).

PERMIAN   The last geological period of the PALAEOZOIC era, following the CARBONIFEROUS period some 280 million years ago, and lasting some 50 million years when it was succeeded by the MESOZOIC era. The land continued to be dominated by several types of reptiles, although amphibians became reduced in both their numbers and in size.

PHALANGES, sing. PHALANX   The small bones in the digits (fingers or toes), linked to each other by hinged joints and articulating with the metacarpal bones of the fore foot or lower forelimb, or the metatarsal bones of the hind foot or lower hind limb. In the typical PENTADACTYL LIMB of five digits, there are two phalanges in the smallest and innermost digit and three in each of the others.

PHANEROGLOSSAL   Possessing a tongue, as opposed to AGLOS-SAL – lacking a tongue – as, for example, in members of the anuran family PIPIDAE.

PHARYNX   The part of the alimentary canal between the mouth and the oesophagus, serving as a passage for both food and respiratory gases. At its anterior end, it has openings from the nasal passages and mouth, and at its posterior end openings to the trachea and oesophagus. In aquatic amphibians, the pharynx is pierced with gill slits through which water flows, supplying the blood in the gill filaments with oxygen.

PHEROMONE   A substance that is produced and secreted by an animal and which stimulates a response in others of the same species. Pheromones have a significant role in the social behaviour of many animals and their uses include marking territories, laying trails, attracting mates etc.

PHOLIDOSIS   The number, shape, pattern, arrangement and location of the scales, plates, shields and laminae of reptiles, factors important in the identification and systematics of these animals.

PHOTOPERIOD   The period of light and dark (day and night) in every 24 hours. Photoperiodism, or the response of organisms to the lengthening or shortening of the diurnal photoperiod, determines the triggering of such activities as migration, hibernation, breeding and other seasonal aspects of their lives. Controlling the photoperiod of captive reptiles and amphibians is often an essential factor in successful breeding.

PHRYNOMERIDAE   Snake-neck frogs. Family of the ANURA, suborder Diplasiocoela, inhabiting Africa south of the Sahara. Three species in a single genera.

PHYLOGENESIS, PHYLOGENY   The entire course of development in a species, genus etc. over successive generations.

PHYLUM   One of the basic classificatory divisions of the animal kingdom and the highest division in TAXONOMY, comprising organisms all having the same general form. Reptiles and amphibians, together with the other vertebrates, are placed within the phylum Chordata, which contains animals that possess a spinal cord.

PHYTOTHELM   Any small body of rainwater occurring in a tree hollow, epiphyte funnel, leaf fold, or similar situation in forest vegetation. Important to many arboreal reptiles as a source of drinking water, and to many tree-frog species for the development of their larvae.

PIGMENT   The colouring substance in the cells and tissues of animals and plants. Melanin, for example, is the pigment responsible for dark brown to black coloration in reptiles and amphibians.

PINEAL COMPLEX   The rudimentary, median, third eye and its associated parts, in many lizards and the tuatara (*Sphenodon*), lying beneath a foramen towards the front of the parietal bone and covered only with skin and connective tissue. The complex consists of two processes projecting dorsally from the diencephalon, the anterior of which is termed the parapineal organ, and the posterior, the pineal organ, terminating at the surface on the top of the head with the pineal eye. In the tuatara the eye is equipped with a lens, retina and nerve fibres linked to the brain, serving as a light-sensitive organ and possibly also responding to solar radiation. Derived from the pineal gland, the structure is thought to have existed in many fossil vertebrates but today its only known living example is the tuatara.

PINEAL EYE   *See* PINEAL COMPLEX.

PINEAL ORGAN   *See* PINEAL COMPLEX.

PINKY   Any newborn rodent that has yet to grow fur.

PINKY-PUMP   A syringe-like device with a blunt tip, used in the force-feeding of snakes which, for one reason or another, will not feed voluntarily. A dead PINKY is inserted into the cylindrical barrel of the pump, the tip or nozzle of which is then introduced carefully into the snake's oesophagus. As the handle of the pump is slowly pressed into the barrel, the pinky is compressed and forced out through the nozzle into the snake's stomach.

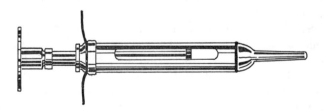

A stainless steel pinky-pump used to force-feed macerated newborn mice to snakes.

**PIPIDAE**   Clawed frogs. Family of the ANURA, suborder Aglossa, inhabiting South America and Africa. 26 species in four genera.

**PIPPING**   In reptiles, the act of slitting the egg by the hatchling inside, prior to its emergence. The reptile-breeder may sometimes have to pip by hand eggs which have gone POST-TERM if it is suspected that the hatchlings are too weak to do it themselves.

**PISCIVOROUS**   Feeding on fish.

**PIT** (LOREAL PIT)   The deep cavity situated on either side of the head, between the nostril and the eye, of crotaline snakes (hence the name PIT VIPER), which is the external opening to a highly sensitive infra-red detecting organ, enabling the snake to locate and strike at prey in complete darkness. *See also* LABIAL PIT.

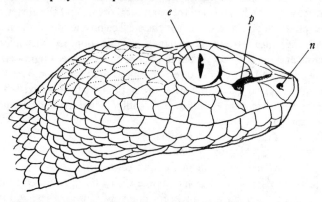

A lateral view of the head of a pit viper (Crotalinae) showing the position of the highly sensitive infra-red-detecting organ: *e*, eye; *n*, nostril; *p*, pit.

**PITH**   To kill a reptile or amphibian by piercing or severing the brain and spinal column, usually by inserting a sharp instrument between the base of the skull and the first vertebra. Often used as a form of EUTHANASIA.

**PIT SCALE**   A scale situated in or on the margin of the PIT in crotaline snakes, such as the FOVEAL or LACUNAL scale.

**PITUITARY GLAND**   A small, ductless gland situated at the base of the brain, the hormonal secretions of which control many important bodily functions and regulate other glands within the body.

**PIT VIPER**   A common classification for any one of the venomous snakes in the VIPERIDAE subfamily, Crotalinae, all of which share the same characteristic feature of a sensitive, heat-detecting PIT.

*Plate   167*

PLACENTA   A spongy, vascular structure, uniting foetal and maternal tissues, through which the foetus receives nourishment and oxygen and its waste products are removed. The development of a placenta (placentation) is known to take place in some reptiles which exhibit VIVIPARITY.

PLAGIOTREME   Having a transversely placed anal slit, or VENT, characteristic of species possessing paired hemipenes, e.g., snakes and lizards. *See also* CYCLOTREME.

PLANTAR   Of, or relating to, the sole or ventral surface (face) of the hind foot. Contrast with PALMAR.

PLANTAR TUBERCLE   A raised, rounded, wart-like protuberance on the ventral surface, or sole, of the hind foot in anurans.

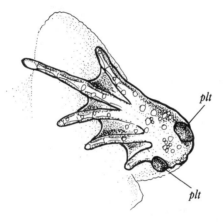

Plantar tubercles (*plt*) on the ventral surface, or sole, of the hind foot of a toad.

PLASTRAL   Of, on, or relating to, the PLASTRON of a chelonian.

PLASTRON, pl. PLASTRA   In reptiles of the order Chelonia (turtles, terrapins, tortoises) the ventral part of the shell consisting typically of nine symmetrically placed plate-like bones, covered on the outside by horny shields. The domed upper part of the shell is termed the CARAPACE.

PLATE   1. Any one of the enlarged units, formed by the fusion of smaller scales, usually on the dorsum, or upper surface, of the head, or on the undersurface of the body where it is termed a VENTRAL scale.   2. Any one of the bony elements that together form

the skeleton of the chelonian CARAPACE and PLASTRON.   3. The OS-
TEODERM lying beneath an epidermal scale in some reptiles.

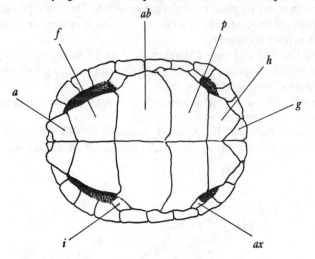

Ventral view of the shell of a chelonian showing the plastron and the
positions of the laminae upon it. *a*, anal; *ab*, abdominal; *ax*, axillary; *f*,
femoral; *g*, gular; *h*, humeral; *i*, inguinal; *p*, pectoral.

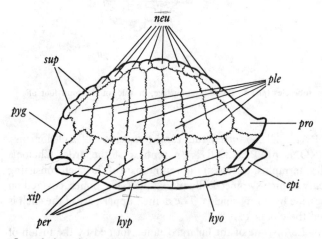

Lateral view of a typical chelonian shell showing the positions of the
bony plates: *epi*, epiplastron; *hyo*, hyoplastron; *hyp*, hypoplastron; *neu*,
neural; *per*, peripheral; *ple*, pleural; *pro*, proneural; *pyg*, pygal; *sup*,
suprapygal; *xip*, xiphiplastron.

PLATYSTERNIDAE   Big-headed turtle. Family of the CHELONIA, suborder Cryptodira, inhabiting South-East Asia. MONOTYPIC.

PLEISTOCENE   The first epoch of the QUATERNARY period, beginning at the end of the PLIOCENE some 2 million years ago, and lasting until the HOLOCENE about 10,000 years ago. Characterized by a series of glacials, it is often termed the 'Ice Age' when advancing ice margins drove many organisms toward the equator, and many others to extinction.

PLETHODONTIDAE   Lungless salamanders. Family of the URODELA, inhabiting North America south to central South America, with species of one genus found in southern Europe. Over 200 species in some 23 genera.

PLEURAL   Any one of the bony plates forming the chelonian CARAPACE, occurring on either side of the NEURAL bones and corresponding with the COSTAL laminae.

PLEURODIROUS   Descriptive of chelonians that are unable to retract the whole of their necks into the CARAPACE due to the presence of well-developed transverse processes on certain of the cervical vertebrae. The neck, which in several species is almost as long as the shell, is bent sideways beneath the front edge of the carapace. Pertaining to any member of the order Pleurodira.

PLEURODONT   Possessing teeth that are situated laterally on the inner edge of the jaw bone, as in many snakes and iguanid lizards.

PLEUROGLYPH   Descriptive of any rear-fanged snake (ECTOGLYPH, sense 1) in which the fang has its venom-conducting groove situated on the side. Contrast with PROECTOGLYPH.

PLIOCENE   The final epoch of the TERTIARY period, beginning at the end of the MIOCENE some 7 million years ago, and lasting about 5 million years until it was succeeded by the PLEISTOCENE.

PNEUMONIA   Acute inflammation of the lungs, in which their normally spongy tissue is converted into a solid mass and the lungs themselves become filled with liquid, making them useless for breathing. In reptiles, pneumonia can be the result of bacterial or viral infections. It can also be caused by heavy infestations of the endoparasitic nematode, LUNGWORM.

POIKILOTHERM (ECTOTHERM)   Any animal in which body temperature varies approximately with that of the surroundings; a cold-blooded species. All reptiles and amphibians are poikilothermic. Contrast HOMOIOTHERM.

POISON GLAND   *See* PAROTOID GLAND, VENOM GLAND.

POISONOUS   In general, used to describe any living organism
having a toxic secretion, or a bite or sting which discharges a poisonous substance, acid or venom, a comparatively small quantity of
which can cause sickness or death. It is, however, becoming more
acceptable to restrict the term to organisms that have a harmful effect on another when partially or completely devoured, and to use
the term VENOMOUS for organisms that introduce venom into the
body of another by means of a sting or, as in certain reptiles, fangs.

POLLEX, POLLYX   The first, or innermost, digit on the forelimb
of a tetrapod vertebrate, containing two phalanges.

POLLYX   A variant spelling of POLLEX.

POLYDONT   Possessing a number of fully functioning teeth.

POLYMORPHISM   The occurrence of more than two types of individual within a species or subspecies, determined genetically or
by the environment. Several reptiles (e.g., California king snake,
*Lampropeltis getulus californiae*) and amphibians (e.g., African reed
frog, *Hyperolius marmoratus*) are polymorphic, all having more than
two pattern or colour types.

POLYPHYODONT   Having teeth that are replaced more than
once during the animal's life.

POLYTYPIC   Containing several forms (taxa) e.g., a genus with
more than two species. Contrast with MONOTYPIC.

POLYVALENT   Possessing antibodies for more than a single particular organism or substance, and a term used commonly for any
antivenom effective against the venoms of a number of different
snake species.

POPE, Clifford H.   1899–1974, American herpetologist. On grad-
uating from the University of Virginia he joined the Department of
Amphibians and Reptiles at the American Museum of Natural His-
tory and, after some five years as a field naturalist with the Central
Asiatic Expeditions in China, he was made Assistant Curator of
Herpetology at the Museum. Joined the Chicago Natural History
Museum in 1940 where he became Curator of Reptiles and Amphi-
bians until 1953. His publications include *Reptiles of China* (1935),
*Turtles of the United States and Canada* (1939), *Snakes alive and how
they live* (1942), *Amphibians and reptiles of the Chicago area* (1944),
*Giant snakes* (1962), and *The reptile world* (1955).

POPPING   The term used to describe the method of sexing
juvenile snakes, involving the application of gentle pressure to the
base of the tail with the ball of the thumb which is slowly rolled

upwards towards the CLOACA. In most species, if the snake is a male, it will evert, or 'pop', its hemipenes.

POPULATION   1. A collection of individuals of the same species occupying a particular space. A population is determined by birth and death rates, male/female ratios, density etc. and is controlled by various environmental factors, disease and food supply etc. 2. The total number of individuals of a given species occurring within a defined area, e.g., the population of the smooth snake (*Coronella austriaca*) in Britain is estimated at around 2000 adults.

PORE   Any small opening or passage in the skin or external covering such as, for example, the FEMORAL and PREANAL PORES of lizards which may, in breeding males, secrete a wax-like substance.

POSTABDOMINAL   The enlarged ANAL scale, or plate, of snakes.

POSTANAL   Behind, or posterior to, the anus or cloacal region.

POSTANAL GLAND   The ANAL GLAND of snakes, often more prominent in the females.

POSTANAL SAC   Either one of the pair of pouch-like hollows situated directly behind the vent on either side of the tail in some lizard families, e.g., ANGUIDAE, GEKKONIDAE and PYGOPODIDAE, and thought to be similar in function to the CLOACAL GLAND of crocodilians and the ANAL GLAND of snakes.

POSTANAL SCALE   In the males of some lizard species, a scale lying posterior to the anus which, in iguanids, is usually enlarged and paired.

POSTANAL TRIANGLE   An often sharply contrasting area of ventral scales in male EUBLEPHARID lizards, the apex of which is in the area of the vent, with the sides of the triangle diverging along the rear margin of the thighs. Also known as the ESCUTCHEON.

POSTANAL TUBERCLES   A seldom used alternative term for the PELVIC, or ANAL, SPURS.

POSTAURICULAR   Referring to the area of the neck behind the ear. Postauricular swellings frequently occur in certain lizards (e.g., *Phelsuma*) especially in reproductively active females, and are thought to play an important role in the metabolism of calcium during egg-shell formation.

POSTAXIAL   Of, or relating to, the posterior side of the forelimb.

POSTCENTRAL   The single or paired SUPRACAUDAL lamina on the rear edge of the CARAPACE in chelonians.

POSTERIOR LOBE   The section, lying posteriorly to the INGUINAL NOTCH, of a chelonian PLASTRON.

**POSTFOVEAL** Any one of the small scales bordering the PIT of crotaline snakes, lying between the LACUNAL and INTEROCULABIAL scales. *See also* FOVEAL, PREFOVEAL.

**POSTLABIAL** In lizards, one or more enlarged scales, or plates, situated behind the LABIAL scales.

**POSTLOREAL** In rattlesnakes of the genus *Crotalus*, any small scale occupying the space between the LOREAL and PREOCULAR scales.

**POSTMALAR** Any one of a series of chinscales in the South American worm lizards (*Amphisbaena*) posterior to the CHINSHIELD and the MALAR.

**POSTMANDIBULAR** Any one of the scales forming a series directly beneath and to the rear of the lower labials in chelonians.

**POSTMARGINAL** The SUPRACAUDAL lamina of a chelonian CARAPACE.

**POSTMAXILLARY** Pertaining to teeth situated in the upper posterior part of the jaw; posterior to the fangs.

**POSTMENTAL** In snakes the single, and in lizards the single, or paired, scale situated directly posterior to the MENTAL scale.

**POSTNASAL** The scale, or scales, situated in front of the LOREAL and behind the NASAL scale.

**POSTNEURAL** An alternative term for the bony SUPRAPYGAL plate on the posterior of a chelonian carapace.

**POSTOCULAR** Behind the eye, as in 'postocular scale' which refers to any scale situated on the rear edge of the eye socket (ORBIT).

**POST-PARTUM** (POST-PARTURIENT) The period of time following birth (PARTURITION).

**POST-PARTURIENT** *See* POST-PARTUM.

**POSTROSTRAL** In some snake species, e.g., rattlesnakes (*Crotalus*, *Sistrurus*), any scale lying between the ROSTRAL and the INTERNASAL scales.

**POST-TERM** After term; after the due date. Said of eggs which have gone beyond the date they were expected to hatch.

**POUCH** *See* BROOD POUCH, MARSUPIAL POUCH.

**POX** (LIZARD POX) A harmless dermal condition of unknown origin, occurring occasionally in both wild and captive lizards, especially *Lacerta*, in which one or more tumours (papillomata) form in the skin. These tumours sometimes develop into enlarged, roughened and grotesquely shaped structures known commonly as 'tree bark tumours'.

PREANAL   In front of the anus or cloacal region.

PREANAL PORE   A structure, identical in function to the FEMO-RAL PORE, situated anterior to the anus or cloacal region, in some lizards. The pore opens to the exterior on the upper surface of the PREANAL SCALE.

The underside of a lizard showing the position of the preanal pores directly above the anus.

PREANAL SCALE   Any one of the row of scales situated in the pelvic region, directly in front of the anus. In some lizards several of these scales may have PREANAL PORES.

PREBUTTON   In newborn rattlesnakes (*Crotalus, Sistrurus*) the small pre-rattle segment on the tip of the tail which is usually lost a short while after birth when the snakes undergo their first skin shedding.

PRECAMBRIAN   The period of geological time extending from the earth's formation, considered to be about 4600 million years ago, to the beginning of the CAMBRIAN some 590 million years ago.

PRECENTRAL   The NUCHAL LAMINA of the chelonian CARAPACE.

PRECILIARY   In rattlesnakes (*Crotalus, Sistrurus*), a small scale occupying the front upper border of the eye.

PREDATION   A relationship between two or more species within a community, in which one (the predator) hunts the other (the prey), which may be vertebrate or invertebrate, for food. Most reptiles, and amphibians and their larvae, are predators.

PREFERRED SUBSTRATE TEMPERATURE (PST)   The temperature of the ground upon, or in which, a reptile chooses to rest, when the substrate of that particular area has a varying thermal gradient.

**PREFOVEAL**  Any one of the small scales in crotaline snakes (pit vipers), bordered by the NASAL, LOREAL, SUPRALABIAL and LACUNAL scales. *See* FOVEAL, POSTFOVEAL.

**PREFRONTAL**  Either one of a pair of large scales directly in front of the FRONTAL.

**PREGULAR FOLD**  Any one of the single, or several, skin folds transversing the throat in some lizards, in front of the GULAR FOLD.

**PREHALLUX**  The vestigial digit on the innermost side of the first toe (HALLUX) of the hind foot in anurans.

**PREHENSILE**  Adapted for seizing or grasping, especially by wrapping around a support. The tail of the nocturnal monkey-tailed skink (*Corucia zebrata*) is prehensile and used for grasping branches from which it hangs during the day whilst asleep.

**PRE-MATING ISOLATING MECHANISM**  The term given to the unique individual CALL of anuran species to which only other members of the same species will respond. Where several species occur together within the same habitat, this auricular 'signature' is vital as it prevents females of one species from mating with males of another, thereby saving valuable energy and time on a sterile mating. The call thus effectively 'isolates' one species from another.

**PREMAXILLA BONE**  Either one of the two, often teeth-bearing, dermal bones that form the front-most angle of the upper jaw in amphibians and reptiles.

**PREMAXILLA TOOTH**  Any one of the teeth found on the PREMAXILLA BONES of the front upper jaw.

**PREMONTANE**  Said of reptile and amphibian species that occur in the foothills of a mountain or mountain range.

**PRENASAL**  A scale situated directly in front of the nostril in some snakes.

**PREOCULAR**  Situated in front of the eye, as in 'preocular scale' which refers to any scale situated on the front edge of the eye socket (ORBIT).

**PRESUBOCULAR**  Any one of the several small scales situated beneath the PREOCULAR and in line with the LOREAL.

**PRE-TERM**  Before term; before the due date. Said of eggs that hatch earlier than expected.

**PRETYMPANIC, PRETYMPANUM**  Any one of the number of

scales situated directly in front of the tympanum, or ear, on either side of the head in lizards.

PREY   Any animal that is hunted or captured by another animal for food. Even though the majority of both reptiles and amphibians are PREDATORS, most of them are also, at some stage in their life, prey not only to other forms of animals but frequently to their own kind as well.

PREY SPECIES SPECIFIC   In reference to feeding, the situation in which a particular food item is eaten in preference to any other. Reptiles that use a specific prey species exclusively are termed 'stenophagous'; the egg-eating *Dasypeltis scabra* is an example.

PROBOSCIS (ROSTRAL APPENDAGE)   The long tubular snout, or ROSTRUM, in the soft-shelled turtles (*Trionyx*), matamata (*Chelus fimbriatus*) and Fly River turtle (*Carettochelys insculpta*) which can be protruded above the water's surface like a snorkel, allowing the chelonian to breath whilst the rest of the head and body remains submerged.

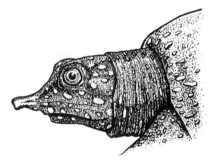

The proboscis of certain aquatic chelonians, such as the soft-shelled turtle (*Trionyx*), can be protruded from the water, enabling the reptile to breath whilst submerged beneath the surface.

PROCAUDAL   *See* SUPRAPYGAL.

PROCRYPTIC   Possessing camouflaging patterns or colours, exhibited in many reptiles and amphibians and helping them to remain undiscovered amongst the surroundings in which they rest.

PROECTOGLYPH   Descriptive of any rear-fanged snake (ECTOGLYPH) in which the fang has its venom-conducting groove situated on its front surface. Contrast with PLEUROGLYPH.

PROLAPSE   The sinking of an organ, or part, from its normal position within the body. In amphibians, it can occur as a rectal and cloacal prolapse, the causes usually being constipation and/or a vitamin or mineral deficiency, and is not uncommon in *Ambystoma* salamanders and giant anurans. In reptiles, it usually occurs as a prolapse of the oviduct, through EGG-BINDING, or the rectum, through constipation.

PROLONGED AMPLEXUS   The system in some anurans in which the male and female remain coupled for days, weeks or, as in certain members of the *Atelopus* genus, several months, whilst they travel the vast distances necessary to reach their breeding sites.

PRONEURAL (NUCHAL BONE)   The central bony plate at the front edge of a chelonian CARAPACE, corresponding to the NUCHAL, or PRECENTRAL LAMINA.

PROPHYLAXIS   Precautionary treatments applied in order to prevent disease or contain its spread. It is often advisable to give prophylactic treatment to any reptile or amphibian that is suspected of carrying disease, or disease-carrying agents, or to newly imported or wild-caught specimens before introducing them to a collection.

PROTEIDAE   Waterdogs and olms. Family of the URODELA, inhabiting North America and Europe. Some five species in two genera.

PROTEROGLYPH   A snake that possesses venom-conducting fangs, usually with a closed groove, connected to a comparatively immobile MAXILLA, preventing them from being folded back against the roof of the mouth. Contrast SOLENOGLYPH.

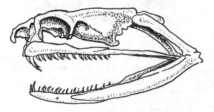

The skull of a proteroglyph snake has immovable fangs situated at the front of the upper jaw.

PROTOZOAN   Any minute, single-celled invertebrate of the phylum Protozoa, including flagellates, amoebas, ciliates, sporozoans etc., some of which occur as ENDOPARASITES in reptiles and amphibians.

PROTOZOONOSIS   Any disease of the digestive tract or blood cells and circulatory system, in reptiles and amphibians, caused by an infestation of Protozoa.

PROVENANCE   The history of an individual specimen, detailing its origin, its parents, diseases and treatments, breeding successes etc.

PROXIMAL   Pertaining to the part of a structure or organ, such as the tail or limb, that is closest to its point of attachment to the body. Contrast DISTAL.

PSAMMOPHILOUS   Of, relating to, or living in, a sandy substrate. Several amphibians and many reptiles are psammophilous in their habits.

PSEUDIDAE   Harlequin frogs. Family of the ANURA, inhabiting the Caribbean coast of Venezuela and Trinidad down to Patagonia, southern Brazil, Uraguay, Paraguay and northern Argentina. Four species in two genera.

PSEUDOMONAD INFECTION   An infectious disease affecting the digestive tract, oral cavity, stomach and tissues of reptiles caused by various bacteria such as *Pseudomonas fluorescens* and *P. aeruginosa*. MOUTH ROT in snakes is a relatively common pseudomonad infection.

PSEUDOTUMOUR   An abnormal swelling in the skin of reptiles and amphibians, caused either by encysting parasites, such as nematode worms, or by an increase in the number of cells (hypertrophy) which may occur in the course of the healing of a wound or during REGENERATION.

PTERYGOID   Either one of the pair of bones that form much of the palate in many species, secured in front to the upper jaw and roof of the mouth and at the back to the QUADRATE. They are supported, in some species, by the two vertical, strut-like EPIPTERYGOID BONES.

PUBIC SYMPHYSIS   A joint created from the fusion of the two pubic bones (PUBES) of the pelvic girdle in many reptiles.

PUBIS, pl. PUBES   One of the three bones that constitute part of the PELVIC GIRDLE. The pubes in many reptiles are fused together forming a joint with a small degree of movement, the PUBIC SYMPHYSIS.

PUPIL   The opening (aperture) in the centre of the IRIS of the eye. In reptiles and amphibians, the pupil can be any one of a number of shapes: circular, vertically elliptical, horizontally elliptical, heart-shaped or triangular, all useful features in the identification of these animals. The size of the pupil can be adjusted by the contraction of the muscles of the iris in order to protect the sensitive cells of the retina.

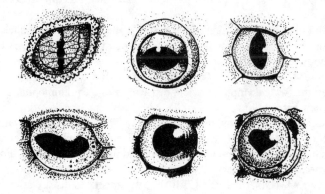

Reptile and amphibian pupils come in a variety of shapes and sizes. Clockwise from the top: leopard gecko (*Eublepharis macularius*), common frog (*Rana temporaria*), reticulated python (*Python reticulatus*), fire-bellied toad (*Bombina orientalis*), leopard snake (*Elaphe situla*), longnosed tree snake (*Dryophis nastua*).

**PYGAL**   The central bony plate at the rear edge of a chelonian CARAPACE, corresponding to the SUPRACAUDAL lamina.

**PYGOPODIDAE**   Flap-footed, or snake, lizards. Family of the SQUAMATA, suborder SAURIA, inhabiting Australia and New Guinea and a few adjacent islands including New Britain. 31 species in eight genera.

# Q

QUADRAT   In ECOLOGY, a square sample area, which can be any size, chosen for detailed study of, for example, the amphibian or reptile POPULATION of a square kilometre.

QUADRATE   1. A large scale situated on the head, forming the hindmost end of the JUGAL group.   2. A bone of the skull, forming the jointed lower jaw surface, more conspicuous in reptiles than amphibians in which it is usually small, or absent altogether.

QUADRATOJUGAL   A dermal bone situated on the BUCCAL area beneath the SQUAMOSAL, and between the JUGAL and the QUADRATE on the lower edge of the skull. Found in crocodiles, chelonians and *Sphenodon* but not in lizards and snakes.

QUADRATOMAXILLARY   In anurans, a bone situated between the QUADRATE and the MAXILLA, in the skull.

QUADRICARINATE   Having four ridges, or KEELS.

QUARANTINE   A period, or place, of isolation for newly acquired specimens in order to prevent the spread of disease or parasites etc. For reptiles and amphibians, the period of quarantine is generally 4–6 weeks, during which time the animals are observed for signs of ill-health and treated accordingly. A preventive drug is frequently given (PROPHYLAXIS) to specimens suspected of having, but not showing signs of, parasites or illness.

QUATERNARY   The second, and most recent, period of the CENOZOIC from around 2 million years ago to the present, and consisting of two epochs: the PLEISTOCENE and RECENT. During the Quaternary, or 'fourth age', man became the dominant terrestrial species.

QUINCUNX  A group of five objects arranged in a rectangle or square with one at each of the four corners and a fifth in the centre. Has been used to describe the laminae arrangement on the CARAPACE of *Chrysemys*.

QUINQUECARINATE  Has been used to describe laminae or scutes bearing five KEELS.

# R

RACE  A group, or population, of a species distinguished from other members of the same species by different physical characteristics, such as colour and markings, and inhabiting a more or less isolated geographical area; a SUBSPECIES.

RACER  Any one of a number of long, slender, non-venomous snakes of the family COLUBRIDAE, subfamily Colubrinae, genus *Coluber*, inhabiting North America, Europe, north-western Africa, the Near East and central Asia. In Europe, they are usually known as 'whip snakes'.

RADIOGRAPHIC DIAGNOSIS  The use of X-rays to confirm the presence of eggs or young, or to determine the nature of an intestinal obstruction or abdominal tumour, in a reptile.

RADIOULNA  The bone of the lower forelimb in anurans formed from the fusion of the RADIUS and ULNA.

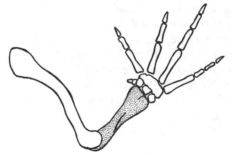

Diagram of the right foreleg of an anuran with the radioulna bone shown stippled.

**RADIUS**  The shorter of the two bones of the lower forelimb (forearm) in tetrapod vertebrates. In anurans it is fused with the ULNA to form the RADIOULNA.

**RAINFOREST**  A humid, evergreen forest with thick and lush vegetation characterized by huge trees, lianas, palms, epiphytes etc., and with a tremendous diversity of reptile and amphibian species. Rainforests occur mainly in lowlands of the tropical wet zone.

**RAKER**  The GILL RAKER of larval amphibians.

**RALE**  The term given to the abnormal crackling sound, heard through a stethoscope, when listening to lungs which have an accumulation of fluid, and frequently heard in snakes suffering from respiratory infections, pneumonia etc. *See also* RHONCHUS.

**RAMUS, pl. RAMI**  Any part, organ or process that branches from another. One half of the lower jaw or MANDIBLE.

**RANIDAE**  True frogs. Family of the ANURA, inhabiting much of the world with the exception of Australia, New Zealand, the southernmost part of South America and small islands. 667 species in 47 genera.

**RAPHE**  An elongated, seam-like ridge along the union of the two halves of an organ, or part of the body, such as that down the centre of the back in certain anurans along which the outer layer of skin (STRATUM CORNEUM) breaks at the start of shedding (ECDYSIS).

**RASPING ORGAN**  The arrangement of rows of numerous minute rasping cusps around the mouth in the majority of anuran tadpoles, with which they scrape particles of food from submerged rocks and other debris.

**RATTLE** (RATTLE-STRING, STRING)  The sound-producing organ on the tail of rattlesnakes (*Crotalus, Sistrurus*), formed from a series of keratinized rings or SEGMENTS, each stacked loosely within the other, a new one being added at each skin shedding. Responsible for the characteristic rattling or buzzing noise when the tail is vibrated during moments of excitement.

**RATTLE-FRINGE**  The posterior caudal scales of a rattlesnake (*Crotalus, Sistrurus*) which extend over the edge of the basal segment of the RATTLE.

**RATTLE-STRING**  An alternative term for a rattlesnake's RATTLE.

**RAY, John**  1627–1705, British anatomist and naturalist. His generalized account of reptiles, *Synopsis methodica animalium quadru-*

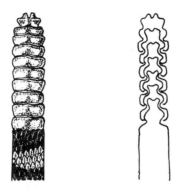

The rattle of the western diamondback rattlesnake and a section (right) showing the interlocking arrangement of six segments.

*pedum et serpentini generis*, in 1693, comprehensive and excellent for its time, distinguished the heart of reptiles from those of mammals and birds, and was the first to precisely describe the tooth structure in venomous and nonvenomous snakes, showing that it was possible to distinguish venomous from harmless species by their dental characteristics.

REAR-FANGED (BACK-FANGED, OPISTHOGLYPHOUS) Possessing enlarged, grooved, venom-conducting teeth situated in the rear of the mouth on the upper jaw (MAXILLA). Rear-fanged snakes are found in the family COLUBRIDAE, in several genera including *Boiga*, *Dispholidus*, *Ahaetulla* and *Thelotornis*, among others.

RECENT (HOLOCENE) The present epoch in the geological time scale, and the second of the QUATERNARY period, extending from the last glaciation of the PLEISTOCENE, some 10 000 years ago, to the present day.

RECEPTACULUM SEMINIS *See* SPERMATHECA.

RECRUDESCENCE Reappearance or regrowth. Used in reference to testicular cycles in male reptiles, following a REFRACTORY PERIOD.

RECTIFORM (LONGITUDINAL TYPE) Descriptive of a particular arrangement in the scalation of snakes; a SCALE ROW forming a straight rather than an oblique series.

RECTILINEAR MOVEMENT (CATERPILLAR MOVEMENT) The method of progress in snakes, in which the reptile proceeds forwards in a straight line by means of complex alternate movements of the ribs, muscles and large ventral scales, in a series of undulations which involve no lateral movement.

RED-LEG   One of the most dangerous bacterial diseases affecting captive aquatic and semi-aquatic amphibians, easily and rapidly spread from one animal to another by the bacterium *Aeromonas hydrophila*, and resulting in a distinct reddening of the undersurfaces of the hind limbs and, in some cases, lower abdomen; a form of severe generalized haemolytic sepsis, from which most victims fail to recover.

REFLEX FEEDING   Pertaining usually to newborn or freshly captured snakes which are reluctant to feed voluntarily and are induced to do so by encouraging them to use their strike reflex, accomplished by provoking them into striking at, seizing and, subsequently, swallowing the item of food.

REFRACTORY PERIOD   In reptiles, the period, usually lasting for several months following mating, in which testicular regression may take place in males, with the production of sperm only recurring again after exposure to a period of cooling followed by a gradual warming. Ovulation in females may also be reduced or halted during this period.

REGENERATION   The regrowth, in a reptile or amphibian, of an organ lost or damaged through injury, AUTOTOMY etc. Urodeles can replace part of, or an entire, limb with an identical one, and lost tails in many reptile species can be regrown.

RELICT   A group of organisms surviving as a remnant of a vanishing, formerly widely distributed race, type or species, usually in an environment different from that in which it originated; of an almost extinct order, such as, for example, the tuatara (*Sphenodon punctatus*) and the Bornean earless monitor (*Lanthanotus borneensis*).

RENIFORM   Having the shape or outline of a kidney, as, for example, the PAROTOID GLAND of some bufonid toads.

REPLACEMENT FANG (ACCESSORY FANG, RESERVE FANG)   In front-fanged venomous snakes, any one of the teeth that lie, in progressive stages of development, within a protective fleshy sheath behind the functioning fang, the next in succession and most developed of which serves as a replacement should the original be lost.

REPRODUCTIVE PERIOD   The interval in time during which

males and females engage in sexual activity. In temperate reptile and amphibian species this may be a defined period in the spring following HIBERNATION. In tropical species, which experience a largely stable climate, the period can occur at any time during the year.

REPTILIA Reptiles. The class of vertebrates that contains the first entirely terrestrial tetrapods, and which consists of the crocodiles and alligators (CROCODILIA), snakes and lizards (SQUAMATA), tuatara (RHYNCHOCEPHALIA), tortoises and turtles (CHELONIA), and the amphisbaenids which form a suborder of the Squamata. Known since the Upper Carboniferous, they number today approximately 6000 species. Most possess a dry skin with a covering of keratinized scales or shields preventing water loss. All are POIKILOTHERMS, and respiration is by lungs only. Fertilization is internal and there is no larval stage or METAMORPHOSIS.

REPTILIARY An open-air enclosure in which reptiles are maintained in near natural conditions.

RESERVE FANG *See* REPLACEMENT FANG.

RESONATING ORGAN The VOCAL SAC of male anurans, situated on the throat or on the sides of the neck.

RESPIRATION The process, in living organisms, of taking in oxygen and giving out carbon dioxide. In reptiles this is achieved by breathing air through the lungs, whilst in amphibians it is effected in several ways: in most adult terrestrial forms, via lungs and, in adult aquatic forms and most larval stages, via gills. All adult and larval amphibians also absorb oxygen through their skin from the air or water around them.

RETICULATE Netlike in form or pattern; a skin pattern consisting of a network of intersecting lines and blotches, as in the reticulated python (*Python reticulatus*), for example.

RETINA The light-sensitive, membranous layer lining the rear wall of the eyeball, and consisting of cones (most numerous in diurnal reptiles and amphibians) and rods (most numerous in nocturnal ones), which are sensitive to colour and light. Images focused on the retina are transmitted, as nerve impulses, to the brain.

RETRACTILE Capable of being drawn inwards, e.g., the head and limbs of many chelonians can be drawn into the SHELL.

RHACOPHORIDAE Flying frogs. Family of the ANURA, inhabiting Africa, Madagascar and the Oriental region. Over 200 species in 10 genera.

**RHAMPHOTHECA**  The sharp, keratinous sheath, or BEAK, on the jaws of a chelonian.

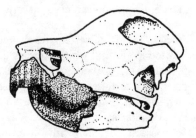

Skull of the green turtle (*Chelonia mydas*), showing the rhamphotheca, or beak, on the jaws.

**RHEOCOLOUS**  Of, situated in, or inhabiting, the waters of streams. Many urodeles are rheocolous, e.g., the spring salamander (*Gyrinophilus porphyriticus*) and brook salamander (*Eurycea bislineata*), among others.

**RHINEURIDAE**  'Worm lizards'. Family of the SQUAMATA, suborder Amphisbaenia, inhabiting central and northern Florida. MONOTYPIC genus.

**RHINODERMATIDAE**  Mouth-brooding frogs. Family of the ANURA, suborder Procoela, inhabiting southern Chile and Argentina. Two species in a single genus.

**RHINOPHRYNIDAE**  Mexican burrowing toad. Family of the ANURA, suborder Opisthocoela, inhabiting Central America from Texas to Costa Rica. MONOTYPIC genus.

**RHOMB**  A lozenge- or diamond-shaped, marking in the skin patterns of snakes, e.g., the rhombic night adder (*Causus rhombeatus*).

**RHONCHUS, pl. RHONCHI**  The term given to the abnormal snapping sound, heard through a stethoscope, when listening to lungs which have an accumulation of fluid, and frequently heard in snakes suffering from respiratory infections, pneumonia etc. *See also* RALE.

**RHYNCHOCEPHALIA**  The order of superficially lizard-like reptiles of the order Lepidosauria, suborder Rhynchosaurida (giant beaked lizards), common during the MESOZOIC but now extinct except for one living species, the tuatara (*Sphenodon punctatus*), characterized by (among other features) a DIAPSID skull, a well-developed PINEAL EYE and a beak-like, toothless upper jaw.

RICKETS  *See* NUTRITIONAL SECONDARY HYPERPARATHYROIDISM.

RICTUS  The gape, or mouth opening.

RING  1. A colour pattern element consisting of a broad, or narrow, solid band of colour that completely encircles the long axis of the body of a snake.  2. Any one of the individual, loosely connected keratinized segments that constitute the RATTLE in rattlesnakes (*Crotalus, Sistrurus*).

RINGHALS, RINKHALS  The much feared spitting cobra (*Hemachatus haemachatus*) of the family ELAPIDAE, subfamily Elapinae, inhabiting Africa south of the Zambezi.

RIPARIAN (RIVERINE)  Of, relating to, or inhabiting, the bank of a river, lake or other body of water.

RITUAL COMBAT  Intraspecific and innate rivalry in male reptiles and amphibians during the breeding season involving two or more participants, in which each attempts to overthrow the other in often elaborate, but rarely injurious fights, usually in order to gain possession of a female.

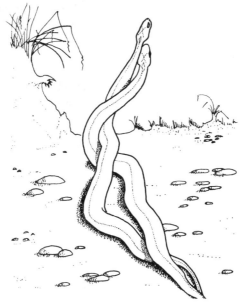

A pair of male European adders (*Vipera berus*), engaged in ritual combat.

RIVERINE  *See* RIPARIAN.

RIVER JACK  The rhinoceros viper (*Bitis nasicornis*), a member of the family VIPERIDAE, subfamily Viperinae, inhabiting rainforests of West Africa east to Uganda, western Kenya and southern Sudan, and southwards to Angola.

ROMER, Alfred Sherwood  1881–1950, American palaeontologist and anatomist, Director Emeritus of the Museum of Comparative Zoology at Harvard University. Author of several publications dealing with the anatomy of reptiles, including *Osteology of the reptiles* (1956), containing a detailed account of the skeleton of both fossil and modern forms, and *Vertebrate paleontology* (1945, 1966).

ROSTRAL (APICAL)  Pertaining to the ROSTRUM (snout), e.g., the rostral scale situated on the tip of the snout between the LABIAL scales that border the upper lip.

ROSTRAL APPENDAGE  The long tubular snout (PROBOSCIS) in certain chelonians (e.g., soft-shelled turtles, *Trionyx*).

ROSTRAL CREASE  A distinct groove or indentation (the LINGUAL FOSSA) in the rostral scale of snakes, allowing the protrusion of the tongue when the mouth is closed.

ROSTRAL HUMP  The enlarged scaly hump on the tip of the snout of the lyre-headed agamid lizard (*Lyriocephalus scutatus*).

ROSTRUM  The beak, or a beak-like part. Used in herpetology for the snout of a reptile.

ROUND WINDOW  *See* TYMPANUM.

RUGA, pl. RUGAE  A wrinkle, crease or fold. In a large number of *Anolis* species, a raised ridge on either side of the top of the head from the snout to the eyelid, between which lies the slightly hollowed area known as the INTERRUGAL SPACE.

RUNT  A dwarfed or undersized hatchling, or newborn reptile; the smallest, least developed of a litter.

RUPICOLOUS  Living on, or amongst, rocks.

# S

SAC   A usually narrow-mouthed, pouch-like part in the body of a reptile or amphibian.

SACRAL DIAPOPHYSIS, pl. SACRAL DIAPOPHYSES   A transverse process on a SACRAL VERTEBRA which can, in some forms, such as anurans, be expanded at its outer margin where it articulates with an ILIUM.

SACRAL HUMP   *See* HUMP.

SACRAL PROMINENCE   The HUMP on the lower back in anurans.

SACRAL REGION   Pertaining to the area of the lower back where certain vertebrae articulate with the pelvic girdle.

SACRAL VERTEBRA   Any one of the strong, large vertebrae that articulate with the pelvic girdle. In reptiles there are two or more, bearing ribs which join with the ILIUM, and in amphibians a single one bearing stout processes (SACRAL DIAPOPHYSES) and ribs.

SACRUM   One or more fused SACRAL VERTEBRAE attached to the ilia and providing support for the pelvic girdle. In the vertebral column of anurans, it is the last single vertebra bearing the SACRAL DIAPOPHYSES which articulate with the ILIUM.

SADDLE   Descriptive of any dorsal blotch of colour in the pattern of certain snakes, that extends down the sides but is wider along the mid-line than it is laterally.

SAHEL ZONE   A region of SAVANNA and scrub lying directly south of the Sahara.

SALAMANDER TOXIN   Any of several secretions (e.g., SAMANDARIN) produced in the skin glands of urodeles, causing cramps, irritation to the mucus membranes and the skin, convulsions and paralysis.

**SALAMANDRIDAE**  Fire salamanders, newts and related forms. Family of the URODELA, inhabiting the HOLARCTIC. Approximately 48 species in some 15 genera.

**SALIENTIA**  The order of the Amphibia, more commonly known as the ANURA, containing the frogs and toads. With the exception of the polar regions and some oceanic islands, representatives of the order are found throughout the world.

**SALIVA**  A watery digestive secretion produced by the salivary glands in the mouth and discharged into the buccal cavity where it performs a lubricatory function, easing the passage of food into the oesophagus. The venom glands of certain snakes are modifications of salivary glands.

**SALMONELLOSIS**  A common communicable disease occurring in reptiles, especially snakes and chelonians, caused by bacteria of the genus *Salmonella*, and often the cause of food poisoning in human beings who have been careless in their hygiene practices following contact with an infected reptile. Many chelonians, especially the semi-aquatic forms, carry the *Salmonella* bacteria without showing any outward symptoms of the disease.

**SALT GLAND**  Any of the glands in reptiles used for excreting concentrated excess salt solutions (OSMOREGULATION). In crocodiles, salt glands are located in the tongue (there are no such glands in alligators or caimans). In certain terrestrial lizards (e.g., *Iguana, Dipsosaurus, Ctenosaura*), the marine iguana (*Amblyrhynchus*) and the marine snakes (Hydrophiidae), they are located in the nasal passages, and in the marine turtles (Cheloniidae, Dermochelyidae), in the region of the eye.

**SAMANDARIN**  A toxic alkaloid secretion produced in the skin glands of *Salamandra* urodeles. Used as a defence mechanism, it can cause muscular cramps and convulsions in predators.

**SAND-SWIMMING**  The term applied to the rapid undulatory movements of many desert-dwelling lizard species (e.g., *Angolosaurus, Anniella, Aporosaura, Uma*) as they burrow their way into sand.

**SAURIA**  The suborder of the SQUAMATA, containing the lizards. It is also known as the Lacertilia.

**SAUVAGE FINISH**  In the commercial skin trade, the term applied to the matt, textured, oiled-leather appearance of a specially processed crocodilian skin.

SAVANNA   A large, open tract of grassland, with scattered trees and bushes, typical of much of tropical Africa, but also occurring in South America and Australia. Reptiles and amphibians inhabiting savannas experience an arid climate with a long dry season and short wet season.

SAXATILE, SAXICOLINE, SAXICOLOUS   Living among rocks; inhabiting rocky locations.

SAY, Thomas   1787–1834, American zoologist and co-founder of the Philadelphia Academy of Natural Sciences. Described many new North American reptile and amphibian species.

SCALATION   Pertaining to the number, shape, pattern, arrangement and location of the scales in reptiles.

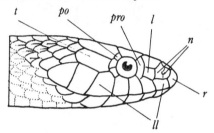

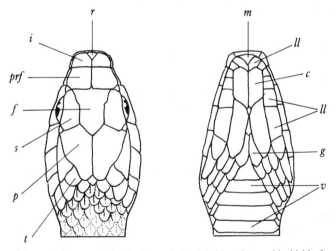

The scalation on the head of a typical colubrid snake: *c*, chinshield; *f*, frontal; *g*, gular; *i*, internasal; *l*, loreal; *ll*, lower labial; *m*, mental; *n*, nasal; *p*, parietal; *po*, postocular; *prf*, prefrontal; *pro*, preocular; *r*, rostral; *s*, supraocular; *t*, temporal; *v*, ventral.

**SCALE** Any one of the flattened, horny, thick or thin, epidermal plates covering the bodies of reptiles. *See also* LAMINA, PLATE, SCUTE, SHIELD.

**SCALE-BOSS** *See* KNOB.

**SCALE-CLIPPING** A method of marking reptiles, especially snakes, by clipping or cutting one or more scales (usually on the VENTER) in a predetermined combination, in order that individuals can be recognized both in the field and in the laboratory. *See also* TOE-CLIPPING.

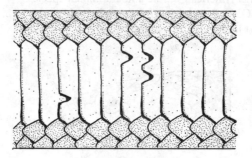

Marking snakes by clipping one or more scales aids the recognition of individuals in the field.

**SCALE FOSSA** *See* SCALE PIT.

**SCALE ORGAN** In lizards, minute structures on the upper surface of the scales consisting of tiny rounded projections and/or hairlike filaments, apparently tactile in function.

**SCALE PIT** (APICAL PIT, SCALE FOSSA) The tiny depressions on the apex of the dorsal scales in snakes and lizards.

**SCALE ROT** A form of DERMATITIS in captive reptiles, especially snakes, usually a result of keeping the animals too wet, or the vivaria too humid. In its early stages, it may appear as small blisters and/or a pinkish or brownish discoloration of the ventral scales. Untreated it very often becomes NECROTIC, i.e., areas of tissue die and slough away.

**SCALE ROW** The DORSAL scales of most snakes are arranged in a continuous series of straight, distinct, longitudinal and oblique rows, the number of which usually varies from one end of the body to the other. When undertaking a scale-row count, the rows at mid-body are those commonly considered. In the longitudinal type of scale row, common to most snakes, the rows run in three directions, one diagonally up from the ventrals and forward to the centre of the back, one diagonally up from the ventrals and backward to the centre of the back, and one extending the length of the body. The number obtained varies from one species to another but usually remains constant within a species. Most scale-row counts result in odd numbers, e.g., 17–19, which signifies either 17 or 19 and not 17, 18 or 19.

SCALE-ROW COUNT   *See* SCALE ROW.

SCANSOR   A modified pad on the tip of the toes of many geckos, made up of numerous microscopic hairlike structures, which permit the lizard to climb apparently smooth vertical surfaces by taking advantage of minute flaws and cracks within those surfaces.

SCANSORIAL   Specially adapted for climbing, as for example, lizards of the family CHAMAELEONIDAE, and many geckos.

SCAP   To capture freshwater or marine chelonians with the aid of a dip net.

SCAPULA, pl. SCAPULAE   The dorsal part of the shoulder girdle.

SCAPULAR CHEVRON   A dark V-shaped bar or band transversing the dorsum above the forelimb insertion, i.e., over the site of the scapulae.

SCAPULAR REGION   The area on the dorsum of a reptile or amphibian, lying directly behind the neck and over the position of the dorsal part of the pectoral girdle, or scapulae.

SCAT (BOLUS)   A small pellet of faecal matter.

SCENT GLAND   The ANAL GLAND situated in the base of the tail of snakes, or any corresponding gland in crocodilians, chelonians, or amphibians. *See* CLOACAL GLAND, MUSK GLAND.

SCENTING   *See* SCENT MANIPULATION.

SCENT MANIPULATION   A method used to encourage a captive reptile to eat a food item which is not its preferred or natural food, by applying the smell of one type of food to another. For example, toads are the principal food of the North American hognosed snakes (*Heterodon*), but in captivity they will take mice which have been rubbed with a toad.

SCENT TRANSFERENCE   *See* SCENT MANIPULATION.

SCHMIDT, Karl Patterson   1890–1957, American biologist and herpetologist at the American Museum of Natural History in New York. In 1922 he established the Herpetological Department in

Chicago's Field Museum of Natural History. Contributed many publications on herpetology including *The American alligator* (1922), *Crocodiles* (1944), *Crocodile hunting in Central America* (1952), *Checklist of North American amphibians and reptiles* (1953), *The truth about snake stories* (1955), and *Living reptiles of the world* (1957) which he co-authored with Robert Inger.

SCIENTIFIC NAME   The title applied to each taxonomic division, understood throughout the world and serving to avoid the complications associated with the usage of many different vernacular names by providing an internationally agreed uniform system. The application of scientific names to organisms is termed NOMENCLATURE.

SCINCIDAE   Skinks. Family of the SQUAMATA, suborder SAURIA, inhabiting the tropics and warmer temperate zones of the world, with the greatest number of species occurring in Australasia, South-East Asia and Africa. Estimated at around 1000 species in some 50 genera.

SCREAM   The distress call, or FRIGHT CRY, of an anuran.

SCREE   An area of weathered rock fragments at the foot, or on the slopes, of a mountain or cliff, offering an ideal habitat for several SAXATILE species of reptile.

SCRUB   An area of arid land covered with bushes, stunted trees and low vegetation.

SCUTE   Any one of the enlarged scales on a reptile and alternatively termed a SHIELD or PLATE.

SCUTELLATION   Pertaining to the number, shape, pattern, arrangement and location of the LAMINAE on the CARAPACE and PLASTRON of chelonians.

SCUTELLUM, pl. SCUTELLA   Any small scale on the body of a reptile.

SEAM   The joined edges of, or border between, adjacent plates or laminae.

SEASONAL BREEDER   A reptile or amphibian species that, in captivity, will only breed during a particular time of the year, as opposed to other species that may breed at any time.

SEASONAL MOVEMENT   The movement, or migration, of a reptile or amphibian population from one area to another, closely associated with the cycle of the seasons and usually in response to increasing or decreasing daylengths (see PHOTOPERIOD). The purpose behind such seasonal movement in reptiles and amphibians is usually linked to either reproduction or hibernation and, in the case of many amphibians and the marine turtles, can often involve long distances as they travel to their breeding sites. In many temperate reptile species, seasonal movement occurs at the onset of winter as they migrate to an established overwintering quarter, or HIBERNA-CULUM.

SEGMENT (BELL, BUTTON)  Any of the parts into which something is separated, e.g., an individual keratinized ring that interlocks with other rings on the tail of a rattlesnake to form the RATTLE.

SELVA  Dense tropical RAINFOREST, especially in the region of the Amazon, characterized by very tall, broadleaved evergreen trees, lianas, epiphytes and vines, and experiencing heavy rainfall most of the year and a dry season lasting only 2 or 3 months.

SEMATIC  Descriptive of the conspicuous coloration typical of many poisonous amphibians and certain venomous reptiles, serving as a warning to other animals.

SEMI-AQUATIC  Descriptive of any reptile or amphibian that occurs in a watery environment, or spends part of its life in water.

SEMI-ARBOREAL  Descriptive of any reptile or amphibian that spends part of its life in trees.

SEMI-ARID  Descriptive of a region characterized by sparse, scrubby vegetation and very limited rainfall.

SEMINAL PLUG  Dried semen that adheres to the invaginated hemipenes of a male snake, verifying that the reptile is reproductively active, i.e., producing sperm.

SEMINAL RECEPTACLE  *See* SPERMATHECA.

SEMI-STERILE MAINTENANCE  Referring to the husbandry of captive reptiles and/or amphibians when housed in vivaria with only essential furnishings, e.g., hide box, water bowl and a very simple substrate, such as newspaper, bark chippings, allowing the maintenance of optimum hygiene conditions.

SEMI-TERRESTRIAL  Descriptive of any reptile or amphibian that spends only part of its life on land or at ground level.

SEPTAL RIDGE  A lateral ridge on the SEPTUM, or dividing wall, of the nostrils, as in the soft-shelled turtles (*Trionyx*).

SEPTUM  A dividing partition separating two tissue masses or cavities, e.g., the vertical tissue separating the nasal passages.

SEROTHERAPY  The application of a serum, such as an antivenin when treating the bite of a venomous snake, for example.

SERPENTARIUM   Any building housing a collection of snakes, but often other reptiles and sometimes amphibians also. It may be a simple public display of various species or a more scientific establishment where specimens are kept and bred for specific purposes, e.g., for venom extraction in the production of serum.

SERPENTES   The suborder of the SQUAMATA, containing the snakes. It is also known as the Ophidia.

SERPENTINE MOVEMENT (UNDULATING MOTION)   The most common method of progress in snakes, in which the reptile proceeds forwards by means of continuous, rhythmic, winding, lateral waves of the body. A method of movement also employed by other legless forms, e.g., certain lizards and caecilians.

SERUM   *See* ANTISERUM.

SEX CALL   A form of VOCALIZATION in male anurans, which acts as a mating invitation to females, and on to which only members of the same species will home in.

SEX DETERMINATION   The ascertainment of sex in a reptile or amphibian. The methods used include superficial examination to detect differences in the size, shape or colour of individuals, or the presence of any one or more structures or appendages associated with male or female sex characteristics, such as crests, vocal sacs, preanal and/or femoral pores, or dewlaps, for example. If no such features are present then it may be necessary, in the case of snakes in particular, to use a CLOACAL PROBE to determine an individual's sexual identity.

SEX RATIO   The number of males in relation to females as they occur in the wild or in captivity. For example, male leopard geckos (*Eublepharis macularius*) are very territorial and may inflict injuries upon each other if housed together, and are therefore usually kept in a sex ratio of one male to two or more females.

SEX SEPARATION   A frequently used method of encouraging reptiles, especially snakes, to breed by first isolating the males from the females for a short period of a few weeks, thereby overcoming the sometimes non-productive 'familiarity' that can occur between animals constantly housed together.

SEXUAL DIMORPHISM   The morphological condition in which the male and female of a species exhibit distinct differences in colour, markings, size and/or structure. Sexual dimorphism is evident, in one form or another, in many reptiles, especially lizards and chelonians, and in some amphibians.

SHED (SLOUGH)   To cast off, or moult, the outermost layer (STRA-TUM CORNEUM) of skin. *See also* ECDYSIS, EXUVIATION.

SHELL   In the majority of chelonians, the hard, rigid structure enclosing the entire body, with the exception of the head, limbs, and tail, although in most species these are retractile to a varying degree, consisting of bony plates overlaid with enlarged scales, or laminae. In a few chelonians (TRIONYCHIDAE), the structure is much softer and covered with skin. The shell consists basically of two parts, the CARAPACE and the PLASTRON, united on either side of the body between the front- and hind limbs by the BRIDGE.

SHELL-BREAKER   The horny outgrowth, or CARUNCLE, on the tip of the snout in baby chelonians, tuataras and crocodilians, for slitting the shell of the egg prior to hatching. Contrast EGG TOOTH.

SHIELD   In reference to chelonians, any one of the large horny plates (LAMINAE) that cover the SHELL or, as used by some authors, the shell itself. Sometimes also used for any one of the enlarged scales, or PLATES, on the head of many snakes.

SHOVEL   The SPADE on the hind foot of the spadefoot toads (*Scaphiopus, Pelobates*).

SIBLING   The progeny of the same parents, but not necessarily of the same litter.

SIDE HIDE   In the commercial skin trade, the term applied to the narrow piece of skin cut from beneath the lower jaw, running backward to transverse the foreleg, extending along the flank, beneath the hind leg, and stopping close to the vent. Such strips are usually taken from the larger adult caimans (*Paleosuchus, Melanosuchus, Caiman*) all of which have belly hides that are of no use as leather due to the presence of heavy osteoderm buttons.

SIDE ORGAN   Any organ on the side of the body of aquatic amphibians, forming the LATERAL LINE SYSTEM.

SIDEWINDING MOVEMENT   The method of progress used by certain desert-dwelling snake species (e.g., *Cerastes vipera, Crotalus cerastes*) when traversing loose sand, by means of sideways looping movements of the body.

SILURIAN   The geological period of the PALAEOZOIC era, beginning some 440 million years ago at the end of the ORDOVICIAN and extending for about 35 million years, when it was succeeded by the DEVONIAN period.

SINCIPITAL   The collective name for any FRONTAL or PARIETAL scale on the heads of reptiles.

SINCIPUT   The anterior upper part of the head, or skull. Contrast OCCIPUT.

SINUS   Any hollow depression or cavity in the body.

SIPHONIUM   A narrow, membranous tube in the head of crocodilians, linking the cavity of the middle ear with the articular bone of the lower jaw.

SIRENIDAE   Sirens. Family of the URODELA, inhabiting the southeastern NEARCTIC. Three species in two genera. Often placed within its own order, the Trachystomata.

SKIN BLISTER   *See* BLEB, BULLA, DERMATITIS, THERMAL BURN.

SKIN FRINGE   Any fleshy or scaly margin on the body of a reptile, especially on the posterior borders of the limbs.

SKITTER   To move rapidly or lightly, especially over water; used to describe the flight of certain anuran species across a body of water when startled or pursued.

SLAP-FEEDING   A technique used to encourage snakes which are reluctant feeders to strike and seize a food item which is tapped lightly against the snake's snout.

SLIDE-PUSHING MOTION   An alternative term for CONCERTINA MOVEMENT.

SLOUGH   The moulted or cast-off outermost skin layer of a reptile or amphibian. *See* ECDYSIS, EXUVIATION, SHED.

SLUG   Any unfertilized ovum passed by a female reptile and frequently pushed away from the main clutch. Slugs are generally yellowish in colour and are merely yolk and shell.

SMALL-SCALE HIDE   In the commercial skin trade, the term applied to soft-bellied crocodilian species possessing 26–35 TRANSVERSE VENTRAL SCALE ROWS. *See also* LARGE-SCALE HIDE.

SMITH, Malcolm Arthur   1875–1958, British physician and herpetologist, and research associate at the British Museum (Natural History), London. Played a significant role in the development of herpetology in Britain, and helped to establish the British Herpetological Society. Over 120 publications, including *Monograph of the seasnakes* (1926), *The breeding habits of the Indian cobra* (1937), and the classic *The British amphibians and reptiles* (1951).

SNAKE ANTITOXIN   *See* ANTISERUM.

SNAKE BITE   Pertaining to any bite of a snake, but especially that of a venomous species, or the condition arising from the bite of a venomous snake.

SNAKE-BITE SERUM   (ANTISERUM, ANTIVENENE, ANTIVENIN,

ANTIVENOM)   A serum, processed from the blood of an animal that has received gradually increasing, immunizing doses of a VENOM and/or ANAVENOM, which has the ability to counteract or neutralize the effects of a specific snake venom.

SNAKE-CHARMER   Any entertainer, especially in parts of Asia (*see* SNAKE WALLAH), who, with swaying movements of the body and by playing music, encourages certain snakes, particularly cobra, in his possession to respond in certain ways, thereby giving the impression that they are being magically charmed.

SNAKE FARM   Any establishment, usually in a tropical or subtropical country, set up to keep and breed snakes, especially venomous species. *See also* SERPENTARIUM.

SNAKE HOOK   An instrument, varying in size and design but generally consisting of a long pole serving as a handle with an L-shaped piece at one end, suitable for pinning snakes to the ground or lifting dangerous species whilst keeping them at arms length.

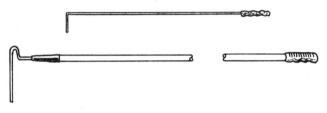

Snake hooks can be used to pin snakes to the ground or to lift potentially dangerous species whilst transferring them from one place to another.

SNAKE MITE   *Ophionyssus natricis*, a minute arachnid of the order Acarina, frequently infesting snakes. They may occur on any part of the snake's body but tend to concentrate around the head, especially the eyes and nostrils. Snake mites suck the blood of their host and heavy infestations can often result in a snake's death.

SNAKE ROOT   Any one of several North American plants (e.g., *Eupatorium urticaefolium*, *Aristolochia serpentaria*), the rootstalks of which have been used to cure SNAKE BITE.

SNAKE STONE   Any poriferous object which, when placed on the punctures of a snake bite, is supposed to draw out and absorb the venom. The BEZOAR STONE found in the stomach of animals is an example.

**SNAKE WALLAH**  A term, used in India and Pakistan, for a person who cares for, or is in charge of, snakes; a snake-charmer.

**SNARING**  *See* NOOSING.

**SNIFFLES**  In reptiles, especially snakes, a discharge from the nasal passages, resulting from inflammation of the mucous membranes, and usually caused by chilling. The watery discharge may also be accompanied by expiratory wheezing noises and nasal bubbling.

**SNORKEL**  The lengthened tubular snout, or PROBOSCIS, of certain aquatic chelonians, which enables them to breathe whilst the rest of their body is completely submerged.

**SNOUT**  The part of the head anterior to the eyes, consisting of the nostrils, jaws and surrounding area.

**SNOUT–VENT LENGTH (SVL, HEAD–BODY LENGTH)**  The straight-line length of an anuran, caecilian, snake, lizard or crocodilian, as measured from the anterior tip of the snout to the posterior margin of the anus or vent. Contrast TOTAL LENGTH.

**SOFT-SHELL**  A deformity in the CARAPACE of a chelonian, as a result of a calcium deficiency (HYPOCALCEMIA) which, in captive animals, is usually linked to incorrect nutrition and/or a calcium: phosphorus imbalance in the diet.

**SOLENOGLYPH**  A snake that possesses venom-conducting fangs connected to a comparatively kinetic MAXILLA bone, enabling them to be folded back against the roof of the mouth. Contrast PROTEROGLYPH.

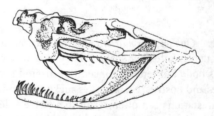

The skull of a solenoglyph possesses movable fangs at the front of the upper jaw. These can be folded back against the roof of the mouth when the mouth is closed.

**SOLENOGLYPHIC TEETH**  The venom-conducting teeth of front-fanged vipers, hollow and situated well forward on the upper jaw.

SOLE TUBERCLE   In many anurans, a METATARSAL TUBERCLE on the hind foot.

SOMATOLYSIS   Disruptive pattern and coloration exhibited by many reptiles and amphibians which, in the animal's normal environment, breaks up its body contours making it difficult if not impossible to see but, when seen against a plain background, renders the animal extremely conspicuous. The gaboon viper (*Bitis gabonica*) is an excellent example of somatolysis.

SOOGLOSSIDAE   Seychelle frogs. Family of the ANURA, inhabiting the Seychelle Islands. Three species in two genera.

SPADE   The enlarged METATARSAL TUBERCLE on the hind foot of spadefoot toads (*Scaphiopus*, *Pelobates*), used for digging. Also, but less commonly, termed the 'shovel'.

SPATULATE   Flat and rounded at the tip; shaped like a spatula, as for example, the large, flattened toe DISC of many arboreal anurans.

SPAWN   The gelatinous mass or string of eggs produced by amphibians. *See* EGG MASS.

SPECIATION   The development of one or more new species from an existing species, as when a geographically isolated population evolves distinctive features as a result of natural selection, and can then no longer interbreed with the parent population.

SPECIES (sp., spp.)   A group of similar individuals that are able to breed among themselves and produce offspring. Individuals or groups belonging to the same species are termed 'CONSPECIFIC'. Each species has a SCIENTIFIC NAME designated in italics by the GENUS name followed by the specific name, e.g., *Python regius* (the royal python). Similar or related species are placed within a genus; many species are divided into SUBSPECIES.

SPECIES DIVERSITY   The different types of species occurring in a particular region or habitat. Species diversity among reptiles and amphibians is greatest within the tropics.

SPECIES ISOLATION   The separation of, or 'barriers' between, different species, serving to prevent members of one species attempting to interbreed with members of another, different, species, which would result in either infertile matings or sterile offspring, both of which would threaten the continued existence of both species. Species isolation is achieved through various mechanisms, including olfactory signals (via glandular secretions), visual signals (species-specific behaviour) and acoustic signals, as in the pre-mating calls of anurans. *See* PRE-MATING ISOLATING MECHANISM.

**SPECIES-SPECIFIC** Restricted to one particular species.

**SPECIFIC NAME** In the SCIENTIFIC NAME of a given reptile or amphibian, the second word in italics, indicating the SPECIES. For example, in the name *Spalerosophis diadema* (the diadem snake), the specific name is *diadema*.

**SPECTACLE** *See* BRILLE.

**SPERMATHECA** (RECEPTACULUM SEMINIS, SEMINAL RECEPTACLE) The receptacle or cavity in the cloaca of female urodeles, that receives the male's SPERMATOPHORE and holds it until fertilization occurs.

**SPERMATOGENESIS** The formation and development of sperm within the male testes.

**SPERMATOPHORE** The gelatinous packet or capsule containing sperm, secreted by cloacal glands and deposited by a male urodele in water or on moist soil, where it is then taken up by a female and retained in a cavity (SPERMATHECA) within her cloaca until fertilization takes place.

**SPERMATOZOON, pl. SPERMATOZOA** Sperm; the mature, motile reproductive cell (GAMETE) produced by the male testes.

**SPERM CAPSULE** The gelatinous packet (SPERMATOPHORE) containing the sperm of a male urodele.

**SPHENODONTIDAE** Tuataras. Only family of the RHYNCHO-CEPHALIA, suborder Sphenodontida, inhabiting a few islands off New Zealand. MONOTYPIC genus.

**SPHENOIDAL TEETH** In skinks of the genus *Eumeces*, teeth situated on the PTERYGOID bone of the skull.

**SPIDER-WEB UMBILICUS** A term used for the network of lines and creases in the soft, scaleless skin surrounding the rear part of the umbilicus scar on the venter of the American alligator (*Alligator mississippiensis*).

**SPINAL** Of, or relating to, the spine or spinal cord. Sometimes used in place of VERTEBRAL when describing scales or markings along the mid-dorsal line of a reptile.

**SPINAL CORD** The part of the central nervous system of vertebrates, connecting the brain and the nerve cells that supply the muscles and organs of the body by means of a series of paired spinal nerves along its length. In reptiles and amphibians it extends from the brain to the tail, enclosed within the neural canal of the vertebral column.

**SPINE** Any firm, pointed structure or process on the body of a reptile (e.g., above the eye in the African horned viper, *Cerastes cerastes*, and on the tail tip of uropeltid snakes) or amphibian (e.g., on the dorsum of the base of the tail in the spine-tailed salamanders, *Mertensiella*, and the skinless innermost digit on the forefoot of some anurans). *See also* TAIL SPINE.

SPINOSE   Bearing numerous spines.

SPIRACLE   The small external opening in the body wall of an anuran tadpole that leads to and from the gill chambers (atria). In most anuran species there is a single spiracle situated on the left side of the body of the tadpole. In the LEIOPELMATIDAE, DISCOGLOSSIDAE and MICROHYLIDAE it is placed mid-ventrally and, in the RHINOPHRYNIDAE and PIPIDAE, it is paired bilaterally.

The spiracle, or breathing tube, of most anuran tadpoles is situated on the left side of the body.

SPITTER   Herpetological slang for any elapid snake species possessing the ability to expel venom from the mouth in a fine stream at an aggressor, e.g., the ringhals (*Hemachatus haemachatus*) and the black-necked cobra (*Naja nigricollis*).

SPLINTER SCAR   Evidence of a wound on the carapace of a chelonian, in which a long thin strip of the bony layer has been exposed between the surrounding keratinous laminae.

SPONTANEOUS FEEDING   The natural, voluntary feeding (i.e., unassisted or unforced) in a reptile, especially a hatchling or newborn individual. Contrast FORCE-FEEDING.

SPOROZOA   Parasitic unicellular organisms which reproduce by forming spores, and commonly responsible for blood and intestinal infections in reptiles, and for small tumours and cysts in the skin and muscles of amphibians.

SPREADING   The flattening of the neck to its fullest extent, characteristic of an angry or excited cobra, but also seen to a slightly lesser degree in a few other species, e.g., the 'false water cobras' (*Hydrodynastes*) and the hognosed snakes (*Heterodon*).

**SPUR** Any sharply pointed, rigid, spinelike structure often on the hind limbs, as in the spur-thighed tortoise (*Testudo graeca*) and certain urodeles (*Euproctus*), or on either side of the vent, as in the vestigial hind limbs of certain primitive snake species. *See also* ANAL SPUR, PELVIC SPUR.

Rear view of the spur-thighed tortoise (*Testudo graeca*), showing the spur on each of the hind limbs which give the reptile its name.

**SPUR FLAP** A succession of enlarged, connected scales along the outer border of the forelimb in the Australian swamp turtle (*Pseudemydura umbrina*), giving the appearance of a flap.

**SPUR STIMULATION** The use, by a male boid snake, of the ANAL SPURS during courtship to stimulate a female into sexual activity. Scratches on the female's body in the region of the cloaca may often be a sign that she has been engaging in mating activity.

**SQUAMA** A scale, or scalelike structure.

**SQUAMATA** Scaled reptiles. The largest order of the Reptilia, containing the most successful living reptiles, the lizards (SAURIA, or Lacertilia) and the snakes (SERPENTES, or Ophidia), and characterized by an external covering of horny scales.

**SQUAMATION** The state of possessing, or developing, scales and, in reptiles, the arrangement, shape and number of scales on the body.

**SQUAMOSAL** Either one of a pair of thin, platelike bones on the side of the skull, overlain by the TEMPORAL scales.

**SQUAMOUS** Scaly; covered with, having the appearance of, or formed from, scales, e.g., the 'squamous HORN' on the snout of the African rhinoceros viper (*Bitis nasicornis*).

SQUIRT GLAND A dermal gland in caecilians producing a liquid, strongly irritant to the mucous membranes, which can be forcibly expelled by muscular contraction.

STABILIZER (BALANCER, HALTERE) Either one of a pair of short, elongated projections or stalks situated on the mandibular arch of certain urodele larvae (e.g., Ambystomidae, Hynobiidae, Salamandridae) during the early stage of their aquatic life, serving to maintain balance whilst swimming and disappearing with the growth of the forelimbs.

STAGHORN GILL The gill of the terrestrial larvae of certain urodeles, named after its striking similarity to the antlers of an adult male deer.

STASIS TADPOLE An anuran larva that has been deprived of food during its premetamorphic stage, resulting in a cessation of, or stagnation in, its development.

STATUS The position of a reptile or amphibian species in a given area, indicating the frequency with which it appears, and frequently described imprecisely by such adjectives as 'common', 'scarce' or 'locally abundant'.

STAUROTYPIDAE Mexican musk turtles. Family of the CHELONIA, suborder Cryptodira, inhabiting Central America from Mexico to Honduras. Three species in two genera.

STEINDACHNER, Franz 1834–1919, Austrian zoologist at the Imperial Museum of Vienna. Published much on the subject of herpetology.

STEJNEGER, Leonard 1851–1943, Norwegian physician and zoologist at the Smithsonian Institution, Washington DC. His many publications include *The poisonous snakes of North America* (1895), *The herpetology of Japan* (1907), and *Checklist of North American amphibians and reptiles* (1917) written jointly with Thomas Barbour.

STENOPHAGOUS Feeding upon a specific type, or limited range, of food items. Stenophagy occurs in a number of reptiles, e.g., the marine iguana (*Amblyrhynchus cristatus*), which feeds on kelp, and the egg-eating snake (*Dasypeltis scabra*), which as its name suggests feeds on the eggs of birds.

STENOTHERMAL Able to exist only within a very narrow range of temperatures. Compare EURYTHERMAL.

STEPPE A vast area of usually treeless grassland in Eurasia, especially the former USSR, characterized by prolonged hot summers, often with extensive drought, and cold winters with heavy snow and long periods of frost. The reptile and amphibian fauna includes several chelonian species, anurans such as bufonid and pelobatid toads, and a number of snake and lizard species.

STERNUM   An unpaired, shield or rod-shaped cartilage or bone on the ventral side of the thorax, articulating with the bones of the pelvic girdle and with most of the ribs when these are present. Commonly termed 'breastbone'.

STILET   Used for the often tiny, sometimes toeless and pointed limb of certain lizards, e.g., the South African large-scaled grass lizard, (*Chamaesaura macrolepis*).

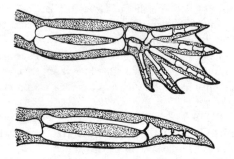

The small pointed limb, or stilet, of the large-scaled grass lizard (*Chamaesaura macrolepis*), below, showing the greatly reduced bone arrangement compared to the limb of a crocodilian. Not to scale.

STILLBIRTH   In reptiles exhibiting VIVIPARITY, the birth of dead, but usually fully developed, young.

STOMATITIS (CANKER, MOUTH ROT, NECROTIC STOMATITIS, STOMATITIS INFECTIOSA, ULCERATIVE GINGIVITIS, ULCERATIVE STOMATITIS)   An infection of the oral cavity in snakes and, less commonly, lizards, usually caused by GRAM-NEGATIVE BACTERIA, as a result of a mouth injury, suboptimal captive husbandry practices, or STRESS, or a combination of these and several other health-weakening conditions.

STRADDLE AMPLEXUS   A type of AMPLEXUS engaged in by certain Malagasy ranid frogs, in which the male sits astride the shoulders of a female whilst both grasp a suspended leaf.

STRATUM CORNEUM (CORNEAL LAYER) The outermost layer of dead, flattened, horny, keratinized cells of the epidermis which provides a protective barrier between the body and the environment. The stratum corneum of reptiles and amphibians is shed frequently during their life to allow for growth (*see* ECDYSIS), and may be sloughed relatively quickly and in one piece, as in snakes and amphibians, or gradually and in numerous pieces, as in lizards, crocodilians and chelonians. A useful source of protein, it is often eaten by many amphibians and certain lizards as it is shed.

STRESS A condition that disrupts the normal biochemical and physiological patterns in the body and which, in captive reptiles and amphibians, can result from any one or combination of several factors, e.g., careless or over-handling, temperatures that are too high, housing together two or more incompatible species or individuals. Stress is often evident in specimens following transportation and in recently collected wild individuals. It is the most frequent cause of illness amongst captive animals.

STRIATE Marked with narrow bands or lines of textures or colours that contrast with the ground texture or colour; ridged, grooved, or striped with parallel markings, as on the scales of many reptiles.

STRIDULATION The production of a harsh rasping or creaking sound in certain snake species, e.g., the saw-scaled vipers (*Echis*) and egg-eating snakes (*Dasypeltis*), when their obliquely positioned keeled scales rub against each other.

STRIKE The lunging, usually swift movement of the head and anterior part of the body with which a snake secures its prey or defends itself by biting an aggressor.

STRIKE REFLEX *See* REFLEX FEEDING.

STRING The sound-producing appendage, or RATTLE, on the tail of a rattlesnake.

STRIPE A comparatively long narrow band of contrasting colour, or texture, running along the length of the body of a reptile.

STRIPING A pattern defect in snakes, in which the normal spots or blotches are joined to form stripes. Most striping results from the accidental exposure of gravid females to temperatures below or, less commonly, slightly above their optimum range.

STUMP-TAIL A term commonly applied to a lizard that has recently lost its tail through AUTOTOMY, or is in the process of growing a new one.

STYLE   Used for the slender, pointed, degenerate limb of certain lizards, as an alternative to STILET.

SUBACRODONT   Teeth, situated in the upper jaw, which are replaced several times during an animal's lifetime.

SUBANGULAR GLAND   A distinct rounded bulge situated on either side of the lower surface of the jaw in species of gopher tortoise (*Gopherus*), swelling during the breeding season and exuding a strong-smelling scent which is used by the males to mark out their territories and their mates.

SUBAPICAL LAMELLA   Any one of the thin single or divided plates, excluding the larger distal plates, that extend across the underside of the digits in many gecko species.

SUBARTICULAR TUBERCLE   A small, rounded, granular protuberance situated between two digital phalanges on the underside of the fore- and hind foot in anurans.

SUBCAUDAL   Any one of the scales situated on the underside, or ventral surface, of the tail from the vent to the tail tip. In most snake species the subcaudals are divided, lying in a double row. In others they may be single, or partly single and partly divided.

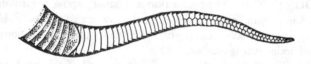

The ventral surface of the tail of a snake in which the subcaudal scales are partly single and partly divided.

SUBCUTANEOUS   Beneath the skin, as in a 'subcutaneous injection' when administering a drug to a reptile.

SUBDIGITAL LAMELLA   Any one of the single or divided scales or plates situated on the underside, or ventral surface, of the digits in most lizard species.

SUBDIGITAL PAD   *See* ADHESION SURFACE.

SUBFAMILY   The taxonomic category, used in the classification of organisms, that consists of a division of a FAMILY, ranking between it and the genus. The SCIENTIFIC NAME of a subfamily ends in '-inae', e.g., Viperinae, the subfamily of the family VIPERIDAE.

The underside of the forefoot of a lizard showing the subdigital lamellae
on the ventral surface of a toe.

SUBLABIAL   Any one of the scales on the lower jaw which, in
snakes, occupy the area between the LOWER LABIAL scales and the
CHINSHIELD and, in lizards, make up the second scale row beneath
the lip.

SUBLINGUAL   Of, related to, or situated on, the area beneath the
tongue, and used by some authors for the scales on the area of the
chin.

SUBLITTORAL   Of, related to, or inhabiting, the shallow-water
zone of a lake, or of the sea between the shore and the continental
shelf. The sublittoral zone of a freshwater lake refers to the depths
of between 6 and 10 m, and that of the sea to depths of between 6
and 200 m.

SUBMARGINAL   Pertaining to the ventral surface of a MARGINAL
scale or LAMINA.

SUBMAXILLARY   An alternative term for the CHINSHIELD of lizards.

SUBMENTAL   Used occasionally for the CHINSHIELD of snakes
and lizards.

SUBMENTAL GROOVE   Used occasionally for the medial furrow on the undersurface of the lower jaw in snakes; the MENTAL
GROOVE.

SUBOCULAR   Pertaining to a scale or scales situated immediately
beneath the eye.

SUBOPTIMAL   Less than favourable or below standard. Frequently used in reference to hygiene, captive husbandry and conditions etc.; for example, 'suboptimal temperatures', meaning
below the temperatures required.

SUBORBITAL BAR   An elevated crease or ridge of skin beneath
the eye usually extending backward to the angle of the jaw.

SUBORDER   The taxonomic category, used in the classification of organisms, that consists of a division of an ORDER, ranking between it and the family, e.g., the Cryptodira is a suborder of the CHELO-NIA.

SUBPLEURODONT   A reptile possessing laterally situated teeth on the inner margin of the jaw, which, when lost, undergo INTER-CALARY REPLACEMENT.

SUBSPECIES (ssp.)   The taxonomic category, used in the classification of organisms, that consists of a division of, and ranks below, a species. Often termed a 'RACE', a subspecies is given a three-part scientific name (TRINOMIAL NAME) which incorporates its genus, species and subspecies.

SUBSPECIFIC NAME   *See* TRINOMIAL NAME, SUBSPECIES.

SUBSTRATE   The surface upon or in which a reptile or amphibian lives, either in its natural environment, or in captivity.

SUBTERRANEAN   (SUBTERRESTRIAL)   Living and functioning below ground. Although many reptile and amphibian species may spend part of their lives below ground during HIBERNATION or AES-TIVATION, some are truly subterranean and are rarely seen above the surface. Examples include members of the CAECILIIDAE, TY-PHLOPIDAE and UROPELTIDAE.

SUBTERRESTRIAL   *See* SUBTERRANEAN.

SUCKER   (SUCKING DISC)   An alternative term for the ADHESIVE ORGAN around the mouthparts of embryonic anuran tadpoles.

SUCKING DISC   *See* SUCKER, ADHESIVE ORGAN.

SULCATE   Descriptive of the grooved side of a HEMIPENIS along which the sperm is conveyed. *See* SULCUS SPERMATICUS.

SULCUS   A furrow, or faintly depressed linear groove.

SULCUS MARGINALIS   In anurans, the furrow extending along the inner margin of the upper lip, in which the rim of the lower jaw sits when the mouth is shut.

SULCUS SPERMATICUS   A distinct groove, or sulcus, which extends along the length and on the surface of the HEMIPENIS in some male reptiles, along which sperm is conveyed during copulation.

SULPHONAMIDE   One of a group of organic bacteriostatic compounds that prevents bacteria from reproducing and often used, with veterinary guidance, in the treatment of a variety of bacterial infections in captive reptiles and amphibians.

SUNGAZER   The giant zonure or girdle-tailed lizard (*Cordylus gi-*

*ganteus*) of southern Africa, named 'sungazer' after the posture it assumes whilst basking.

SUPRA-ANAL KEEL  In the males of some coral-snake species (e.g., the Nayarit coral snake, *Micrurus proximans*), a strongly defined keel on the lateral scales of the posterior part of the body in the region of the vent, or anus. In other species (e.g., Stuart's coral snake, *M.stuarti*) they are indistinct, and in others are absent altogether. Supra-anal keels do occur occasionally on very large adult females in certain species.

SUPRACAUDAL (ANAL, CAUDAL, POSTCENTRAL, POSTMARGINAL) In chelonians, the single or paired posterior laminae on the edge of the CARAPACE.

SUPRACEPHALIC  Of, related to, or situated on, the top of the head, e.g., the FRONTAL or PARIETAL scales of a snake.

SUPRACILIARY  Any one of a number of small scales situated on the outermost margin of the SUPRAOCULAR scale above the orbit of the eye.

SUPRALABIAL  An enlarged scale situated on the edge of the lip of the upper jaw.

SUPRALABIAL GLAND  In most species of frog of the genus *Rana*, a well-defined secretory area on the upper lip extending back from below the nostril to a point posterior to the angle of the jaw.

Profile of a male edible frog (*Rana esculenta*), in which the pronounced supralabial gland on the upper lip extends backward to the angle of the jaw.

SUPRALITTORAL  Of, related to, or inhabiting, the shore of a lake or sea above the high-water mark.

**SUPRAMARGINAL**   In some chelonian species, any one of the laminae situated between the mid-lateral or COSTAL laminae and the MARGINAL laminae of the carapace.

**SUPRANASAL**   Any scale or scales situated directly above the NASAL scale in snakes and lizards.

**SUPRAOCULAR**   Any scale or scales situated above the eye and referring in particular to, in lizards, any one of the scales situated on the back of the eye socket (ORBIT) or, in snakes, the often enlarged scale, or PLATE, directly above the eye which may, in certain species, project outwards slightly to form a SUPRAOCULAR RIDGE.

**SUPRAOCULAR RIDGE** (SUPRAORBITAL RIDGE)   The prominent elongated margin of the SUPRAOCULAR scale which overshadows the eyeball in a number of snake species, especially vipers.

**SUPRAORBITAL RIDGE**   *See* SUPRAOCULAR RIDGE.

**SUPRAORBITAL SEMICIRCLE**   Used mainly in reference to a curved row of small scales situated between the SUPRAOCULAR scales and the other centrally positioned head scales.

**SUPRAPYGAL** (EPIPYGAL, POSTNEURAL, PROCAUDAL)   The term applied to either of the second and third hindmost bony NEURAL plates directly above the PYGAL bone on the mid-line of the chelonian carapace.

**SUPRATYMPANIC**   Pertaining to the area directly above the TYMPANUM, or eardrum.

**SUPRATYMPANIC FOLD** (SUPRATYMPANIC RIDGE)   In many anurans, a fold or ridge of skin directly above, and overlying, the TYMPANUM (eardrum), sometimes extending posteriorly to cover the shoulder. Especially well developed in the Australian White's tree frog (*Litoria caerulea*).

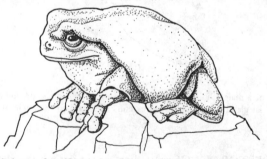

A White's tree frog (*Litoria caerulea*), a species in which the females in particular develop heavy supratympanic folds over their ears.

SUPRATYMPANIC RIDGE   *See* SUPRATYMPANIC FOLD.

SUTURE   The seam or crease formed from the joining together of two surfaces, and used in herpetology for the grooved boundary occurring between adjacent laminae, plates or scales.

SYMBIONT   Any one of the individual organisms involved in a symbiotic relationship with other different organisms. *See* SYMBIOSIS.

SYMBIOSIS   In general, the close association between two or more individuals of different species that are in some way dependent upon each other, as seen in parasitism, for example, but referring in particular to a relationship in which the interactions are mutually beneficial to all the individuals (SYMBIONTS) concerned. For example, in the symbiotic relationship that occurs between the Galapagos giant tortoise (*Geochelone elephantopus*) and some of the island's finches, the birds obtain nourishment in the form of ticks picked from the bodies of the reptiles, which assume a particular posture to enable the birds to reach otherwise hidden places, whilst the tortoises are freed of troublesome parasites and, at the same time, warned by the birds' behaviour of any approaching enemies.

SYMPATRIC   Said of closely related species that coexist within the same, or overlapping, area or region, but which do not interbreed due to one or more factors, e.g., having different breeding seasons, behavioural differences and various SPECIES ISOLATION mechanisms. Compare ALLOPATRIC.

SYMPHYSIS   A type of joint articulating by means of smooth layers of cartilage and fibrous ligaments, allowing only minimal movement, e.g., the joint formed between the two halves of the lower jaw of a chelonian.

SYNAPSID   A skull type, found in extinct mammal-like reptiles, possessing a single, low temporal opening.

SYNDACTYL   An animal possessing hands, or feet, in which two or more of the digits are growing fused together, as in the feet of chameleons (CHAMAELEONTIDAE).

SYNONYM   1. A term having the same or nearly the same meaning as another term, such as 'thoracic' and 'pectoral'. 2. A SCIENTIFIC NAME of a taxon, no longer considered valid and rejected or succeeded by another.

SYSTEMATICS   (TAXONOMY)   The area of biology concerned with the study of the classification and diversity of reptiles and amphibians (and all other living organisms), and the natural associations and interactions between them.

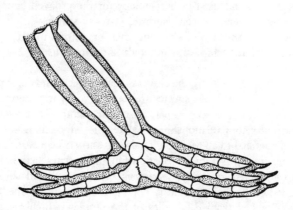

A cross-section of the lower hind limb of a chameleon in which the rear-facing and forward-facing digits are syndactyl, or fused together.

# T

TACTILE ALIGNMENT (TA)   The form of behaviour in courting snakes, in which the male attempts to position its tail with that
of the female so as to bring their cloacae into line. The cloacal
spurs, or ANAL SPURS, of male boids may be used to assist alignment, which precedes INTROMISSION and COITUS.

TACTILE BRISTLE (APICAL BRISTLE, TACTILE HAIR)   In certain
lizards, a single, short, sensitive filamentary 'hair' situated in the
centre of the APICAL PIT on the dorsal scale.

TACTILE CHASE (TC)   The form of behaviour in courting
snakes in which the male follows, and attempts to mate with, the
female. The male accompanies or closely follows the female, his
tongue frequently flicking over her as she proceeds forward. He
becomes excited as he tries repeatedly to locate her cloaca with his
own (TACTILE ALIGNMENT) and his movements become spasmodic.
Should the female show little or no interest and attempt to escape
the male's attentions, he may try to restrain her with his jaws. If
she is receptive, the male will follow up the chase with a TAIL-
SEARCH COPULATORY ATTEMPT.

TACTILE HAIR   *See* TACTILE BRISTLE.

TADPOLE   The larva of an anuran, although the term is sometimes
used to include the larvae of urodeles. A tadpole is characterized by
a rudder-like, finned tail and, in the early days, external gills, on an
egg-shaped body.

TAIL CREST   The cutaneous ridge on the upper surface of the tail
of certain lizards, e.g., *Basiliscus plumifrons*, anuran larvae and
many breeding male urodeles.

The plumed basilisk (*Basiliscus plumifrons*), has a particularly
well-developed tail crest.

**TAIL-CURLING**   A reaction in some lizard species, e.g., *Leio-
cephalus carinatus*, to various external stimuli, in which the tail is
rolled or curled vertically up and down.

**TAIL-DROPPING**   The automatic defensive habit of many lizards
in which the tail breaks off when seized (AUTOTOMY).

**TAIL FILAMENT**   A fine, short, bristle-like appendage projecting from the centre of the usually truncated tail tip in the male palmate newt (*Triturus helveticus*) during the breeding season.

The bristle-like tail filament of the male palmate newt (*Triturus
helveticus*) in breeding condition.

TAIL GLAND (ANAL GLAND) The usually paired sac-like structure within the base of the tail in many reptiles, producing an odorous liquid used mainly in defence.

TAIL LENGTH In snakes and lizards, the distance from the rear margin of the ANAL PLATE to the tip of the tail.

TAIL-SEARCH COPULATORY ATTEMPT (TSCA) The form of behaviour in courting snakes in which the male attempts to locate the female's tail with his own in order to unite their cloacae. He coils his tail once or twice around her tail, moving the coils back and forth along its length so as to bring their cloacae into line. If the female is receptive she may elevate her tail in response to this action. If she is unreceptive, however, the male may raise her tail with his before giving up the attempt. The tail-search usually follows the TACTILE CHASE and precedes TACTILE ALIGNMENT.

TAIL SPINE 1. The NAIL on the tail tip of certain chelonians, e.g., *Testudo hermanni.* 2. The terminal scale on the tail tip of snakes which, in most species, is quite long and sharp but, in others, short and blunt. 3. The prominent thornlike vertical protuberance on the base of the tail of male spine-tailed salamanders (genus *Mertensiella*), tactile in function and used to stimulate the female during mating.

TAIL TREMOR The quivering and wriggling of the tail in certain lizards, especially geckos, when excited, as for example, when stalking insects.

TAIL-VIBRATING The rapid shaking of the tail tip in many snake species (e.g., *Pituophis, Elaphe*) when aroused or disturbed, producing a loud buzzing or rattling sound when the reptiles are amongst dried leaves or other debris.

TAIL WALK In some lungless salamanders (PLETHODONTIDAE), a stage in the sequence of behaviour displayed during courtship in which the female walks behind the male in response to the constant flicking and waving of his sharply bent tail.

TAIL-WAVING In a number of juvenile snakes, especially those of the arboreal pit vipers (e.g., *Trimeresurus*), the raising and waving around of the often bright and contrastingly coloured tail tip, which attracts inquisitive prey to within striking distance.

TAIPAN *Oxyuranus scutellatus*, of the family ELAPIDAE. The largest and most dangerous snake in Australia, attaining some 4000 mm in length and found in a variety of habitats in Queensland and the northernmost parts of the Northern Territory.

TAPEWORM    *See* CESTODA.

TARSAL    **1.** Any one of the bones in the distal region of the hind
limb between the TIBIA and/or FIBULA and the METATARSAL BONES
in tetrapods. In anurans, these bones are greatly elongated and
form the section of the hind limb between the shin and the foot.
**2.** A scale in reptiles, situated between the digits and the joints of
the tibia and/or fibula (ankle) of the hind foot.

TARSAL FOLD (TARSAL RIDGE)    A prominent fold or ridge of
skin along the margin of the tarsal region of the foot in many anurans.

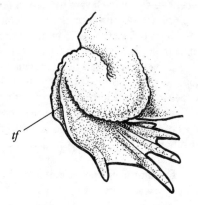

The tarsal fold (*tf*) on the lower hind limb of a toad.

TARSAL RIDGE    *See* TARSAL FOLD.

TARSO-METATARSAL ARTICULATION    The joint between the METATARSUS and the TARSUS.

TARSUS    The bones (astragalus and calcaneum in anurans) of the
hind limb which form the ankle.

TAXON, pl. TAXA    A group, or rank, in TAXONOMY. The taxa
*Bitis*, Viperidae, Squamata, Reptilia and Chordata are examples of
a genus, family, order, class and phylum respectively.

TAXONOMY (SYSTEMATICS)    The branch of biology concerned
with the scientific classification of living things into groups, based
upon all that is known or suspected of the evolution of the organisms concerned and on anatomical similarities etc.

TECHNOPHAGY    The act, witnessed occasionally in some reptiles, in which the female eats her own eggs. It has been observed

in skinks of the genus *Eumeces* and in certain snakes which may devour unfertilized ova. The exact reasons for this behaviour are uncertain but they could include removing odours which would otherwise attract predators or utilizing a valuable source of energy or, in captive reptiles, be the result of stress and/or suboptimal temperatures etc.

TEETH   Hard and, in many species, dense structures situated on the jaws and/or over the palate in reptiles and amphibians, used primarily for biting, seizing and holding prey and, in some species, for partially masticating food. In many snakes, and one family of lizards (the HELODERMATIDAE), some of the teeth, the fangs, have been modified for the conduction of venom. Depending upon the way in which the teeth are attached to the jaw, their various types include ACRODONT, THECODONT and PLEURODONT. Those which possess some form of venom-conducting groove include AGLYPHIC, OPISTHOGLYPHIC, PROTEROGLYPHIC and SOLENOGLYPHIC TEETH.

TEIIDAE   Whip-tails, tegus and allies. Family of the SAURIA, inhabiting North and South America and the West Indies. Approximately 225 species in some 40 genera.

TEMPERATE   Having, or experiencing, a well-defined seasonal variation in temperature; a region, or any species from that region, which experiences mild or moderate climates intermediate to those of the polar and tropical regions.

TEMPERATURE-DEPENDENT  SEX  DETERMINATION (TSD)   The phenomenon in some crocodilians, chelonians and lizards, in which the sex of the eventual hatchlings may be determined by the temperature at which the eggs are incubated. Sex in snakes is generally determined genetically rather than by temperatures experienced during incubation.

TEMPERATURE-INDUCED   PATTERN   ABERRANCY The phenomenon in certain GRAVID female snakes which, when exposed to temperatures slightly above or, more commonly, below the recommended gestation temperature, produce young with varying degrees of pattern abnormality.

TEMPORAL   Of, on, or relating to, the region of the temple on the side of the head, e.g., any one of the more or less enlarged scales situated behind the POSTOCULAR scales, beneath the PARIETAL and above the upper LABIAL scales at the angle of the jaw in snakes and lizards.

TEMPORAL HORN   Any one of the large, often long, hornlike

spines on the posterior margin and sides of the head in the horned lizards (*Phrynosoma*).

**TERATOGENIC** Causing birth defects or malformations. Teratogenesis in captive reptiles may result from a number of factors, including the use of X-rays in determining whether a specimen is GRAVID, or incorrect temperatures during gestation or egg incubation.

**TERENT'EV, Pavel Victorovich** 1903–70, Russian herpetologist, professor of vertebrate zoology at Leningrad University. Contributed over 150 scientific works, including the *Key to the reptiles and amphibians of the USSR*, co-authored with S. A. Chernov (published in Russian in 1949 and translated into English in 1965), *The frog* (1950 in Russian), and *Herpetology–a manual on amphibians and reptiles* (published in Russian in 1961 and translated into English in 1965).

**TERMINAL PHALANX** The distal bone in each of the digits of the forefoot (hand) or hind foot.

**TERRACED** Descriptive of the prominent ridge situated below the lip in some lizards of the AGAMIDAE, resulting from the difference, in both shape and size, between the inner and outermost scales of the chin.

**TERRAPIN** Any one of various semi-aquatic freshwater chelonians, forming the family EMYDIDAE.

**TERRARIUM, pl. TERRARIA** A generally closed container of any shape or size and usually furnished with plants, in which amphibians, reptiles or other small animals are housed.

**TERRESTRIAL** Living upon the land, as opposed to the sea or air; dwelling largely at ground level.

**TERRITORIAL BEHAVIOUR** Any type of action or response associated with the establishment, possession or defence of an area from which rivals are driven by means of visual threats and/or ritualized combat. Such behaviour occurs in many reptiles and amphibians, e.g., dendrobatid frogs, crocodilians and many lizard species.

**TERTIARY** The larger and older geological period of the CENOZOIC era, following the CRETACEOUS, some 65 million years ago, and extending to the beginning of the QUATERNARY, about 2 million years ago. The Tertiary is made up of the Palaeocene, Eocene, Oligocene, Miocene and Pliocene epochs, and characterized by the emergence of modern mammals.

TESTICULAR REGRESSION  *See* REFRACTORY PERIOD.

TESTIS  The male reproductive organ in which spermatozoa are produced. Reptiles and amphibians have two testes, as do all vertebrates.

TESTUDINIDAE  Tortoises. Family of the CHELONIA, suborder Cryptodira, inhabiting America, Europe, Africa and Asia. Not found in Australia. 41 species in 9 genera.

TETRADACTYL  Having four digits, as in the hind foot of a crocodilian, for example.

TETRAPOD  Any four-limbed vertebrate animal including reptiles, amphibians, birds and mammals. The limb skeleton of all tetrapods is based upon the PENTADACTYL LIMB of five digits.

THANATOSIS  The act of playing dead, in which the locomotory muscles become totally relaxed. Thanatosis occurs in a number of snakes and anurans when threatened, disturbed or manhandled.

THECA  A membranous cup-shaped envelope or sheath. The term has been used in herpetology for the BROOD POUCH of marsupial frogs (*Gastrotheca*).

THECODONT  Possessing teeth each located within a bony socket, as in crocodilians.

THERMAL BURN  In general, any burn resulting from body contact with a naked (unprotected) heat source. In reptiles and amphibians such burns usually occur on the ventral surface of the animal.

THERMORECEPTOR  Any device, or organ, that is sensitive to heat or variations in temperature, such as the LABIAL PIT of many boid snakes and the PIT of crotaline vipers.

THERMOREGULATION  The maintenance of the OPTIMAL TEMPERATURE RANGE in POIKILOTHERMS. In reptiles and amphibians, which are unable to produce metabolic heat to raise their body temperature, thermoregulation must take place by basking when too cool and seeking shade when too warm, in order that bodily functions, such as respiration, digestion, shedding etc., can continue normally.

THIRD EYE  *See* PARIETAL EYE, PINEAL COMPLEX.

THIRD EYELID  *See* NICTITATING MEMBRANE.

THORACIC  Of, on, or relating to, the anterior region of the body trunk of vertebrates containing the heart and lungs within the rib cage (the thorax).

THORACIC LAMINA (PECTORAL)  Either one of the third pair of horny epidermal scutes on a chelonian PLASTRON.

**THORN**   The terminal spinelike scale on the tail tip of blind snakes (TYPHLOPIDAE).

**THREADWORM**   *See* OXYURIDAE.

**THREAT BEHAVIOUR**   Any type of innate, species-specific action or response associated with aggressive, intra- and interspecific combat over territory, females, food etc., and used frequently in the intimidation of potential enemies, predators and aggressors. Threat behaviour amongst reptiles and amphibians occurs in many forms and includes flattening the body, inflating the neck or the whole body, opening the mouth to reveal vivid and brightly coloured interiors, raising and stiffening the legs and arching the back, hissing, biting and displaying brightly coloured parts of the body.

**THROAT FAN**   The DEWLAP on the throat in several lizard genera, especially of the family IGUANIDAE.

**THROATS**   In the commercial skin-trade, the V-shaped pieces of skin taken from the sides of the neck and beneath the chin of very large adult caimans (mainly *Melanosuchus*, occasionally *Caiman*).

**THUMB PAD**   A NUPTIAL PAD, situated at the base of the first, or innermost, digit of the forefoot in some male anurans.

**THYROID DISEASE**   *See* GOITRE.

**TIBIA**   The large innermost bone of the lower hind limb of tetrapod vertebrates, extending from the knee to the heel or, in anurans, the corresponding part of the leg.

**TIBIAL**   Any one of the scales situated on the hind limb of a lizard, between the knee and the heel (ankle).

**TIBIAL GLAND**   A large, swollen gland on the upper surface of the lower hind limb (TIBIA) in some toads of the genus *Bufo*.

**TIBIOFIBULA**   The bone of the lower hind limb in amphibians,

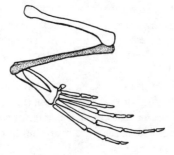

The bones of the hind limb of a frog in which the tibiofibula is indicated by stippling.

formed from the fusion of the TIBIA and the FIBULA.

TIBIO-TARSAL ARTICULATION   The joint, in the hind limb, between the TIBIA and the TARSUS.

TICK   A blood-sucking ECTOPARASITE of the order Acarina, frequently found infesting the skin of reptiles, especially snakes, chelonians and varanid lizards.

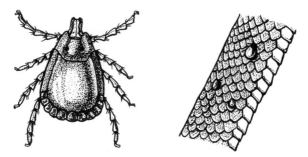

Ticks, of the order Acarina, often occur on the skins of reptiles from where they feed upon the blood of their hosts.

TOADFLY   A fly (*Bufolucilia bufonivora*) which deposits its eggs within the nasal openings of toads. The larvae feed mainly upon mucus but, as they grow, they frequently penetrate into the eyes and brain of the toad with usually fatal consequences.

TOADLET   A newly metamorphosed toad.

TOE-CLIPPING   A method of marking lizards by clipping one or more toes in a predetermined combination in order that individuals can be recognized both in the field and in the laboratory.

TOE DISC   *See* DISC.

TOKEN AMPLEXUS   A brief, somewhat ritualized, form of AMPLEXUS in certain anurans which deposit their eggs in situations other than in water, e.g., *Mantella aurantiaca*, *Rhinoderma darwini* and several *Dendrobates* species.

TONGUE-FLICKING   The protrusion and, in some species, the up-and-down movement of the tongue, in many snakes and lizards, during which scent particles adhere to the moist upper surface and are transferred to the JACOBSON'S ORGAN in the roof of the mouth for analysis. In snakes, the tongue is extended for a few seconds while the mouth is closed, by means of a V-shaped indentation (the LINGUAL FOSSA) in the underside of the ROSTRAL scale, and the flicking increases during the pursuit of prey, or a mate, or when the reptile is agitated or annoyed. In certain lizards, such as the blue-tongued skinks (*Tiliqua*), the brightly coloured tongue is protruded for several seconds, sometimes through an open mouth, as a form of threat behaviour towards an aggressor.

TONGUE WORM   A modified worm-like arachnid that, either as a larva or a 120-mm adult, inhabits the respiratory tract of amphibians and reptiles, especially crocodilians.

TOPOGRAPHY   Description of the external features of a reptile or amphibian.

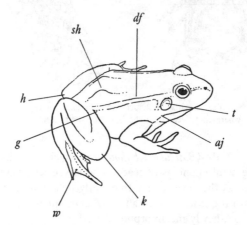

The topography of a frog: *aj*, angle of jaw; *df*, dorsolateral fold; *g*, groin; *h*, heel; *k*, knee; *sh*, sacral hump; *t*, tympanum; *w*, web.

TOP PREDATOR   *See* FOOD CHAIN.

TORPOR   An energy-saving period of inactivity, in which bodily functions are greatly slowed, exhibited by many reptiles and amphibians during adverse climatic conditions. *See* AESTIVATION, HIBERNATION.

TORTOISESHELL   The horny, semi-transparent, yellow and dark brown mottled laminae from the shell of the marine hawksbill turtle (*Eretmochelys imbricata*).

TOTAL LENGTH (TL)   The greatest, combined, straight-line length of a reptile (with the exception of chelonians), caecilian or tailed amphibian, measured from the tip of the snout to the tip of the tail. *See also* HEAD–BODY LENGTH, SNOUT–VENT LENGTH.

TOXICOLOGY   The branch of science concerned with the study of naturally occurring poisonous substances (toxins), their nature and effects upon living organisms, and antidotes effective against them. Compare TOXINOLOGY.

TOXIN   *See* TOXICOLOGY.

TOXINOLOGY   A subdivision of toxicology that is concerned specifically with the toxins produced by organisms (e.g., the venom of snakes and the poisonous secretions of amphibians). Compare TOXICOLOGY.

TRACHEA   The membranous tube, or windpipe, in air-breathing vertebrates, stiffened by incomplete cartilaginous rings and leading from the throat to the lungs allowing the passage of air. In many snakes, the anterior part of the trachea is thrust forwards on the floor of the mouth to allow the reptile to breath whilst in the process of swallowing large prey items.

TRACTABLE   Said of any reptile or amphibian that is easily controlled or managed; inoffensive.

TRANSFORMATION   A noticeable and usually sudden change (METAMORPHOSIS) in the shape and structure (and usually also in the habits) of most amphibians as they progress from larval to adult form, e.g., tadpole to frog.

TRANSILLUMINATION   The technique, commonly called 'candling', used to determine the viability of eggs, through which a strong light is directed briefly in a darkened room during the early stages of incubation. Viable eggs clearly show blood vessels which appear as a web-like network of red lines. An absence of blood vessels indicates that the embryo has died or that the eggs have not been fertilized.

TRANSLOCATION   The moving of reptiles and/or amphibians from one area to another and releasing them there. Colonies of sand lizards (*Lacerta agilis*) and smooth snakes (*Coronella austriaca*), for example, have been translocated in southern England from districts where they were under threat to new, less disturbed areas.

TRANSVERSELY DIVIDED   Pertaining to a scale, on the head of some crotaline vipers, that is divided across its long axis to form two smaller scales, e.g., the first INFRALABIAL in *Crotalus ruber* and the upper PREOCULAR in *C. lepidus*.

TRANSVERSE VENTRAL SCALE ROW   The arrangement of the ventral scales in crocodilians, situated in transverse rows, with the number of rows between the neck and vent varying from one species to another. The rows are counted from that directly behind the collar up to, but excluding, the row bordering the vent.

**TREMATODA**  Class of parasitic PLATYHELMINTHES known as flukes, that attach themselves to a HOST by means of hooks and suction discs. They occur throughout the alimentary canal and other internal organs of both amphibians and reptiles.

**TRIAD**  A group of three. A term commonly used for the trio of black rings in the pattern of some coral snakes (*Micrurus*) and their mimics (*Erythrolamprus*), in which successive arrangements of black–yellow (or white)–black–yellow (or white)–black rings are isolated from the others by red rings.

**TRIASSIC**  The oldest period of the MESOZOIC era, beginning some 230 million years ago at the end of the PERMIAN and extending for about 35 million years until it was succeeded by the JURASSIC. It is characterized by an increase in the number of primitive amphibians and reptiles, including phytosaurs, dinosaurs and chelonians.

**TRICARINATE**  Descriptive of a scale, lamina or chelonian carapace bearing three ridges or keels.

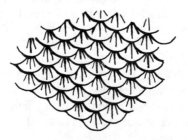

Scales bearing three keels are termed 'tricarinate'.

**TRICOLOUR**  A convenient grouping term for any of the snakes of the genus *Lampropeltis* which have patterns of three alternating rings or bands of black, red and yellow (or white). Includes most of the *L. triangulum* group, commonly known as 'milk snakes'. The term has been used occasionally, although rarely, by some authors for certain coral snakes of the genus *Micrurus*.

**TRICOLOUR DYAD (TD)**  A pattern in certain snakes characterized by red rings or bands, each isolated from the other by a group of alternating rings or bands of black–light–black, i.e., two black between two red.

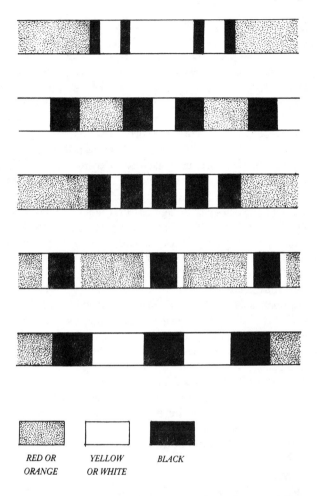

RED OR          YELLOW          BLACK
ORANGE          OR WHITE

Diagrammatic patterns of tricoloured snakes. From the top: tricolour
tetrad – *Erythrolamprus bauperthuisii*; tricolour dyad – *Lystrophis
semicinctus*; tricolour pentad – *Micrurus tschudii*; tricolour monad –
*Micrurus corallinus*, and tricolour triad – *Micrurus frontalis*.

**TRICOLOUR MONAD (TM)**   A pattern in certain snakes characterized by red rings or bands, each isolated from the other by a
group of alternating rings or bands of light–black–light, i.e. one
black between two red.

**TRICOLOUR PENTAD (TP)**   A pattern in certain snakes characterized by red rings or bands, each isolated from the other by a group of alternating rings or bands of black–light–black–light–black–light–black–light–black, i.e. five black between two red.

**TRICOLOUR TETRAD (TTE)**   A pattern in certain snakes characterized by red rings or bands, each isolated from the other by a group of alternating rings or bands of black–light–black–light–black–light–black i.e. four black between two red.

**TRICOLOUR TRIAD (TT)**   A pattern in certain snakes characterized by red rings or bands, each isolated from the other by a group of alternating rings or bands of black–light–black–light–black, i.e. three black between two red.

**TRIDACTYL**   Possessing three digits on the fore- or hind foot.

**TRINOMIAL NAME**   The three-part scientific name of a reptile or amphibian that incorporates its genus, species and subspecies, e.g., *Python molurus bivittatus* (a subspecies of the Asiatic rock python). The system of giving a scientific name to a subspecies in which a third name is added to the genus and species is called trinomial nomenclature. *See also* BINOMIAL NOMENCLATURE.

**TRIONYCHIDAE**   Soft-shelled turtles. Family of the CHELONIA, suborder Cryptodira, inhabiting most temperate and tropical regions of the world with the exception of Central and South America, Madagascar and Australia. 28 species in 6 genera.

**TROGLODYTIC**   Cave-dwelling. Although many reptiles and amphibians venture into caves either by accident or in pursuit of prey, only a few urodeles are true troglodytes, characterized by their loss of pigmentation and vision, e.g., the olm (*Proteus anguineus*) and several members of the genus *Eurycea*.

**TROGONOPHIDAE**   Family of the SQUAMATA, suborder Amphisbaenia, inhabiting north-western Africa, Somalia, the Arabian peninsula and Socotra Island in the Indian Ocean. Six species in · four genera.

**TROPICAL**   Of, relating to, or inhabiting, the tropics; occurring in regions between the latitudes of $23\frac{1}{2}°$ N (tropic of Cancer) and $23\frac{1}{2}°$ S (tropic of Capricorn) of the equator.

**TROPICAL ARID FOREST**   A sparse vegetation type, occurring at elevations of between 100 and 600 m on the leeward side of high ground, in the path of rainbearing winds, receiving normally no more than 1000 mm of rain annually, and characterized by scattered cacti, stunted trees and scrub, and several types of grasses.

TROPICAL DECIDUOUS FOREST   A vegetation type, typical of low-lying, semi-arid regions of the tropics, with trees and shrubs that shed their foliage in the dry season.

TROPICAL EVERGREEN FOREST   A vegetation type, typical of low-lying, semi-humid regions of the tropics, with trees and shrubs that bear foliage throughout the year.

TROPICOPOLITAN   Confined in distribution to regions within the tropics. Contrast COSMOPOLITAN.

TRYPANOSOME   Any one of a number of parasitic protozoans of the genus *Trypanosoma*, found in the blood and intestines of amphibians and reptiles and transmitted by certain insects (Diptera) and possibly mites (ACARINA). Leeches (Hirundinea) are largely responsible for the transmission of trypanosomes in aquatic reptiles and amphibians.

TUATARA   *Sphenodon punctatus*, a lizard-like reptile of the order RHYNCHOCEPHALIA, inhabiting certain small islands off New Zealand, and the sole surviving representative of a group common during the MESOZOIC.

TUBERCLE   A small knoblike projection or elevation on the skin, e.g., the PALMAR TUBERCLE on the ventral surface, or palm, of the forefoot in anurans.

TUBERCULATE   Having small, raised, rounded nodules on the skin; covered with tubercles.

TUBERCULOSIS   A communicable bacterial disease caused by *Mycobacterium* micro-organisms, occasionally affecting the respiratory or intestinal system or, less commonly, the skin, of reptiles and amphibians. Usually occurs as a secondary disease in animals already weakened by other conditions, e.g., suboptimal husbandry, poor nutrition, injury etc.

TUMOUR   Any abnormal swelling or tissue growth forming as a result of the uncontrollable development of new cells, occurring occasionally on the skin, bones or internal organs of reptiles and amphibians. Such tumours may be malignant (e.g., thyroid carcinoma, black melanosarcoma) or, more commonly, benign (e.g., papillomata).

TUNDRA   An immense treeless zone extending between the ice cap and the timber line of Eurasia and North America with a permanently frozen subsoil as a result of the prevailing climate, allowing only minimum vegetal growth in the form of dwarf shrubs and bryophytes. No reptiles or amphibians occur within the tundra.

TUSK   *See* DENTARY PSEUDO-TEETH.

TWIN-EGG   Two eggs which have adhered together in the oviduct of a reptile. Such an egg may be the cause of dystocia, or EGG-BINDING.

TWINNING   The presence of two embryos within the same egg, resulting from two separate embryos being unintentionally enclosed in the same shell during their progress through the oviduct.

TYMPANIC   Of, or relating to, the region of the TYMPANUM; a scale situated directly above the tympanum in some lizards.

TYMPANIC DISC   *See* TYMPANUM.

TYMPANIC MEMBRANE   *See* TYMPANUM.

TYMPANUM   (EARDRUM, TYMPANIC DISC, TYMPANIC MEMBRANE) The membrane separating the middle ear from the outer ear, vibrating in response to sound waves and communicating them, by means of the OSSICLE of the middle ear, to the site of hearing. In many amphibian and reptile forms the tympanum is exposed at the skin surface, while in others it may be hidden or completely lacking. It is particularly well developed in many anurans and often larger in males than in females.

TYPE   The original specimen used for naming and describing a species or subspecies. If this specimen is the one collected by the author who first published a description of, and gave a scientific name to, the species, it is termed a 'holotype'. The place of origin of the type specimen is termed the 'type locality'.

TYPE GENUS   The genus chosen as a standard of reference for a family. For example, the lizard genus *Lacerta* is the type genus of the family LACERTIDAE.

TYPE LOCALITY   *See* TYPE.

TYPE SPECIMEN   *See* TYPE.

TYPHLONECTIDAE   Aquatic caecilians. Family of the APODA, inhabiting tropical and subtropical South America. Six species in five genera.

TYPHLOPIDAE   Blind snakes. Family of the SQUAMATA, suborder SERPENTES, infraorder Scolecophidia, inhabiting most of the warmer parts of the world. Over 180 species in some four genera.

TYPICAL RACE   A subspecies that bears a specific name identical to that of the species, e.g., *Epicrates cenchria cenchria* (the rainbow boa) or *Chelydra serpentina serpentina* (the snapping turtle).

# U

ULCERATIVE GINGIVITIS   *See* STOMATITIS.
ULCERATIVE STOMATITIS   *See* STOMATITIS.
ULNA   One of a pair of bones in the forelimb of TETRAPODA, or four-limbed animals.
ULNAR   1. Located to the rear of the body axis.   2. In relation to the hindmost part of a vertebrate limb, often in reference to anurans.

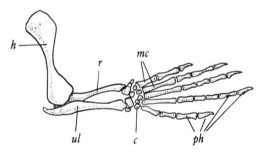

The bones of the forelimb of a lizard showing the position of the ulna: *c*, carpal; *h*, humerus; *mc*, metacarpal; *ph*, phalange; *r*, radius; *ul*, ulna.

ULTRASOUND-SCANNING   High-frequency sound waves given off by a transducer which is moved over an animal's body to determine if it is pregnant or GRAVID. The presence of the comparatively dense ovarian FOLLICLES is determined by the pattern of reflected sound waves. Ultrasound is completely harmless to the

developing embryo, unlike X-rays which can produce certain CON-
GENITAL conditions.

ULTRAVIOLET RADIATION (UVR)   Lying beyond the violet
end of the visible spectrum, ultraviolet is important in the successful husbandry of many reptiles, particularly desert-living tortoises
and lizards, as it is necessary for calcium metabolism and the
stimulation of pigment cells and sex glands. It is also essential for
vitamin D synthesis. Reptile-keepers can obtain most of the ultraviolet radiation needed from various forms of mercury-vapour
lamps.

UMBO   The slightly convex or rounded hump in the centre of an
individual LAMINA of a juvenile chelonian PLASTRON.

UNCIFORM   The small bone in an anuran hand, formed into a
single component by the union of the fourth and fifth CARPAL
BONES.

UNDULATING MOTION   *See* SERPENTINE MOVEMENT.

UNGUIS   A claw, or the part of the DIGIT from which it develops.

UNKEN REFLEX   Particular actions employed by certain amphibians, e.g. *Bombina* and *Dendrophryniscus*, in response to threat or
disturbance and which form an APOSEMATIC display. In the fire-
bellied toad (*Bombina orientalis*), the back is flattened and arched,
with the head help up and back, and the palms of the hands and
feet are raised and reversed, exposing the vivid red-and-black flash
coloring on the ventral surface and generally accompanied by an
increase in skin secretion.

UREA   Nitrogen-containing substance excreted by some animals,
e.g., fish, amphibians and mammals.

UREOTELIC   Excreting nitrogen in the form of UREA. Amphibians
are ureotelic.

UREOTELISM   The condition, found in terrestrial chelonians and
amphibians that dwell in damp situations, in which UREA is the
main product of kidney excretion.

URETER   One of a pair of ducts occurring in reptiles (and birds
and mammals) that carries URINE to the CLOACA from the kidneys.
Linked with the METANEPHROS, it replaces the WOLFFIAN DUCT occurring in amphibians.

URIC ACID   A white, odourless and virtually insoluble crystalline
product of protein metabolism, transformed from nitrogenous
waste by animals that inhabit arid areas. The substance, in terrestrial reptiles, that is produced from the breakdown of purine and

which is the most significant form in which metabolic nitrogen is excreted.

URICOTELIC   Relating to those animals that excrete URIC ACID rather than UREA and characteristic of many terrestrial animals in which the conservation of water is essential. Reptiles are uricotelic.

URINE   The slightly acid fluid discharged through the CLOACA. It is produced in the kidneys and contains UREA (in amphibians) or URIC ACID (in reptiles), and many other substances in small amounts.

URODELA   The tailed amphibians, comprising the salamanders and newts and related forms. *See also* CAUDATA.

UROPELTIDAE   Shield-tailed snakes. Family of the SQUAMATA, suborder Henophidia, inhabiting southern India and Sri Lanka. Approximately 44 species in eight genera.

UROSTEGES   The enlarged scales on the ventral surface of the tail; SUBCAUDAL scales.

UROSTYLE   A pointed rod of bone at the hind end of the vertebral column of frogs and toads. Greatly elongated, it reaches from the middle of the back to the posterior end of the body and is formed by the fusion of several caudal vertebrae.

URUTU   *Bothrops alternatus*, a PIT VIPER of the family VIPERIDAE, subfamily Crotalinae, inhabiting Brazil, Paraguay and northern Argentina. Responsible for a large number of bites each year.

UTERINE MILK   A creamy, paste-like substance produced in the OVIDUCT wall of viviparous caecilians, consisting largely of emulsified fats and orally assimilated by the developing foetuses.

# V

**VAGINA DENTALIS**   The term for the sheath-like membrane of tissue that covers and protects the FANG of venomous snakes.

**VARANIDAE**   Monitors. Family of the SQUAMATA, suborder SAURIA, inhabiting Africa, South-East Asia and Australasia. Approximately 30 species in a single genus (*Varanus*).

**VASCULAR SYSTEM**   The specialized network of veins, arteries and lymph vessels for the circulation of fluids throughout the body tissues. The blood-vascular system of animals enables the passage of nutrients, excretory products, respiratory gases and other metabolites into and out of the cells. The arterial system transports blood to different parts of the body from the heart, the venous system returns the blood to the heart, and the lymphatic system transports the fluid which permeates into the tissues from the blood.

**VAS DEFERENS**   One of the main pair of ducts that carry sperm from the TESTES to the exterior.

**VAS EFFERENS**   In reptiles, any of a number of various small ducts that carry sperm from the seminiferous tubules of the testis to the EPIDIDYMUS.

**VECTOR**   Any animal, such as a tick or mite, that can convey a disease-producing organism from an infected animal to a healthy one, either within or on the surface of the body.

**VELUM PALATI**   The upper of two muscular folds, or plicae, located on the palate in the rear of the mouth of a crocodilian. Its function, in combination with the lower fold (BASIHYAL VALVE), is to prevent water from entering the glottis when a submerged animal opens its mouth.

VENOM   The substance secreted by specialized glands of certain animals, such as poisonous reptiles, that is capable of bringing about a toxic reaction when introduced into the tissues of another animal. A white, greenish or yellow viscous fluid, venom is a complicated mixture of substances. Dried, it consists of 90–95% various proteins with varying degrees of toxicity and effectiveness, including proteins with enzymatic features and non-toxic proteins. Snake venoms frequently contain small quantities of other organic compounds, e.g., carbohydrates, lipids and free amino acids, and metals, such as potassium, manganese, sodium and calcium.

VENOM DUCT   The canal that extends from the VENOM GLAND to the entrance of the FANG in venomous snakes. The duct passes beneath the eye, pit (if present) and nostril, and over the upper bone of the jaw (the MAXILLA).

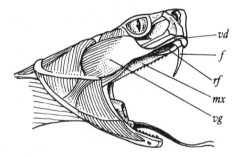

Diagram of the head of a viper in which the skin has been removed to show the different parts of the venom apparatus. *f*, fang; *mx*, maxilla; *rf*, replacement fang; *vd*, venom duct; *vg*, venom gland.

VENOM GLAND   A gland in reptiles, evolved from one of the salivary glands. Located between the eye and the angle of the mouth, the gland carries venom through the VENOM DUCT to the FANG which, depending upon the species concerned, is either grooved or hollow. In the HELODERMATIDAE (beaded lizards), the venom gland is the inferior labial salivary gland which has become specialized for the production of venom, which is secreted through the mucous membrane of the lower jaw and collects at the base of the teeth.

VENOMOUS   Relating to an animal that possesses venom. Until recently, the term 'venomous' was used as an alternative to POISON-

OUS (e.g. a poisonous snake, venomous frog) but today the term 'poisonous' is normally used in reference to those animals which have a noxious or harmful effect on another when partially or completely devoured, and 'venomous' for animals that introduce venom into the body of another by means of specialized teeth (fangs) or a sting.

VENT   The hind opening located on the undersurface of the body at the beginning of the tail; the external entrance/exit of the CLOACA.

VENTER   The abdomen or belly of an animal; the complete undersurface.

VENT LOBES   Fleshy lobes occurring in certain male urodeles, usually behind and on each side of the VENT.

VENTRAL   Any one of the enlarged scales on the undersurface, or VENTER, of a snake, from the head to the tip of the tail but generally used in reference to those ventral scales between the head and the ANAL PLATE.

VENTRAL COLLAR   In the majority of crocodilians, a distinctive row of enlarged scales across the throat just anterior to the forelimbs. One species has two rows of enlarged scales, forming a double collar, and a few species are without the row of enlarged scales altogether, so their collar is not obvious.

VENTRAL COUNT   *See* SCALE COUNT.

VENTRAL KEEL   A prominent ridge on the middle of the ventral scales of certain snakes, especially certain members of the HYDROPHIIDAE.

VENTRICLE   A lower chamber of the heart, having thick, muscular walls and receiving blood from the upper chamber (atrium), which it pumps to the arteries. The hearts of reptiles have two ventricles but those of amphibians have one.

VENTROLATERAL   Relating to the part of the body where the side unites with the undersurface.

VERMICIDE   Any substance employed to kill and eliminate intestinal worms.

VERMICULATE   Decorated with irregular or wavy tracery or markings resembling the tracks of worms.

VERMICULITE   A form of expanded mica which is produced for the insulation of buildings, fireproofing and as a bedding medium for young plants. For reptile-keepers it is an ideal, sterile incubation medium for snake and lizard eggs.

VERTEBRA   One of the bones of the spinal column (backbone) of a VERTEBRATE.

VERTEBRAL   Commonly used, when describing pattern or scaling, for the area covering the spinal column, e.g. any one of the scale rows along the mid-dorsal line on the bodies of lizards and snakes; also a LAMINA on the CARAPACE of a chelonian.

VERTEBRAL LINE   A stripe running the length of the centre of the back, lying over the spinal, or vertebral, column.

VERTEBRAL PROCESS   An elevated ridge running the length of the centre of the back of certain species of snakes, e.g. *Crotalus durissus*, in which it is especially noticeable.

VERTEBRATE   An animal characterized by a bony or cartilaginous skeleton, a well-developed brain and a backbone or vertebral column consisting of a series of ring-like structures (vertebrae) which protects the spinal chord. The group contains mammals, birds, fishes, reptiles and amphibians, each of which form a class and which together form the subphylum Vertebrata within the PHYLUM Chordata.

VERTICAL   Describing the pupil in certain frogs, lizards and snakes which, in bright sunlight, has an elliptical, slit-like opening with its long axis running vertically from top to bottom of the eye.

VERTICILLATE   Arranged in, or having, verticils (i.e., whorls), and normally used to describe the position of the scales on the tail of certain lizards, such as the spiny-tailed iguana (*Ctenosaura*).

VESTIGIAL   Relating to a vestige, or remnant, of a member or organ which at one time was more fully developed and which, during the evolution of the species, has become reduced in size and function, e.g. the vestigial PELVIC GIRDLE of a snake.

VIABLE   Capable of normal growth and development; capable of living, as in viable eggs.

VILLUS   Any one of the many finger- or hairlike projections of the mucous membrane lining the small intestine of many vertebrates. There are also villi in the CLOACA of certain male urodeles and coating the tongues of many lizards.

VIPERIDAE   Vipers. Family of the SQUAMATA, suborder SERPENTES, inhabiting most of the world except the Australasian region. Over 130 species in 11 genera in three subfamilies.

VIRUS INFECTION   Any one of several diseases caused by one of a group of submicroscopic intracellular bodies, many of which are PARTHENOGENIC, capable of reproduction only within the cells of other organisms, including reptiles and amphibians. Normally, virus infections show common infection symptoms, such as listlessness and lack of appetite, or abnormal skin growths and tumours. Secondary bacterial infections, such as *Aeromonas*, then frequently bring about changes that are necessary for the continued development of the disease.

VISCERA   The soft, large internal organs of the body; the entrails, particularly those in the abdominal cavity (COELOM). Post-mortem examination of amphibians and reptiles will often expose a cause of death which would not have been apparent from external examination alone.

VISCERAL GOUT   *See* GOUT.

VITTA   A band or stripe of colour. Generally used for the dark stripe running from either the snout or the eye, along the side of the head to the tympanum or shoulder in many anurans, e.g. HYLIDAE. When a vitta is particularly broad it is often termed MASK.

VIVARIUM, pl. VIVARIA   A tank, cage or enclosure in which live animals (generally reptiles and/or amphibians) are kept under natural conditions for research, study etc., or a building containing a collection of such tanks and cages.

VIVIPARITY   A kind of reproduction in animals in which the embryo develops within the body of the mother and receives its nourishment directly via some form of placenta, resulting in the eventual birth of live young. Viviparity occurs in many reptiles and amphibians, as well as in some invertebrates, certain fishes, and most mammals, all of which are termed 'viviparous'. Compare OVIPARITY, OVOVIVIPARITY.

VOCALIZATION   Vocal intercourse within, and between, species, the most well-known examples being the noisy breeding calls of frogs and toads. Certain lizards can also vocalize and in some, such as the Asian Tokay gecko (*Gekko gecko*), the call is so loud it can be heard over a considerable distance.

VOCAL POUCH   The VOCAL SAC.

VOCAL SAC   An elastic, thin-walled, inflatable pouch on the throat, or at the sides of the neck, in male frogs and toads. In the majority of species there is a single sac lying beneath the throat or chin, whilst in others it is paired, swelling out between the TYMPANUM and shoulder. During VOCALIZATION the sac is filled with air from the lungs and acts as a resonating chamber. A few species have thoracic and abdominal vocal sacs.

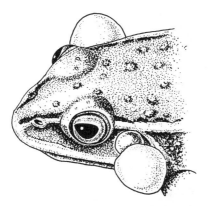

The vocal sacs of male frogs and toads serve to amplify their calls during courtship.

VOLAR   Of, or relating to, the sole of the foot or the palm of the hand.

VOLUNTARY MAXIMUM   The highest possible temperature that a POIKILOTHERM can withstand before it is forced to seek shade or move below ground.

VOLUNTARY MINIMUM   The lowest possible temperature that a POIKILOTHERM can withstand before it is forced to seek the sunlight, either direct or diffused, in order to bask, or to move below ground in order to HIBERNATE.

VOMER   The thin, flat bone in the roof of the mouth, located directly behind the PREMAXILLA, that forms part of the palate.

VOMERINE TEETH   Short, conic projections lying on the VOMER, in the palate of amphibians close to the internal nasal openings. Occurring in many species, vomerine teeth are often a useful guide to their identification.

# W

WAGLER, Johann Georg  1800–32, German zoologist and medical practitioner whose several herpetological works include *Naturliches System der Amphibien* (1830). Author of several taxa.

WALLACE'S LINE  The imaginary boundary passing between Bali and Lombok, Borneo and Celebes, and east of the Philippines, separating the Asiatic and Australasian fauna. The line was named after Alfred Russel Wallace, English naturalist and traveller who, with Darwin, co-founded the theory of evolution.

WALTZ  The 'dance' participated in by male and female *Ambystoma* as they encircle each other whilst attempting to engage their snouts with each other's CLOACA. *See* TAIL WALK.

WARNING CALL  *See* MALE RELEASE CALL.

WARNING COLORATION  The obvious or showy marking or

Warning coloration in reptiles and amphibians indicates to potential enemies that they are dangerous or noxious, as in the case of these two dart-poison frogs, *Dendrobates lehmanni* (left) and *D. quinquevittatus*.

colouring by which an animal advertises to potential attackers that it is dangerous or noxious. Many venomous snakes have conspicuous markings, as do poisonous and foul-tasting amphibians. *See also* APOSEMATIC.

WARNING CROAK  *See* MALE RELEASE CALL.

WARNING DISPLAY  The display in cobras and related species involving neck spreading and usually accompanied by hissing and an erect strike posture. Similar warning displays are seen in certain non-venomous species also, some of which can be classed as MIMICS.

WART  Any well-defined, cornified raised area on the skin of certain amphibians, particularly toads of the genus *Bufo*, of which they are characteristic.

WATCHGLASS  An alternative term for the SPECTACLE in snakes and some lizards.

WATER MEADOW  An area of low-lying grassland that borders a river and which is regularly flooded. Improved river management is leading to the rapid disappearance of this special type of habitat which, at present, is important to many species of amphibian and reptile.

WATERSPOT  A physical irregularity in the calcification of a reptile egg shell, appearing as a slightly elevated star-shaped mark, not unlike a snowflake crystal, on the surface.

Waterspots on reptile eggs appear as slightly raised star-shaped marks on the shell's surface.

WATTLE  A loose fold of skin hanging from the neck or throat of certain lizards and employed by males during courtship, when it can often be erected or extended by means of the HYOID BONE and used in display.

WAXWORM  The larva of the waxmoth (*Galleria melonella*), a member of the Lepidoptera, family Pyralidae. Commonly called tebos, waxworms are cultured as a nutritious food item for many reptiles and amphibians.

WEB   The thin sheet of skin joining the digits of many amphibians and reptiles.

WEDGED PREOCULAR   In snakes of the genus *Coluber* (the racers and whipsnakes), the condition in which the lower PREOCULAR projects downward between the adjoining LABIAL scales.

WERNER, Franz 1867–1939, Austrian herpetologist who published many papers, particularly on snake systematics (1912, 1924, 1929), and was responsible for the much admired revision of the reptiles and amphibians in Brehm's *Tierleben* (volume 4).

WETLAND   Any area of marsh or fresh water, including canals, streams and rivers etc., which is home to many types of reptiles and amphibians. Much attention and effort has been directed at the conservation of this kind of habitat, which is under constant threat from drainage and reclamation.

WETTSTEIN-WESTERHEIMB, Otto von 1892–1967, Austrian herpetologist. Published *Herpetologica Aegaea* (1953) in which he resumed the research of Werner on the reptiles and amphibians of the Aegean.

WHIPSNAKE   Any of several long, slender, fast-moving non-venomous snakes of the COLUBRID genus *Coluber*, such as *C. viridiflavus* of Europe. Also any of several other slender non-venomous snakes, such as *Masticophis flagellum* of North America.

WHORL   Term given to the scales, in lizards, that surround a single portion of the tail in a symmetrical set, and used generally in reference to sets that are obviously quite different, as in the tail of the spiny-tailed iguanas (*Ctenosaura*), where rows of enlarged spiny scales alternate with several rows of small, flat, overlapping scales.

WIEGMANN, Arend Friedrich August 1802–41, German zoologist at the Berlin Natural History Museum. Compiled the first standard work on the HERPETOFAUNA of Mexico: *Herpetologia Mexicana* (1834).

WINDOW   The area of transparent skin on the lower eyelid of certain lizards, particularly members of the SCINCIDAE, which enables the animals to see when the eyes are closed. In the ocellated skinks (*Ablepharus*) of south-eastern Europe and west Asia, the upper eyelid has fused firmly to the lower one, forming a snake-like SPECTACLE, or permanent window over the eye.

WING   1. The wide, delicate sheet of skin that stretches from the forelimb to the hind limb in the so-called 'flying dragon' (*Draco*). Supported by several long false ribs, the membrane is used for gliding between trees of up to 30 m apart. At rest, the 'wings' are folded fan-like against the flanks. **2.** The sideways extension of separate sections of the chelonian PLASTRON which form the BRIDGE.

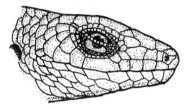

The lower eyelid of certain lizards has a transparent area, or window, allowing the lizards continued vision when the eye is closed.

The thin skin membrane or wing on either side of the flying dragon lizards (*Draco*) enables the reptiles to glide considerable distances.

**WOLFFIAN DUCT** Either of the pair of ducts found in amphibians, that carries URINE to the CLOACA from the kidney. In males, it has a dual purpose and also carries spermatozoa from the testes. It is replaced by the URETER in reptiles and is found only in males, where it forms the EPIDIDYMIS and vas deferens.

**WOLTERSTORFF, Willy** 1864–1943, German herpetologist and zoologist. Produced many herpetological papers many of which were on urodeles in which he specialized. An important collection of this group was started by him at the Magdeburg Museum but was lost during World War 2.

**WORM**   The pale, fleshy, worm-like lure on the tongue of the alligator snapping turtle (*Macroclemys temmincki*) used to entice prey into its open jaws.

**WRIGHT**, Albert Hazen   1879–1970, American herpetologist, author of numerous significant papers on anuran distribution and development. In 1949 he co-authored *Handbook of frogs and toads of the United States and Canada* and later, in 1957, the two-volume *Handbook of snakes of the United States and Canada*, with his wife Anna Allen Wright.

# X

XANTHISM, XANTHOCHROISM An ABERRANT condition involving the presence of an excessive quantity of yellow pigment. A xanthic specimen is a colour MORPH that has yellow as its dominant colour.

XANTUSIIDAE Night lizards. Family of the SQUAMATA, suborder SAURIA, inhabiting southern North America, Central America and the West Indies. Some 12 species in four genera.

XENOPELTIDAE Sunbeam snake. Family of the SQUAMATA, suborder SERPENTES, infraorder Henophidia, inhabiting South-East Asia from Burma to southern China. MONOTYPIC.

XENOSAURIDAE Knob-scale lizards. Family of the SQUAMATA, suborder SAURIA, inhabiting Mexico and China. Four species in two genera.

XERIC Relating to hot and dry conditions, or to the animals living in areas where those conditions occur.

XERIC PATTERN A type of BREEDING PATTERN occurring in certain types of frogs, which is effected greatly by the outside surroundings, the main influence being rainfall. Species having a xeric breeding pattern do not usually have a fixed breeding season but instead breed throughout the year in reaction to rain.

XIPHI- A prefix meaning shaped like, or resembling, a sword.

XIPHIPLASTRON, pl. XIPHIPLASTRA Either one of the hindmost pair of bones in a chelonian PLASTRON.

# Y

YAWN  The wide stretch of the jaws that precedes the start of EC-
DYSIS in snakes and lizards or which, in snakes, follows the swallowing of a large prey item to realign the jaws.

YOLK  The spherical mass of normally yellow nutritious substance
that maintains the developing embryo within the YOLK SAC.

YOLK PLATELET  Any one of the somewhat large and flattened
granules of yolk occurring in the eggs of amphibians.

YOLK SAC  The membranous sac, linked to the ventral surface of
the embryo, that contains the YOLK in reptiles. Upon hatching
from the egg, the yolk sac is drawn into the abdomen and provides
the young reptile with nourishment during its first few days of life
until it can feed itself.

# Z

ZONARY   Term used to describe the concentric pigmented areas occurring on the SCUTE of a chelonian shell.

ZOOGEOGRAPHICAL REGIONS   The six geographical divisions of the world, sometimes called 'faunal regions', contrived in conformity with the distribution of land animals. The regions comprise PALAEARCTIC, NEARCTIC, NEOTROPICAL, ORIENTAL, ETHIOPIAN (or Afrotropical) and AUSTRALASIAN, and each has its own unique collection of animal species.

ZOOGEOGRAPHY   A branch of zoology concerned with the geographical distribution of animals and the primary causes of this.

ZOOLOGICAL RECORD   An important annual publication which contains precise sources of reference for all new reptile and amphibian taxa validated during a specific year.

ZOONOSIS   A disease or infection that can be passed to man from lower vertebrates. Only very few reptilian diseases are transmittable to man.

ZOOTOXIN   A poisonous secretion produced by an animal and, in herpetology, refers to the toxic skin secretions of amphibians and to snake venoms.

ZYGODACTYL, ZYGODACTYLOUS   Having the toes in pairs, two facing forwards and two facing backwards, as in birds of the Picidae family (the woodpeckers), but also used in herpetology when relating to the feet of the CHAMAELEONIDAE. The fused toes of chameleons have been modified into claws for climbing and grasping: the fore limbs having three inner toes and two outer ones, and the hind limbs having two inner toes and three outer ones.

**ZYGOTE**   A fertilized female GAMETE, resulting from the union of a SPERMATOZOON and an OVUM, or the individual organism resulting from such a cell.